Yesterday's

Volume Six.

Life on the Island in the Sixties.

*From the pages of
The Isle of Wight County Press.*

by

Alan Stroud

Now and Then Books

ISBN 978-0-9565076-3-1
Typesetting and graphics by Alan Stroud
© Alan Stroud 2011

Printed by Short Run Press, Exeter.

Acknowledgements

As this is to be the last book in this series I want to thank my wife Sue, and children Tom and Kate for all their help and suggestions over the last four years. Their encouragement, as always, means so much to me.

I also want to thank my friend Richard Brimson who not only provided his usual stirling editorial help but who actually makes an appearance in the book this time. Thanks also go to Fay Brown, Colin Fairweather, John Groves and Charlie Taylor for their assistance. I'm also indebted to Roger George Clark, who kindly agreed to the use of a marvellous photograph from his book, "Perfect England - The Isle Of Wight in the 1960s," and Martin Mitchell, who permitted the use of photographs of HMS Arethusa from his website.

Over the last four years the County Press could not have been more helpful and I would like to thank the following - Managing Director, Robin Freeman, who literally opened doors for me by allowing me out-of-hours access to the County Press archive every Saturday morning. In the County Press shop, I'd like to thank Barbara, Debbie, Sue, and especially Gloria, who all looked after me week after week. David Owen, shop manager until his recent retirement, provided words of wisdom and much appreciated publicity, and thanks also go to Richard Wright, for his generous and thoughtful reviews of the books. I also want to thank Keith Newbery for his invaluable advice and kind words, both much appreciated.

Finally, I want to give special thanks to Ray Foulk, co-promoter of the original Isle of Wight festivals with his brother Ronnie, for his invaluable help over the last year. In the summer of 2010 Ray kindly agreed to a lengthy interview for an Isle of Wight Radio documentary about the festivals, produced by Tom, and over the following months he patiently answered all my many follow-up queries. In addition, he has allowed the use of extracts from the interview to appear in this book, where they provide a unique and informative running commentary to the festival articles. Tom's encyclopaedic knowledge of the festivals also proved invaluable, saving me from myself on more than one occasion and guiding me when sometimes I couldn't see the wood for the trees.

Ray's contribution to this book has enabled the publication of a full account of the birth pains and death throes of the Island's first festivals. It has also provided an opportunity to correct some of the myths, untruths and plain absurdities that have plagued so many previous accounts of the Island's first festivals.

Published by Now and Then Books Isle of Wight
E-mail: nowandthenbooksiw@googlemail.com

Please note : Volumes 1, 2 and 3 are published by The Oakwood Press, Usk, Mon. NP15 1YS and are available
www.oakwoodpress.co.uk or local bookshops.

Contents

The County Press and The Festivals

The Sixties was an eventful decade. As Britain's televisions went from black-and-white into colour, so did the public in a lot of ways. Britain took a giant social leap forward and ideas and attitudes that were unthinkable at the beginning of the decade became commonplace by the end. However, the ashes of the Sixties can only stand so much raking over and even though previous volumes have included a potted history of the times in the introduction, it seems unnecessary on this occasion. Unlike Victorian times, the 1960s are well within living memory and many readers, like the author, may well have grown up during that decade and need no history lesson. Suffice to say, as this collection of articles will hopefully demonstrate, the changing times and attitudes of the Sixties made a distinct mark on the Island. At the beginning of the Sixties, a family emigrating to Australia or an account of a family's holiday in Canada was deemed interesting enough to be a news story for the County Press but by the end of the decade the paper would be publishing photographs of naked festivalgoers at Compton Bay, such was the pace of change. The advert pages, especially, also provide an interesting barometer of the rapidly changing attitudes towards sex in Britain during the 1960s.

The Sixties saw the end of many institutions that had become a part of Island life. The closure of all the military barracks came first, a process that had begun in the late 1950s. Albany Barracks, the largest military establishment on the Island, closed in 1960, the buildings being demolished in 1963 to make way for Albany Prison, and in 1962 the Army finally said farewell to the Island with the closure of Fort Victoria. The Fort was purchased by the Council, most of the buildings were demolished and the site took on a new lease of life to become today's popular leisure park. Local traders could only regret the departure of the soldiers, particularly from Newport where they had become a welcome spending force.

Equally damaging to the local economy was the unemployment caused by the closure of J.S. White's shipyard at Cowes. Completely undercut by foreign manufacturers, White's had ceased to be competitive and in 1965, HMS Arethusa became the last ship to leave White's yard. In the following December, the company threw in the towel and the shipyard closed, leaving White's to concentrate on marine manufacturing.

What was left of the Island's steam railway service was also to disappear. The closures of the 1950s had left just two lines intact, the Cowes to Ryde, and the Ryde to Ventnor line. In 1966 more closures took place, leaving just today's stretch of line between Ryde and Shanklin. The Princess flying boat, cocooned at Cowes, finally disappeared after death throes lasting more than 10 years, when in the small hours of a dark and stormy night in 1967, it was towed across the Solent to a waiting scrapyard, with Harry Spencer directing operations while standing on top of the hull, 60 feet above the waves.

Two elegant castles disappeared at the beginning of the Sixties, Steephill and East Cowes. Perhaps if they had managed to survive until the end of the decade, when public attitudes had changed, they might still be here today. Plans for a nuclear power station at Hamstead were dropped following a public outcry, and shortly afterwards much of Newtown passed into the ownership of the National Trust. The days of telephone operators connecting calls by hand came to an end in 1969 with the closing of the Island's last manual telephone exchange at Ventnor.

1969 also saw the end of Mew Langton, the Island's largest brewer. A family concern, it owned and supplied most of the pubs on the Island and their sign depicting a huntsman quaffing a pint were a familiar sight. In 1965, Mew Langton was bought by Strongs, a mainland brewer, who in turn were taken over by Whitbreads in March 1969, and in October, Mew's Newport brewery produced its last ever pint. Shortly afterwards, Whitbreads began a radical programme of pub closures and many of the Island's smaller, idiosyncratic pubs were to disappear.

The rock 'n' roll of the 1950s had given way to pop music by the mid-sixties and aided by pirate radio, all-day pop music had become a way of life for millions. Nationally known jazz acts had appeared occasionally on the Island in the early 1960s but from about 1964 onwards, Island promoters only had eyes for pop groups, and over the next five years more than a hundred 'Top 40' acts appeared here. Throughout the Sixties, the Island, particularly Ryde, was spoilt for musical choice. Every Saturday night throughout the summer season, a well-known pop group would be appearing somewhere on the Island. The roll call of groups who made their way here is an impressive one. Those who trod the boards at Ryde include The Small Faces, The Nice, The Moody Blues, The Bonzos and even the Rolling Stones. The Island pop boom ended abruptly in 1969. The explanation for its sudden end may lie in the fact that since 1967, music festivals had sprung up across Britain, and performers increasingly found they could earn a four figure sum for just one short appearance. Overnight, earning a hundred pounds for a show on the end of Ryde Pier was no longer the attractive proposition it had once been. As a result, by 1970, musical acts appearing on the Island were confined to just a nine week season, mostly at one venue, the Music Box at Westridge, where lesser-known and, correspondingly, cheaper acts such as Black Widow, Audience, and the Keef Hartley Band became the order of the day.

Finally, the 1960s saw the beginning of the end for Mark Woodnutt, the Island's MP since 1959. He appears to have been a genuinely hard-working constituency MP, closely involved in attracting some sizeable businesses to the Island over the years and he was a man who could literally be found visiting hospital patients on Christmas Day. He was also a very close friend of the County Press where his activities were always guaranteed to receive full and generous coverage, but with one notable exception - his involvement in the Bembridge Harbour Affair - a business deal which eventually came to haunt him.

Mr Woodnutt had acted as broker in the 1962 sale of the harbour and potentially lucrative surrounding land, but his subsequent involvement with the syndicate who purchased it became the subject of widespread gossip and speculation. It did not extend to the County Press, however, who chose not to publish any details of the allegations. That was their prerogative; a newspaper is free to print, or not print, whatever they choose, but whether this 'selective reporting,' was helpful or damaging to Mr Woodnutt's cause is a moot point. In time, it appeared the practice of selective reporting would also come to be used against the Island's festivals.

The 'Bembridge Harbour Affair' was a major event in the life of the Island. Rumours, speculation, and a catastrophic television interview, saw an MP in one of the safest seats in the country defeated in a dramatic election result which destabilised the Island's politics for the next three decades. A full account of events surrounding the sale of the harbour has yet to appear, so in an attempt to shed some light on the subject for the first time a generous account of the affair is included, using some newly uncovered material.

There is one subject that received more coverage in the County Press than any other in its entire history - the phenomenon that was the Isle of Wight festivals, when for two years the Island hosted two of the biggest musical events in the world. The subject would animate the County Press like no other, before or since. In terms of quantity, the coverage of the festivals stands alone, the photocopied cuttings of 1969 and 1970 filling well over a hundred A4 pages. To reflect that vast amount of coverage, this volume includes a 60 page appendix of County Press coverage of the festivals which offers a full account of the uneasy relationship between the newspaper and the festival promoters.

The festivals were organised by Totland brothers Ronnie and Ray Foulk, both in their twenties. While countless articles have been penned over the years by 'festival experts', the Foulk brothers themselves have remained largely silent but in the summer of 2010, Ray Foulk agreed to an extensive interview for use in an Isle of Wight Radio documentary produced by Tom Stroud, the author's son. Both travelled to Oxford and spoke at length with Ray, who subsequently agreed to the use of extracts from the interview appearing in this volume. These extracts provide the perfect accompaniment to the articles and give Ray an opportunity to tell the other side of a story that over the years has been bedevilled by ill-informed comment and absurd myths.

Although not directly involved in creating any of those myths themselves, the County Press reporting of the festivals is not their finest hour. In 1960 Walter Sibbick, by then in his early seventies, had retired as editor and was replaced by Ernest Ash whose arrival marked a significant change in the tone of the paper. News reports became more worthy and the light-hearted items which had been a staple part of the County Press for so many years all but disappeared. Mr Ash lacked the light touch of Walter Sibbick's gentle and considered writing style and favoured no-nonsense headlines such as "Isle of Wight Car Headlight Realignment Campaign Begins," "Wroxall Bus Shelter Gets New Roof," and "Shanklin Gas Board Showroom Now Open Six Days a Week." Like most of his generation, Mr Ash was no fan of rock music, especially when accompanied by nudity and drug taking, and he would certainly have regarded the perceived lifestyle and morals of festivalgoers with equal distaste. The County Press owners and management certainly seemed to share the same opinion and so, as it happened, did that good friend of the County Press, Mark Woodnutt, MP.

Between them, Mr Woodnutt and Mr Ash represented the middle-class, conservative values of their respective constituents and readers, and both were unashamedly anti-festival. The two men were able to voice their disapproval of the festivals within the pages of the paper - Mr Ash in editorials, and Mr Woodnutt in interviews and press statements. For Mr Ash, alienating young people in the process was of no consequence since the County Press had no young readers to talk of, and for Mr Woodnutt, the fact that 18-20 year-olds were to get the right to vote just eight weeks before the 1970 festival, was of no concern to him. He made no attempt to moderate his views on the festival in order to attract any youth vote, and his judgement was proved correct when he went on to retain the seat with a record majority.

International Times, a leading 'underground' magazine of the day, began its coverage of the festival with the words, "The Isle of Wight County Press was established in 1884 - and is still the same." It was a criticism the County Press could take on the chin. In a sense the paper had not changed. From its very first days it had seen itself as a paper of record (albeit a selective one at times) and had not allowed its news pages to be tainted by opinion or bias. It was a stance they still maintained but there were some notable exceptions - the reporting of the festivals being one of them.

While their coverage is largely accurate and unsensational, many of the accounts are tinged with innuendo, inference and sarcasm, and are interspersed with exaggerated headlines such as 'Law Unenforceable,' 'Genuine Fans Upset,' 'Frightening Experience,' 'Threatened Battle etc.' On occasion 'selective reporting' led to petty, almost vindictive omissions. When Bob Dylan ended three years of seclusion with a world-famous press conference at Seaview, almost every national newspaper attended, but the County Press ploughed its own furrow and chose neither to attend nor to report the event. The following year, when one of the world's biggest musical line-ups performed at Afton in one of the most significant events in recent Isle of Wight history, the County Press chose to print not a single name of any of the acts appearing.

Mr Ash, though, was quite happy to print uncompromising readers' letters that ranged from the wildly inaccurate to the completely absurd. One reader, referring to the festivalgoers at Afton, wrote, "A proportion of the faces were depraved almost beyond belief, and in many cases clearly drug-ridden; scores had such faces as might be seen in a criminal lunatic asylum." Another described them as "creatures" and "gullible beatniks," while the hope was expressed by a Wootton reader that, "the area will be 'crop-sprayed' with strong disinfectant to prevent the usual diseases that arise from overcrowded insanitary conditions."

In a highly political move, Mark Woodnutt was allowed an extensive editorial following the 1969 festival in which he roundly criticised both promoters and festivalgoers. His essay plays to his readers preconceptions and on occasion is less than factual. For whatever reason he chose not to put his name to the article, simply signing it 'M.W.'

However, the County Press coverage needs to be seen in context. Times were different. The counterculture movement was in full swing and teenagers and parents had grown apart like never before. The County Press was a Conservative newspaper with no allegiance to youth. It was a middle-class newspaper for middle-aged people. Its opposition to the festival did no more than reflect what it rightly or wrongly assumed to be the views of its readers and it would have been remarkable if it had been otherwise - but of course, not everyone was a County Press reader. The fact is, whether the County Press liked it or not, many Islanders did not share the views of Mr Woodnutt et al and actually welcomed the festival, a possibility confidently dismissed in its pages.

However, in fairness, the County Press was not the only newspaper to wear its politics on its sleeve. At the 1970 festival, the national underground magazines jointly produced a daily free-sheet, Freek Press. A lofty passage from issue 6 reads, "The dialogue between Fiery Creations and the White Panthers and other radical groups is totally unworkable as their aims and ethics bear no relationship to each other... There can be no dialogue until the basic problem of the evaluation of capital against humanity has been resolved ....."

As usual, compilations under the titles "The Week's News" and "Town and County Notes" are undated for the most part, as in most cases a date is superfluous, but they are always placed within five or six weeks of their original appearance. Where the date of an item has been considered relevant it appears in brackets.

For the most part the items are in their entirety and appear exactly as they did when they were originally published. Some longer items required editing for space considerations, and where this has occurred it is indicated by dotted lines. Titles used for the articles are those that accompanied them on the day they first appeared in the County Press; none have been altered or modified in any way.

As to the paper itself, priced four old pence, the County Press had grown in size since the mid-fifties, when an average issue consisted of 10 or 12 pages. By 1965, the paper, now selling 31,000 copies a week, had grown to 20 or on occasion, 24 pages in length, the increase being almost entirely due to the growth in advertising.

The County Press of the 1960s was liberally scattered with photos, and many of them appear in this volume. Copying photographs from the pages of newspapers from the 1960s is not without its problems, as some of the illustrations demonstrate, but as their historical interest outweighs these shortcomings they are presented warts and all.

Photographs credited "IWCP" have been taken from the pages of the County Press. Photographs from other sources are marked accordingly.

The entire County Press archive, from the first issue in 1884 through to the current day, is available on microfilm, either at the County Press offices at Pyle Street, Newport, or at the County Records Office at Hillside, Newport.

1960

A tornado which caused severe damage to parts of Cowes and Northwood in 1862 is very well documented and several impressive photographs of the damage exist. Much less well known, despite it occurring well within living memory, is the devastating whirlwind that struck St Helens on Boxing Day, 1959 ...

January 5th, 1960

WILDEST CHRISTMAS WEATHER IN LIVING MEMORY
ST HELENS HOUSES DEVASTATED BY WHIRLWIND

The final Christmas of the fifties will long be remembered in the Island for a violent weather mixture without parallel in living memory. During the holiday period a series of gales brought torrential rain, hail storms, and the first thunderstorms to be experienced in the Island at Christmastide for years. The thunderstorms occurred mainly at night when many people were awakened by hail rattling like marbles against their windows, and deafening thunderclaps. Most alarming of all was the whirlwind which struck the village of St Helens while Boxing Day family parties were gathered. Severe and widespread damage was done to property when the whirlwind, accompanied by a vicious hailstorm, passed over the village and grazing land to Nodes Point before taking a seaward course over St Helens Roads. In some cases roofs were ripped off above their heads, and apart from the severely damaged houses in the track of the storm, many others required structural repairs to make them weathertight again. Miraculously, no one was injured and it was providential that the whirlwind struck during daylight, otherwise there must have been casualties in the upper rooms which suffered most heavily ...

Residents' accounts of the whirlwind show that it lasted over a given spot only a very few seconds, during which everything seemed to be sucked up into the atmosphere accompanied by a loud and intense rushing sound. It was the worst storm experienced in the village in living memory ... The whirlwind struck at about 3.15 p.m. and tore through the Upper Green Road before turning in a north easterly direction over the houses near the Upper Green Methodist Church, then passing through fields and a coppice in the direction of Nodes Point, where it blasted its way through the Beach-Acre Holiday Camp before turning out to sea. Mr. Richard Wade, manager of the camp, told our correspondent that they watched the whirlwind approach from the marshes. It was like a big white cloud and it came curling and rolling down the valley at an incredible speed. They were fascinated by its behaviour and could only watch and wait. When it came upon them there was a terrific noise and a blinding, boiling storm of hail. It lashed the chalets, tearing off the roofs of several, which in turn were blown through others .. Passing by Guildford Park Camp the whirlwind lifted one of two hay ricks, leaving the other. With fearsome vigour it tore the rick to pieces and scattered them as it sped on down to the main road, blowing down a lean-to greenhouse at Fakenham Cottage. On the further side of the road, three elm trees were felled and then down across the field at the rear of St Helens House, five more trees in the small copse fell victims. Of these, a large oak and a large ash both had the appearance of having been severely twisted before the trunks were completely severed. Mr. Charles Wade, of Four Winds, West Green, said the scene from his sitting room was most awesome. The whirlwind approached with a terrific howl and he saw tiles, slates and debris being blown along like clouds of autumn leaves ... Throughout the afternoon, rain was falling almost incessantly and fortunately, people had been kept indoors. In many homes what had been a happy Christmas party was, without warning, turned into a scene of confusion and alarm. After recovery from the initial shock, residents who ventured out to discover the cause found large pieces of roofing and masonry wrenched off, leaving gaping holes through which the rain poured. Even more depressing scenes awaited them on inspecting upstairs rooms ...

◆

Until October 1971, Embankment Road, linking St Helens and Bembridge, was a toll road. Owned and operated by British Railways, it was a leftover from the days of the Bembridge to St Helens railway line. A toll booth at the Bembridge end was manned by a British Railways employee who stopped every passing car to issue a ticket on receipt of the toll fee. The toll keeper's hut was the original one built by the railway company over 80 years before and it was time for a new one. The County Press took the opportunity to reminisce ...

Jan 16th, 1960

BEMBRIDGE EMBANKMENT TOLL HOUSE
HISTORIC BUILDING REPLACED

The picturesque ivy-covered little toll house which had stood at the Bembridge end of the Embankment Road since 1881 and was originally part of the works undertaken by the ill-fated Liberator Group, disappeared on Friday week. The disappearance of the toll hut does not mean, however, that there is any intention of freeing the embankment from tolls, and the little house is being replaced by a new building a little smaller than its predecessor but with larger windows and improved accommodation for the toll keeper. Until now the building has been illuminated by gas, including the outside lamp, and no firm decision has been taken as to whether to substitute electricity. The Embankment Road was the first permanent reclamation of a large part of Brading Haven. It was completed in 1881, and in the summer there was a gala sports day and cricket match, Bembridge v. St. Helens, on the reclaimed ground, and the illumination at night of the entire new highway. The fairy lights were hung on the pipe, also used as a handrail, running along the mile-length of the embankment and through which water was supplied to a point in the vicinity of the toll house where steamers were supplied. It is an irony of fate that, 80 years after financial disaster overtook the Liberator Group, the Embankment Road, which is the main remaining result of the group's activities, should be providing a lucrative source of income for British Railways, their eventual successors. The railway pleasure-steamer services to Bembridge, and the extensive activities at St. Helens Quay are now no more, and the Royal Spithead

Hotel has long since passed from the ownership of the Liberator Group, for whom it was built by Messrs. H. Ingram and Sons, of Ventnor. The first toll keepers were Messrs. Albert Jones and J. Hodd, who worked a 24-hour day! There was then another toll house at the St. Helens end of the embankment on the site, where Brading Haven Yacht Club now stands. The hours of duty were reduced after a few years, and the all-night shift was abandoned. Mr. James left the embankment to become caretaker at Carisbrooke Castle, where he remained for several years. A date '4-6-83' scratched in pencil in an old till in the hut probably indicated that it had been here since that date, two years after the opening of the road. It is a remarkable fact that the tolls have remained the same as the original charges first imposed in 1881, cars paying on the same basis as carriages in those days. The names of other toll-keepers were Messrs. Wheeler, Weekes, and Wetherick, and the present keeper, Mr. R. Townsend, of St. Helens, has 44 years' service as a railwayman in the Island.

———————————◆———————————

Decca Radar came to Cowes in 1959, taking over the Somerton site previously home to Cowes Airport. Despite some name changes along the way, the manufacture of radar continues there to this day, providing hundreds of jobs on the Island. In the 12 weeks since they had arrived, the company had transformed the Somerton site and the promised jobs were beginning to appear ...

Jan 16th, 1960

DECCA RADAR, LTD.
SATISFIED WITH SOMERTON VENTURE

Three months ago Islanders welcomed the announcement that Decca Radar, Ltd., had taken over buildings on the former aerodrome at Somerton, Northwood, as the nucleus of a factory for making some of their world-renowned radar equipment. The announcement was welcomed as a step towards meeting the need for more light industry in suitable places in the Island. We were informed by a representative of the company this week that so far the venture has proved most satisfactory. Production has been commenced well within the scheduled time, and 50 people are now employed, as promised at the outset. Almost all are skilled engineering workers who were resident in the Island and temporarily unemployed, or men who were anxious to move from the mainland because of local associations. "So far," said the spokesman, "everything has gone according to plan. Local authorities and others concerned have been most cooperative, and thanks to the help of the Red Funnel Company we have had no transport difficulties."

TRAINING SCHOOL SOON

Asked about the proposed training school, he said it was hoped to build it and have it in operation by the middle of next summer... The future development of the factory at Somerton would naturally depend on contracts secured, but there was every prospect that as a long-term aim, employment would be available for at least 400 workers.

In the 19th century several private banks flourished on the Island, among them one
operated by the Kirkpatricks, a prominent and well-known Island family. Like most private
banks at that time, the business eventually foundered and the Kirkpatricks were left to look
to their extensive lands and property for an alternative source of income. Their estate
remained in the family until 1960 ...

Jan 23rd, 1960

AN ISLANDER'S NOTES
[By VECTENSIS]

Captain G. E. C. Barton, harbourmaster at Cowes, sends me the following notes
on the Kirkpatrick family, mentioned in recent references in this column to the
private banks which flourished and failed in Newport at the end of the 18th
century. They are taken from reminiscences of a forebear of his at Seaview in about
1880. James Kirkpatrick was originally a draper in Newport. His shop was
extensively patronised by the people from the country, and he frequently ran short
of small change. To meet this difficulty he gave his customers small slips of paper
for the amounts, bearing his signature. These were circulated, and when taken to
Newport were duly acknowledged, until he conceived the idea of circulating
notes. Notes were in circulation at that period, and his bank at Newport became an
established institution, but I understand that there never was a sufficient amount
of capital to cover the notes in circulation. More than twenty years after the death
of James Kirkpatrick (he died in 1819), and many years after the death of his sons,
the notes still circulated with only the name of James Kirkpatrick, jun. on them
until matters connected with the bank came to a crisis about the year 1842, when
it was found that James Kirkpatrick, jun. had so improved the position of the bank
that, had it been left unmolested, he would have worked it into a payable concern.
The directors allowed him enough to live comfortably during the remainder of his
life, but the failure of the bank was a great blow to many in the Island, and this was
unfortunately followed by the failure of Roland Blachford's Joint Stock Bank,
which was nearly as disastrous as the other. In about 1780, Kirkpatrick purchased
the salterns, between Seaview and Springvale, on the site recently purchased by
the Westridge Construction Co. to develop as a holiday centre, over which there
has been so much controversy. He afterwards built Seafield House as a country
residence. Whether the Salterns were bought for the purpose of salt making before
he purchased, or whether he conceived the idea of forming salt works in the
neighbourhood, is not known. He did, however, erect the necessary building and
machinery for the manufacture of salt, and, being in want of a competent man to
run the business, he engaged a John Matthews who resided at Newtown and had
been engaged in the salt business there. Salt making was carried on for some years
by John Matthews, his son, and grandson, until the salterns, with the marshes and
the estate, including Seafield House, were sold and the making of salt abandoned.
The buildings were changed into cottages. Salt, in consequence of the duty, was a
guinea a bushel. At that time there was the windmill just beyond the Salterns,
which pumped the sea water at high tide into the pond which fed the trenches out
to the reservoirs near the boiling house. The water was then pumped by hand into
the large iron pond, where the fire was constantly kept up during the summer. It
yielded 60 tons of salt each year. The winter time was spent in forming the
embankment on the Duver, and in looking to the sluices, and gathering wood for

are
you
a Jaeger girl?

The more questions you can answer 'yes' to, the more important it is that you should see all the autumn clothes at the new Jaeger shop.

1. Do you hate people to know how much you spend on your clothes?
2. Are you between five-feet-two and six feet tall?
3. Are you prepared to invest at least 10½ guineas on the most outstanding suit you've ever owned?

4. Do you tend to like well-cut, colourful casual clothes?
5. Are you prepared to come out quickly with a new fashion if it suits you?
6. Are you between the ages of sixteen and sixty five? Best of all are you in your late teens and early twenties?

the JAEGER shop in Ryde is now open

24 UNION STREET, RYDE

You're as Lovely as Spring in *Laeta Ramage* MODEL

in 'Moygashel' fabrics
made from
Courtaulds fibres

FASHION NOTES
reading from the left

Spring Fashion Parades

We are showing a collection of

SPRING FASHIONS

next Wednesday and Thursday

in the fashion department Ryde

Pack & Culliford
LIMITED

The Island's Leading Fashion House

UNION STREET · RYDE

SHANKLIN   TOTLAND BAY   YARMOUTH   SEAVIEW

fuel to boil the salt water. The Kirkpatrick family were deservedly held in remembrance. The old gentleman was accustomed to preaching at times in a room opened at the Salterns, and his daughters, Mary, Martha, and Louisa, used to teach in the Sunday-school at Seaview.

TOWN AND COUNTY NOTES

"Pretty Blue Eyes," the latest recording by Craig Douglas, was unanimously voted a "hit" by members of the B.B.C. "Juke Box Jury" on Saturday. Jack Payne, well-known bandleader and disc-jockey, praised the Newport singer's record on his " Record Round-up" the same day.

T.V. MAST AS NESTING SITE — Jackdaws are annoying B.B.C. engineers responsible for the maintenance of the 500 ft. TV mast at Rowridge. Twice this week they have had to climb to the portion of the mast where the aircraft warning lights are displayed to remove nests from inside the perspex covering of the lights. Although the openings are netted, the jackdaws still get in. Apparently the reason why this nesting site is so attractive to the birds is that it is wind and rain proof, and kept at a temperature of 80 degrees.

After examining the collection of colour transparencies of West Wight beauty spots at the Industries Fair on Thursday one woman visitor commented, "That's not the Isle of Wight — It says Ilford."

Queen Victoria's small pony cart, which she used in the grounds of Osborne House, was seen again this week in the showroom of a Ryde motor-cycle dealer (Mr. Derek Pickering). He bought it from Mr. G.H. Guttridge, of Whiteley Bank, Wroxall, who has owned it for nearly 30 years. Mr. Guttridge acquired the cart, one of the smallest ever made, in a farm sale at Osborne.

After years of wasted discussions and fruitless deals, the end had come for Cowes Pier. The visiting steamers had long since gone and the pier had suffered severe damage at the hands of the Army who had requisitioned it during the war. Since then it had remained closed and had slowly fallen into disrepair. The town's businessmen wanted to see the pier restored at public expense, arguing that the refurbished pier would bring tourists and their money to the town, but local residents were not in favour, declaring that "ratepayers should not be subsidising local traders" ...

March 19th, 1960

COWES VICTORIA PIER TO BE DEMOLISHED

The future of the derelict Victoria Pier at Cowes has been decided. At the monthly meeting of Cowes Council at Northwood House on Tuesday, it was agreed to proceed with demolition after the 1960 season. Mr. L.G. Daish (chairman of the Works Committee) reported that Mr. W. Dobson, a private individual, who had intended to repair and use the pier, was no longer interested because of illness. For 11 years, to his knowledge, attempts had been made to save the old pier. It was not a glorious edifice by any means, but it was the only deep sea landing in the yachting port. It would be extremely costly and impractical to attempt to adapt it as a landing stage for pleasure steamers. This idea, and several alternative suggestions, had been fully discussed by his committee, but they had reluctantly decided that demolition was the only answer. Mr. F.W. Callaway said he was concerned at the cost of demolition. More than a year ago, before negotiations with Mr. Dobson started, they received an estimate for this work which had been very high. Mr. S.L. Glossop, J.P., C.C., said it was their own fault if it was going to cost a lot to pull it down, because they had all been guilty of procrastination. A recommendation that the council should proceed with plans for the demolition of the pier, and that tenders be invited for commencement of the work in the autumn, was carried.

———————————◆———————————

Craig Douglas, former Newport milkman, was now firmly established as a pop star but he still couldn't keep away from the milk crates ...

May 28th, 1960

AN ISLANDERS NOTES
BY VECTENSIS

18-year-old local singing star Craig Douglas, all of whose records have been in the hit parade, returned to his home on the Pan Estate, Newport, last week for a few days' rest before another strenuous continental tour, and for a few days he threw off the mantle of a teenage idol and became once again Terry Perkins, milk roundsman. When Craig took up vocalism he gave up his job with Mr. Bill Strickland, of Pitts Farm, Calbourne, and his younger brother, Roger, became the assistant milk roundsman in his place. The day after he came home last week, Terry rose before dawn to accompany his brother to the farm. "I'll give you a hand today, so you can get finished early," he said. Mr. and Mrs. Strickland were not surprised. Mrs. Strickland said, "Terry has not changed, nor will he, no matter how much the teenagers swoon. He's still the same unspoiled boy." So the morning delivery of milk went on, but Terry's help did not work out quite as expected. In Newport he was frequently recognised as the singing star, and the delivery took longer than usual because his former customers wanted to chat with him. So, to catch up on lost time, in the afternoon he donned dungarees and rubber boots and helped to clean out the dairy! Craig is leaving shortly for Monte Carlo to start another round of continental appearances, but before he goes he is making a long playing record. His engagements in this country and abroad are becoming so numerous that he intends to learn to fly, so that he can save travelling time. He will be having his first lesson at Bembridge airport on Wednesday.

As this next item makes clear, the Solent, at that time, was referred to as "a sewer," so the presence of a salmon in the River Medina was quite an event ...

July 2nd, 1960

SALMON IN THE SOLENT
AND ONE IN NEWPORT HARBOUR

Salmon are known to be fastidious fish, choosing the freshest rivers for spawning and keeping away from any form of pollution but this week salmon have been caught in the Solent (recently described at a medical conference as "a sewer") and one was stranded by the tide and captured in Newport harbour on Wednesday morning. In the first three days of the week, Mr. H. Legg, former licensee of The Robin Hood, East Cowes, who nets fish in the Solent, caught 421b, of salmon off East Cowes. On Wednesday morning, as the tide receded, workmen engaged in unloading a vessel at Newport Quay saw what they thought was a large bass struggling in shallow water about 100 yards away. Two hours later, Mr. F. Thomas picked up the fish. It weighed 10 lb., and judging it to be too coarse to eat, he gave it away. Mr. A. Chessell, a crane driver employed by the Vectis Shipping Co., later identified the fish as a salmon, worth about £5! Many years ago salmon regularly entered the Medina and were often taken. They were commonly seen lying in the sluice at the Cement Mills. Salmon peel (younger fish) are occasionally netted in the Medina.

TOWN AND COUNTY NOTES

ISLAND NUDIST CAMP TO CLOSE — For more than 28 years, sun worshippers from all parts of the world have spent holidays at Woodside House, Wootton Bridge, but the property has been sold and the nudists are without a camp in the Island. The camp, which has been run by the Rev. Arthur Critchard and his wife, has been bought by a neighbour — Mr. Charles Duley, of Lisle Court. Woodside House can accommodate between 120 and 150 people. The grounds cover a 23-acre site and there is 800 feet of private beach. Mr. Duley said he hopes to develop the site as a conventional holiday camp. The nudists had asked him whether he could possibly keep the camp in its present form, but Mr. Duley said that was out of the question.

A SWARM IN THE POST — Hundreds of people gathered in front of the Newport Guildhall on Wednesday afternoon when a swarm of bees chose the pillar box which stands beneath the clock tower, as a convenient place to settle. The incident started at about quarter to five, when passers-by and motorists found the street filled by the swarm. Following their queen, they started to settle on the pillar box and within 10 minutes the front was thickly covered and more and more were seen crawling into the aperture to join the swarm inside ... Local beekeepers dealt with the swarm.

An octopus caught at Sandown in 1927 was given a train ride to Waterloo, where it was then handed over to London Zoo to go on permanent display. What would happen to one caught at Freshwater Bay in the enlightened Sixties? ...

September 17th, 1960
OCTOPUS CAUGHT AT FRESHWATER BAY

An octopus with a tentacle span of nearly five feet was captured alive in a lobster pot at Freshwater Bay on Tuesday by Messrs. C. Newbury, of The Star Inn, and R. Legg, of The Red Lion Inn, Freshwater. Crowds gathered on the beach to examine the unusual capture, which was brought ashore in a large bucket of seawater and later exhibited to their interested customers by the two licensees. Mr. Newbury told a "County Press" representative that during the time the octopus was trapped in the pot it had eaten the whole of the head and most of the tail of a lobster, which he estimated would weigh about 1 ¾ lb. As the octopus was easily the largest caught in the days since the war, and the first to be landed for several years, the landlords offered it to Sandown Zoo, but the zoo authorities were not in a position to accept such a specimen and passed the offer on to Brighton Aquarium. There it was stated that the octopus was not required as there had been a glut of such specimens along the south coast this season. So the octopus was killed, cut up, and used as lobster bait!

———————————◆———————————

The Island experienced one of its worst ever floods one Saturday morning in October 1960. Newport suffered the most, disappearing under several feet of water for several hours when millions of gallons of rainwater coming down from the hills, met a high spring tide coming up the River Medina. Blame was variously attached to narrow bridges and culverts, inadequate sluice gates, and ancient and disused mill wheels on both the Medina and Lukely streams but it was generally agreed that the flood had not been preventable.

It was to have a lasting effect on Newport. The Medina was, up until that time, still an attractive, natural river where it flowed through the town centre, but following the floods the river was 'canalised' and large concrete riverbanks were installed. The result is that today, what could be a pretty river passes through central Newport largely hidden from view, a town centre asset awaiting rediscovery ...

October 8, 1960
WIDESPREAD FLOODING
WONDERFUL ACTS OF NEIGHBOURLINESS ALLEVIATE DISTRESS

The worst flooding in living memory occurred in the Island on Saturday morning following a cloudburst after a severe thunderstorm. Streams and brooks were swollen into raging torrents of chocolate-coloured destructive water, which caused thousands of pounds worth of damage. Newport was the worst hit area and was isolated for some hours, all roads into the town being impassable to ordinary traffic, although a bus service was maintained to Carisbrooke. Many people were unable to reach their places of employment until later in the day.

The storm broke over the Island in the early hours of Saturday - ironically, the last day of summer time. The noise of the thunder and the tremendous downpour woke most residents, but those in the low-lying areas had little idea at the time of the terror and misery in store. At Chillerton, three inches of rain fell between 3 a.m. and 4 a.m. Carisbrooke is thought to have had more rain but the rain gauge of Carisbrooke Water Works was submerged by the torrent which swept down from

Bowcombe Valley at about 7 a.m. and no accurate figure can be obtained. Water Board officials estimated it at about 3.5 inches. Subsequent freak flooding conditions were due to the fact that high tide at Newport harbour was about 8 a.m. and this added to the trouble. Storm water sewers were unable to carry the water away as exits were blocked by the rising tide.

The first alarm was given by Capt. Gray of the Church Army's Anchorage Home, Hunnyhill. At about 5 a.m. he heard shouting from the downstairs dormitory in which five old men were sleeping and when he stepped off the stairs he found himself knee deep in water. He took the men and their bedding upstairs to safety but by the time he got down again, the water had risen and was waist high. Mr. D.T. Sibbick, milkman, of Carisbrooke Road, whose new house is on the banks of the Lukely stream, had almost completed the morning milk delivery when he and his wife found that the water level was rising at the foot of Cedar Hill and pouring unchecked through the village. They decided to return to their home and found the water lapping the back doorstep. "In a matter of minutes," he said, "the water rose nearly three feet." Mr. Sibbick lost all his chickens (value £200) and the damage to his house ran into hundreds of pounds. Mr. F.O. Boyes and his family were amazed to see from the bedroom windows of their home in Crocker Street, a pig swimming by. Many other residents lost their livestock. The Lukely Engineering Works were at one time under three feet of water and the Island Dairies factory at Westminster Place could not be used. There was a milk shortage in the town as a result and 5000 gallons of bottled milk were brought from Portsmouth.

Newport isolated

For several hours Newport was isolated from the rest of the Island. At some points on the outskirts of the town the flood water was too high for traffic. Some people who tried to drive through found themselves stranded in their cars and had to be towed out. A car at Town Gate Bridge was completely submerged. Shops at the Coppins Bridge end of High Street were flooded to a considerable depth and a substantial amount of stock was damaged.

Turn of the tide

Fortunately, with the turn of the tide, there was a rapid fall in the level of water and by 2 o'clock all roads were clear of flooding, but many were blocked by landslides. The worst was at Froglands Lane... In the town, piles of sodden furniture and bedding were spread out in the roadways. Hour by hour, more and more damage was revealed. At the Island Dairies premises, 60,000 lb. of butter was spoiled by contamination by flood water; the parapet of the Towngate Bridge collapsed; many walls were razed by the pressure of water and light buildings in its path had collapsed.

At Messrs. W. B. Mew, Langton and Co., the depth was an estimated 20 feet when the pressure eventually tore away the side of the building housing the mineral water plant. The maelstrom swept through the entire brewery and a thousand tins of crisps, barrels, crates, bottles, and masses of other loose equipment was swept away. Some of the casks, understood to contain beer and primings were picked up miles out in the Solent. Police and employees of the firm were kept busy preventing a secondary loss by "beachcombing bands" who thought the flotsam and jetsam were fair pickings. Other damage to the brewery

On the morning of Saturday October 1st 1960, the upper reaches of the Medina were swollen by recent torrential rain. The huge body of water reached Newport at the same time as an incoming high tide, and completely flooded the lower parts of the town...

WIDESPREAD FLOODING

"At Messrs. W. B. Mew, Langton and Co., the pressure eventually tore away the side of the building housing the mineral water plant. The maelstrom swept through the entire brewery and a thousand tins of crisps, barrels, crates, bottles, and masses of other loose equipment was swept away. Some of the casks, understood to contain beer and primings were picked up miles out in the Solent."

...everal hours, Newport was isolated from the rest of the Island. At some points on the outskirts ...town the flood water was too high for traffic. Some people who tried to drive through, found ...elves stranded in their cars and had to be towed out. A car at Town Gate Bridge was completely ...rged."

[Photographs by Reg Davies]

was to the cellars and there was a tremendous loss of stock. Nearly 100 telephone calls were received by the firm on Monday morning telling them of articles such as crates, barrels, tins of crisps, and other articles which had been salvaged and were being held for collection. Mr. Joe Mew, of the brewery, said he had 4ft. 6in. of water in his house in Crocker Street and he and his wife had to be rescued by boat. The plight of the town was featured on the BBC lunch-time news, and in later television broadcasts.

Shanklin octogenarian saved by handbell

Of the many incidents in the Shanklin district, the most alarming befell Miss Lily Colenutt, aged 84, who lives in the picturesque old cottage on the beach at the foot of Shanklin Chine. Swollen by the 45 minute deluge, the Chine stream became a raging torrent, carrying before it trees, bushes, earth and boulders. This debris eventually built up a barrier that diverted the waters literally through the windows of her cottage. Mr. Charles Spencer of the nearby Chine Inn saw the stream change course and by the time he reached the cottage there was almost five feet of water inside the kitchen, where Miss Colenutt was trapped against the back door by the force of the flood. She had managed to get her hands and a foot through the door but could get no further, and was nearly up to her neck in water. Mr. Spencer battered the door from the outside with a boulder from the beach, when suddenly, without warning, the entire doorframe collapsed and they were both washed several yards down the beach by the torrent, as furniture and other belongings were carried away.

Island havoc

In Cowes and East Cowes, nearly 100 houses were damaged by flooding. At Cowes drains were unable to cope and torrents of water rushed down the sloping streets to converge on the lower lying areas. The force of the water threw heavy manhole covers aside and scoured road surfaces. The High Street was flooded to a depth of nearly two feet in places. At Morton Common hundreds of acres of marshland were underwater on either side of the Sandown-Ryde main road. The railway tunnel at Wroxall was flooded to a depth of about nine inches and the force of water undermined the ballast. Early trains proceeded with great caution but services were maintained until the line was closed because of flooding in the Ryde Tunnel. There was little flooding in Ventnor but the force of the water was too much for some of the drains and was spouting four feet into the air. The raging torrent pouring over the cascade waterfall was particularly spectacular.

590 million gallons of water

The National Press, reporting the incident on Monday, made reference to comments by some residents that the effect of the storm might have been minimised had the flood gates at Messrs. Mew, Langton's been opened but Lt. Col. Mew said that the gates were opened the night before. All county and local officials, and the staff of the river and water boards are agreed that the gates made no material difference. The quantity of water which fell could not have been handled by any storm gates or sluices. Embittered householders, sadly eyeing the wreckage of their homes - some were not insured against flood - were inclined to blame the county planning authority for having allowed the Lukely stream to be considerably narrowed. At the Island Dairies the stream is taken through a culver under the building; at Westminster Mill the flow has been reduced again. Mr

...arooned crowds gather to see the River Medina crossing Newport High Street for the first time in ...ing memory.

...he other side, at the bottom of Snooks Hill, equally frustrated travellers gathered to look back ...em.   *[Photographs by Reg Davies]*

Baines (clerk of the River Board) also refuted the allegations. "No action of ours, he said on Monday, "brought this about." Mr. Adams (River Board engineer stated on Tuesday that the flooding was to some extent a result of buildin operations along the banks of the Medina and the Lukely streams long before th advent of local councils, planning authorities, or water and river boards. The tim must come when the now disused mills and their hatches, which forme obstructions, would have to be under the control of one authority.

River flow recording equipment was recently installed at Upper Shide on th River Medina. The low-water flow at this point during the summer was no mor than 6 cubic feet a second. At three o'clock on Saturday morning it was flowing a 27 cubic feet and then in the next 1½ hours rose to 150 cubic feet a second befor the recording needle ran off the chart and the gear became flooded in the recorde house... Mr Baines estimated that 590 million gallons of water had flowed throug Newport.

AFTER THE FLOOD

At Carisbrooke, a man went to see if his chickens were safe and had to swim t the chicken house. All the birds were drowned.

Passengers in a bus from Carisbrooke overtook a car as they went through th flood waters and were amazed to find that there was no driver in it. The force o the water was taking it along.

At Newbridge Mill a batch of dough ready for the bakehouse was ruined, and henhouse, containing 30 laying birds, was swept away and dashed to pieces.

The Water Board announced on Thursday that it was no longer necessary to bo drinking water anywhere in the Island.

A lady's silver watch, which had been completely submerged in 3 foot of wate in a house at Lower St James's Street, Newport, when wound up, was found to b in working order. It was made in 1870!

THE WEEK'S NEWS

Over 40 years ago, the late Mrs Celia Collins, of 21 Stephenson Road, Cowes, lo her engagement ring. At the time it was thought that it had come off her fing while she was doing some washing. On Tuesday her husband, Mr. Harold Collin was digging in the garden when the ring was found by his six-year-old grandso Leonard Pullinger. When taken indoors and cleaned, the ring was found to be perfect condition.

CINEMA MANAGERS' STATEMENTS. — The manager of the Theatre Roya Ryde, stated that apart from rowdyism the cinema was free of trouble. At th Commodore, the manager said there had been many cases of seats being damage and about six months ago things were very bad. The cinema ran a "blacklist" people who are not admitted. The manager of the Scala stated that seats had been cut to pieces by knives, and rubber stuffing thrown on the stage; lighted cigarette ends were thrown about and gangs of youths would climb over the backs of seats instead of walking to their seats through the aisles.

Following a petition signed by all the residents of Hassells, on the Pan Estate, Newport, the name has been changed to Downs View.

UNDERGROUND CONVENIENCE TO BE CLOSED. — A plan to close the underground public conveniences at Mill Hill Road was favoured by all but two of the councillors. The others were unanimous in their condemnation of what was described as "a noisome spot," and "a monstrosity." (Oct 22)

Although the wildfowling season opened six weeks ago, mallard are still breeding in the Island, and at Shorwell a wild duck is sitting on a clutch of eggs, the ninth of which was laid on Tuesday! (Oct 22)

———————————◆———————————

When the recent floods subsided, many items were found far away from their original home - including a lucky pig ...

October 15, 1960

A PIG IN A POKE

One of the more remarkable incidents connected with the floods in Newport came to light on Tuesday. Mr. Albert Kent, proprietor of Kent's Furnishing Stores, found a young pig on his premises, still alive after being trapped for 10 days without food. The store, at the foot of Hunnyhill, was flooded to a depth of six feet, and the pig had evidently been swept in on the flood-stream through the window broken by the force of the water (or by the pig) and subsequently boarded up. Mr. Kent cleared out his main store on Tuesday, and was tackling the smaller adjoining premises when he found the animal trapped between furniture in an area about six feet square. Its sustenance for the last few days could have only been an inch or two of mud and water. Mr. Kent recognised the animal — a young pig of some 100lb. - as belonging to Mr. Moul, of Brookfield, whom he notified and who arranged collection.

———————————◆———————————

A large part of Newtown, formerly the property of the Swainston Estate, became National Trust property just at the precise moment the site was threatened by the construction of a nuclear power station ...

December 10, 1960

NATIONAL TRUST TAKEOVER AT NEWTOWN RIVER ESTUARY
AREA CIRCLES THE SITE OF PROPOSED NUCLEAR STATION

The National Trust have taken over the whole of the Newtown River estuary for the benefit of the nation in perpetuity. The four miles of foreshore and 16 miles of tidal lakes virtually encircle the site proposed for the nuclear power station at Hamstead. Mr. F.W. Bright, on behalf of the National Trust, said that negotiations had been completed with the Swainston Estate Company and covered almost the whole of the beautiful estuary. The property includes rights in the bed of the river, certain of the saltings, quays and land at Shalfleet and the foreshore of the Solent coast extending from Bouldnor to Thorness Wood. The area includes four miles of coast between high and low watermarks, and about 16 miles of tidal lakes reaching into the Island for about two miles. These are the Western Haven, Shalfleet Lake, Causeway Lake and Clamerkin Lake and the minor ones of Corfe Lake and Spur Lake. The fishing rights include the Newtown Oyster fishery, which is being revived and is said to be the Island's oldest industry. During the year the trust have acquired other properties at Newtown — Town Copse and the former public house in the centre of the village. This property is being restored and leased as a private house in connection with the oyster fishery. The boundaries of the western end almost encircle the site at Hamstead which has been suggested as a site for an atomic power station, and at the eastern entrance to Newtown Creek the shore and saltings almost entirely surround the area which the Natural History and Archaeological Society are hoping will become a nature reserve.

———————————◆———————————

Whether the two events were connected or not is a matter of conjecture, but no sooner had the National Trust taken possession of Newtown estuary, than the CEGB announced they were deferring a decision on whether or not to build a nuclear power station there. The deferment was widely and correctly seen as an admission that the scheme was dead in the water ...

December 17, 1960

HAMSTEAD NUCLEAR POWER STATION SCHEME DEFERRED
CENTRAL GENERATING BOARD CONSCIOUS OF AMENITY VALUE

The Central Electricity Generating Board have deferred a decision on seeking consent to use a site at Hamstead as a nuclear power station. They find that Hamstead is an excellent site, but conscious of the amenity value of the West Solent, the board are considering an alternative way of providing more power in southern England at reasonable cost ...

"VICTORY FOR PROGRESS"

The Earl of Huntingdon, president of the Solent Protection Society, issued the following statement on Thursday, "We are delighted to hear that the C.E.G.B. have had second thoughts about the building of a nuclear power station at Hamstead and that they may not go ahead with it after all. No amount of landscaping could have merged such gigantic buildings into the countryside as it exists at Newtown. They would have dominated the scene for miles around, besides ruining the immediate neighbourhood, one of the most beautiful in the Solent. But for the unrelenting efforts of the Solent Protection Society ... the whole of this part of England would have been laid wide open for further large-scale industrialisation and urban sprawl. As it is, we are now determined that the whole of the Solent should be designated a National Park. It is the first time that amenity interests have triumphed over such seemingly overwhelming odds. We consider it to be a victory for progress and a prelude to intelligent planning and recognition of the value of our heritage in the 20th century."

After 200 years Albany Barracks was to close and Newport would no longer be a garrison town. As the County Press noted, the military presence had contributed in no small way to the economic, social and sporting life of the town ...

December 24, 1960

ALBANY BARRACKS, PARKHURST
CLOSE OF TWO CENTURIES OF MILITARY OCCUPATION
[By VECTENSIS]

The recent announcement by the War Office that Albany Barracks has ceased to be a military station, and the proposal to use the buildings as the site for a third prison at Parkhurst, brings to a close Newport's long history as a garrison town, extending over two centuries.

It also marks a notable change in the life of the Island, as the succession of famous regiments who have been stationed at Parkhurst, particularly during the last 80 years, have contributed in a marked degree to the economic, social and sporting life of the community.

Newport has valued the trade which the military gave to the town, famous regimental bands have enlivened many public functions, military football and cricket teams have given a philip to local competitions, and the officers of the various regiments have been valued supporters of hunting.

LINK WITH BRITISH INDIA

The building of the prison, the old poor law institution, and the original barracks took in large portions of Parkhurst Forest, which at one time extended to the west bank of the Medina River and southward to the outskirts of Newport. The original barracks were constructed by the Honourable East India Company in the late 1700s ... It consisted of wooden hutments, described in old records as "rough constructions with rabbet-tiled roofs." The barracks were eventually taken over by the War Office as a regular military station and in 1894 the huts had become so dilapidated it was decided to demolish them and build the present barracks .... When the new barracks were completed the "County Press" made the following comment: "While, as in other walks of life, it is not all beer and skittles in the Army, ample provision has been made for our military neighbours to indulge their tastes in both directions, at the commodious canteen and at the skittle alley nearby." .... Doubtless there are many memories of the regiments at Parkhurst in the minds of my older readers. They will be a reminder of the pride which Newport had in being a garrison town, and as an indication of the regret felt that this honour is no longer enjoyed.

Princess Elizabeth, the daughter of Charles I, had been imprisoned in Carisbrooke Castle with her brother Henry following the execution of her father. Within a few weeks the Princess died from a chill or influenza, and was quietly laid to rest in the vault of S Thomas's Church. In 1854, when the church was being rebuilt, her coffin was briefly removed from the church and her remains were examined by a Newport doctor in the hop of discovering her cause of death (See Vol 1, page 61). The doctor appears to have kept a ri bone and lock of hair of the Princess, both items eventually ending up in the ownership c

Mr. Ledicott, a Newport antiques dealer. The exact details of what happened when the Princess's coffin was opened by the doctor are lost to time but over 100 years later, a little more light was shed on the matter ...

December 31, 1960

AN ISLANDER'S NOTES
[By VECTENSIS]

My recent note about a lock of hair and a rib bone of Princess Elizabeth, daughter of Charles I, being at one time in the possession of Mr. W.E. Ledicott, a former Newport curiosity dealer, has brought me further information as to this unsavoury incident in the history of the ancient borough. It is obvious that when the tomb of the Princess, who died at Carisbrooke Castle, was moved from the chancel of the old St Thomas's Church, Newport, in 1854 to its present position, these grim relics of the ill-fated King's daughter were taken from the coffin.

Mr. S.F. Moody, of Fairlee Villa, formerly in business as a jeweller in Lower St James's Street, has shown me a brooch containing a portion of the princess's lock of hair. He tells me that as a lad, when he was apprenticed to the late Mr. J. H. Heal, who then carried on the business, a local antiquarian named Pierce, familiarly known as "Quaker Pierce," came into the shop one day and jubilantly produced a wisp of the princess's hair which he had persuaded Mr. Ledicott to part with. Mr. Moody was given the job of inserting the hair into a locket for Pierce's watch chain, and he retained a small portion which he inserted into the brooch .... The princess's coffin was removed to a nearby shed during the demolition of the church and the building of the new one in 1854, and was then returned to the tomb at the east end of the north aisle, where it now rests below the handsome marble recumbent figure of the princess erected by Queen Victoria. While it was in the shed a local surgeon, Doctor Ernest Wilkins, had the coffin secretly removed to his house, in order that he might examine the body with a view to ascertaining the cause of death, which had been the subject of considerable controversy. In a report afterwards published by Mr. Ledicott (and suppressed by the corporation because of its disturbing revelations), the doctor stated that the misshapen bones proved that the princess was a victim of rickets. He solemnly affirmed that the remains were replaced in the coffin intact, but after his death the lock of hair and rib bone were found in a jar at his house, with a written statement that they were from the remains of Princess Elizabeth.

Eventually they were secured by the curio dealer Ledicott, who refused to return them to the vault in the church when ordered to do so by the Home Secretary and also refused to hand them over to the vicar of St Thomas's. However, Mr. Ledicott "submitted to the gracious influence of Queen Victoria and surrendered the relics, the hair being deposited in the I.W Museum, while the rib bone, enclosed in a silver casket, was reverently restored to the tomb." Apparently Mr. Ledicott could not resist keeping part of the lock of hair, as Mr. Moody's information proves.

I have had letters from the curio dealer's son (Mr. C.F. Ledicott, of Rayleigh, Essex) and grandson (Mr. P. Ledicott, of Newport), in which they confirm most of the facts stated above. The former mentioned that he believed that the lock of the Princess's hair was still in the Carisbrooke Castle Museum. Mr. J Jones, curator, tells me this is so.

Mr. C. F. Ledicott enclosed with his letter a cutting from "The Gentleman's

Journal" of about 60 years ago, headed, "The Olde Curiosity Shoppe," describing an interview with William Smith Ledicott, "a character who might have stepped bodily from the pages of Charles Dickens."

1961

Three huge flying boats had been manufactured by Saunders-Roe at East Cowes on behalf of the British government. The development of sufficiently powerful engines for the aircraft had bedevilled the project, delaying it by several years, and during that time the jet engine had arrived. It immediately rendered the flying boats out of date and left them virtually unsaleable. The government decided to cut their losses and sell them, "as they are, where they are, and for what they will fetch." ...

January 7th, 1961

THREE PRINCESS FLYING BOATS TO BE SOLD
MINISTER'S DECISION

The three giant Princess Flying Boats, built by Messrs. Saunders-Roe at a cost to taxpayers of more than £10 million, are to be sold — possibly for scrap. This was revealed in a statement by Mr. Peter Thorneycroft (Aviation Minister), who has ordered that they be sold "as they are, where they are, and for what they will fetch."

For the last six years the aircraft have been in cocoons — one at Cowes and two at Calshot. The 140-ton flying boats were constructed on Government contract to give Britain the lead in air travel in the immediate post-war years, and were designed to carry 85 passengers in luxury. The one now at Cowes was the only one ever to fly and it caused a sensation when it appeared in 1953 at the Farnborough Air Show. Because of engine difficulties, however, airlines were reluctant to take up this new craft. Since 1953 several schemes have been suggested for their use, but none has materialised.

The "Princesses" will now be advertised in national newspapers and technical journals by the Disposals Branch of the War Office.*

———————————◆———————————

The article about the Princess and her coffin brought more letters ...

January 14, 1961

AN ISLANDER'S NOTES
[By VECTENSIS]

The recent references to the locks of hair and a rib bone being taken from the coffin of Princess Elizabeth continues to bring me correspondence. Mr. W.G Stapleton, proprietor of the Holyrood Art Galleries, in Holyrood Street, Newport has shown me a letter written by Thomas Orde, Governor of the Island to the private secretary to George III, reporting the discovery of the remains to the King He purchased the letter, with a sketch of the coffin and vault, and rubbing of the inscription on the coffin, from a London bookseller, with other old documents, an

---

* The three flying boats remained unsold.

proposes to place them on view in his shop. The letter, addressed from Carisbrooke Castle on October 24, 1793, reads : "The Sexton of the Parish Church of Newport, taking up a part of the pavement near the altar with a view to opening a grave for the late Mr. West, brother to Lord Delaware, struck into a small vault, coarsely bricked on all sides without being plastered, in which lay a simple leaden coffin, raised from the ground up on some rough stones placed under it at both ends, and with three strips of brass across the widest part, with the inscription 'Elizabeth, 2nd daughter of ye late King Charles, dec'd Sep. 8th, MDCL' upon them ... You may, perhaps, not think it improper to mention the circumstances to the King, and to receive any command which His Majesty may be pleased to give in regard to them. I have thought it my duty in the meantime to order the vault to be temporarily closed, that no mischief may be done within the vault, in which, indeed, a very short person could not stand upright. There is a small niche at the bottom of the rough brickwork, in which there seems to have been placed something made of wood, which now lies there in many fragments, wet and rotten. The coffin is perfect. It is my intention unless any other order should be signified, to cause to be placed over the vault a large, plain, flat stone, with a simple inscription ... Your most obedient and humble servant, Thos. Orde."

The governor's intentions were carried out and the coffin remained there until it was removed to its present resting place in the north aisle, when the present church was built in 1854.

———————————◆———————————

On a Sunday night in Yarmouth in March 1961, a late night reveller bet that he could hit the clock face of Yarmouth church with a dart. As the County Press put it, "Unfortunately, he succeeded." ...

March 18th, 1961
DAMAGE TO YARMOUTH CHURCH CLOCK

There will always be a difference of one minute between the times shown on the north and west faces of the 282-year-old Yarmouth Parish Church clock as a result of damage caused by an irresponsible act on Sunday night. Apparently a mainland visitor wagered that he could hit the clock face, 40 feet above the ground, from a distance of 50 yards with an ordinary lightweight dart, as used in the familiar game. Unfortunately, he succeeded and when the minute hand came up against the dart it stopped the clock and strained the mechanism to an extent which has caused the 60 seconds difference.* It is understood that the darts were fired from Pier Square by means of a powerful catapult. The trouble was noticed on Monday, and on Tuesday the rector (the Rev. E. T. Lang) and a helper, working with a 30-foot length of jointed cleaning rods from the top of the tower, managed to dislodge the dart. Another dart, which had penetrated deeply into the stonework near the clock face was also dislodged. The fine old clock is inscribed "Nicholas Paris in Warwick, 1679." The last time the Church fabric was damaged by missiles was during the last war, when two machine gun bullets fired by a low-flying German raider pierced the gilded ball, below the weather vane.

---

* Mark Whatson, the current Vicar of Yarmouth, says the difference no longer applies. The repair work involved was relatively minor and was probably carried out shortly afterwards.

The reason that St Helens Duver resembles a golf course is because until 1961, that is exactly what it was. By then, the club had fallen on hard times, with dwindling membership and competition from other clubs on the Island and despite generous financial help from one of the members, the end had come. It did, however, mean more good news for the National Trust ...

March 18th, 1961

OLDEST ISLAND GOLF CLUB RELINQUISHES COURSE.
LINKS GIVEN TO NATIONAL TRUST

The Royal Isle of Wight Golf Club on St. Helens Duver will become the property of the National Trust and be retained as an open space for all time as the result of a recommendation adopted by a special meeting of the club on Sunday. The recommendation, submitted by the council responsible for conducting the club, virtually means the end of the club, although a decision remains to be taken as to whether members will still be allowed to play over the course. The property will be a gift to the National Trust. It extends over 20 acres and comprises practically the whole of St. Helens Duver adjacent to Bembridge Harbour.

Mr. Louis H. Campbell, of Bembridge, the senior member of the club, presided, supported by Mr. A. R. Mellor, M.B.E., of St. Helens (the local member of the National Trust), who has been largely responsible for the conception of the scheme which will ensure the preservation of an Island beauty spot.

For several years the club has been faced with stringent times, largely the result of the economic situation after two world wars and competition now offered by half-a-dozen other Island golf clubs, whereas for many years previously the St. Helens club was the only one in the Island. After nearly 80 years' existence the situation has changed considerably. The club and its first-rate artisans' section has faded from the picture, and it was only through the generosity of one of its senior members about six or seven years ago that it remained in being. Mr. Richard Peto, of Bembridge, decided to buy the golf links, which he handed over to the club as a gift with a further donation of £2000 for upkeep.

At a meeting of the club in October it was indicated that the money was practically exhausted and that membership had fallen to fewer than a dozen and it was proposed, with Mr. Peto's agreement, that the club should approach the National Trust. Mr. Mellor subsequently received a letter from them agreeing to accept the gift and, if the Club wished, that the use of the course should remain available to members. This point will be settled at a further meeting this week-end.

---◆---

THE WEEK'S NEWS

FAIRLEE HOUSE TO BE DEMOLISHED — Frequently described as "the most expensive white elephant Newport Council ever acquired," Fairlee House Newport, is to be demolished. In the years since the council took it over with farmland they bought for the town's sewage works, there have been several attempts to use the building—as a school and as a factory. The council have spent large sums of money on maintenance and it was unanimously agreed that notice be served that the council wish to demolish the property; and that tenders be invited for the work. (February 4)

REDUNDANCY AT COWES SHIPYARD — Redundancy is being felt at Messrs. J. Samuel White and Co.'s shipyard, Cowes, where 143 men completed a week's notice yesterday. This is the largest single group of workers to be made redundant at one time. Throughout the week Mr. G. Thomas (manager of Cowes Employment Exchange) and other Ministry of Labour officials have been interviewing the men concerned. As a result, some men who came to the Island from the north of England and Scotland during the year will be returning to their homes ... The Ministry of Labour yesterday confirmed that 27 electricians had received a week's notice this week-end. (March 25)

FAMOUS TREE REPRIEVED AT FRESHWATER — The famous Wellingtonia tree planted by Garibaldi during a visit to Farringford, the former home of the poet laureate Tennyson, in April 1864, and condemned to be felled as dangerous to the public about a year ago, has been reprieved. Mr. D.M.J. Coulson, manager of the Farringford Hotel, told a "County Press" representative that a Forestry Commission expert had decided that no danger existed and, as a result, he had no intention of having the tree felled. That meant that the tree would certainly achieve its century and might even live to be 200.

◆

The Island's oyster trade has always suffered from fluctuating fortunes. The business had just gone through another of its periodic downturns when, in 1961, another revival was attempted ...

May 27th, 1961

ISLAND'S OLDEST INDUSTRY REVIVED

Newtown, the Island capital that became a village, sprang into the news again recently when it was selected as a possible site for a nuclear power station. It is in the news again today, but for a very different reason. 1000 or more years before man split the atom, Islanders at Newtown were splitting open oyster shells and treating themselves to one of the sea's rarest delicacies. From then on oyster beds have been laid at Newtown with varying success. Frost, pollution, or seabed enemies have from time to time ended the oyster's life, but always someone has come along to revive what is probably the Island's oldest industry. Today it is a 35-year-old freelance scriptwriter, Mr. Cyril Lucas, who is carrying on the tradition. He purchased the Newtown Oyster Fishery Co. Ltd., a year ago, with the idea of combining the jobs of script writing and oyster rearing. But he quickly realised the oyster industry is a full-time job, and now, more often than not, his pen lies idle while he prepares for a rich oyster harvest. Mr. Lucas, who lives with his wife and two children in the Noah's Ark, Newtown's public house until 1916, prepared the old oyster beds last spring. He imported 50,000 two-year-old oysters from Brittany and these were laid immediately. This spring he has added another quarter of a million oysters to his beds, and now he tends his "fields" as carefully as any dry land farmer ... It is largely playing a waiting game in the oyster industry - none should be picked until it is between four and five years of age ... Mr. Lucas spoke of the hazards which face the oyster farmer. A large volume of fresh water sweeping down Newtown Creek in the winter accounted for some of his young stock. There is the ever-present danger of frost, starfish, and the oyster's particular enemy - the tingle.* This is a type of sea snail which feeds on the oyster by boring a hole in its shell. Mr. Lucas hopes to develop a local market for his oysters ... and also hopes to renew the contract with shipping companies at Southampton, who used to purchase the Island oysters for their liners. His first target is a production of 100,000 oysters a year, but eventually this could well exceed half a million.

For many years the Simeon family were instrumental in keeping the oyster industry flourishing at Newtown ... and in 1877 it was estimated that there were between five and 6 million oysters in the Newtown and Medina rivers. Tragedy overtook the enterprise in 1880, when a severe frost, lasting six weeks, killed the stock. Later the oyster beds were taken over by Messrs. Paskin Bros., of Cowes, but once again disaster overtook the fishery when oil pollution from the Solent during the First World War was blamed for the loss of almost the whole stock. Paskins continued to operate on a small scale until midway through the last war, when the lease was returned to the Swainston Estate ... The next company to be formed was the Newtown Oyster Fishery Co. Ltd., which managed the beds until 1957. Since then they have lain idle until Mr. Lucas bought the company a year ago ... With the traditional glass of stout and brown bread and butter, the Newtown oyster will find many a willing buyer, and the pleasure it will give to the consumer will be matched only by the pleasure it has given the Island in seeing one of its oldest industries thriving again ...

◆

TOWN AND COUNTY NOTES

NO FIVE-DAY WEEK FOR COWES COUNCIL WORKERS — A recommendation that Cowes Council manual employees should have a five-day week was defeated by the casting vote of Mr. F. J. Petty (chairman) on Tuesday. (March 25)

CRAIG DOUGLAS — The Island's singing personality Craig Douglas stars in a specially recorded Easter Monday morning broadcast entitled "Steppin' out" on the B.B.C. Light programme. Craig's latest record, which will soon be available, is called "A hundred pounds of clay." This record is to be played in 450 cinemas throughout Britain. He has recently been to Luxembourg and Cologne to take copies to the disc-jockeys. The original record has been banned by the B.B.C., but a special version has been cut to satisfy their tastes.† (April 1)

A Freshwater man who cracked a large hen's egg while preparing his breakfast was surprised to find that it contained no trace of a yolk.

---

* In the summer of 2010, the business had all but ceased due to another infestation of the tingle, a mollusc which drills a hole through the oyster shell to suck out the contents.

† The song tells of how God created a woman for Adam out of a hundred pounds of clay. The BBC did not approve and demanded amendments before it could be played on air. As a result, the line "He rolled his big sleeves up, he created a woman, and made some lovin' for a man" became "He created old Adam and a woman for the man." Twenty years later the song gained a new lease of life when it appeared on the Kenny Everett LP compilation, 'The World's Worst Record Show.'

George, the old goose whose home was at the Shanklin Manor Pond, is dead. On Tuesday he became impaled on the spiked railings around the pond when trying to fly over, and died shortly afterwards.

CUT POUND NOTES MYSTERY — Police at Ventnor are investigating an unusual discovery - a quantity of pound notes deliberately defaced by scissors. A dozen notes were found between the Esplanade wall and the back of some bathing huts last week and others have been found in Grove Road and in a litter basket near the Canoe Lake. Numbers and the chief cashier's signature have been cut from most of the notes and others have been defaced with squares and strips cut out of them. So far £17 has been found.

◆

For nearly a hundred years, Ryde's Theatre Royal stood on the site occupied by today's NatWest Bank. It was a popular venue from the outset and became one of the South's premier theatres, attracting London productions featuring household names. It had survived the coming of the cinema in the 1920s by eventually becoming one itself but like most cinemas across the land, the arrival of television was rapidly taking its toll on customer numbers. However, the question of whether or not the theatre could survive this latest threat became academic when the building was consumed by a major fire...

May 27th, 1961

THEATRE ROYAL DESTROYED
DISASTROUS BLAZE AT RYDE

The Theatre Royal in the heart of Ryde became a smoking shell within a few hours on Friday week after the fiercest and most spectacular fire seen locally since the Town Hall conflagration of June, 1933. The 600-seat cinema was cleared of patrons at 10.25 p.m., and the staff left some minutes later. Mr. Jack Pugh, licensee of the Turk's Head, in the Colonnade, Lind Street said "I looked through the bar window and saw a shower of sparks burst from the rear (screen) end of the Theatre Royal like a firework display. I telephoned for the brigade." As the firemen were being summoned, flames burst through the roof and soon the building was ablaze from end to end. Two jets were played on the cinema, which had become a blazing torch. A cooling jet was directed on the Crown Hotel, and another on the Colonnade. Nearly 40 holidaymakers sleeping in the Crown Hotel, including several children, were evacuated ... A water tender arrived from Newport enabling two more jets to be directed on the cinema and a screening jet on Pack and Culliford's building. Even so, intense heat and showering fragments gave cause for alarm. The shop blinds were holed, and the top of the premises grew extremely hot. The upstairs windows of Mrs. Violet Pugh's florist's and fruiterer's business in the Colonnade were cracked and the paintwork blistered, even on the inside ... Eventually the wall on the Crown Street side began to bulge outwards and all firemen were withdrawn from that part of the building. Soon afterwards a huge portion of the 40 foot wall collapsed, and many tons of bricks cascaded into Crown Street.

THEATRE ROYAL DESTROYED BY FIRE.
DISASTROUS BLAZE AT RYDE

"The Theatre Royal, in the heart of Ryde, became a smoking shell within a few hours on Friday week after the fiercest and most spectacular fire seen locally since the Town Hall conflagration of June, 1933... At the front, posters still advertised the last film shown, "The Rebel," starring Tony Hancock, and on the Lind Street wall was a poster announcing a forthcoming film at the Scala, entitled 'Too Hot to Handle.'"... (May 27)   *[Photo IWCP]*

The interior of the Theatre Royal from a Ryde Town Guide of 1905.

EMBERS ON PIER

Burning embers were flung far into the night sky by the leaping flames. These fragments, principally of charred wood, drifted on the wind and showered over the town, some even being found on Ryde Pier. On Saturday morning the interior of the cinema was a smoking mass of rubble and blackened, twisted girders. Poised high up above the entrance could be seen the ruined film projectors, still pointing down to where the screen had once stood. At the front posters still advertised the last film shown, "The Rebel," starring Tony Hancock, and on the Lind Street wall was a poster announcing a forthcoming film at the Scala entitled "Too Hot to Handle." ... The task of demolishing the walls which threatened surrounding streets and property began at 2 p.m. on Saturday ... With the aid of the fire brigade turntable ladder, a steel hawser was secured through windows in the 50 foot rear wall and when the strain was taken by a tractor many tons of bricks crashed into the building and on to Lind Hill in a dense cloud of dust. The dangerous north-west corner followed later but it was almost dark before the Lind Street wall, which had swayed perilously during the operations, was finally reduced as a source of danger ...

SECOND THEATRE ON THE SITE

The original building on the site was a market house erected in 1816 by a joint stock company, but the venture failed through lack of custom in the same way as another a few yards away on the site of the Town Hall. Its conversion for use as a theatre took place after the building changed hands in 1838. Generally regarded as an ugly structure, this theatre was pulled down in 1871 to make way for the Theatre Royal. For a theatre, the new building was on the small side, yet with its pit, dress circle, upper circle and gallery, its rows of ornate boxes and lofty embellished ceiling, it was unique in the Island ... Despite intense competition in recent years for the custom of the dwindling cinema-going public and modernisation several years ago which saw the disappearance of the boxes and other nostalgic trappings of the theatre beloved by an older generation, the "Royal" somehow preserved its intimate atmosphere and was always regarded by the management as a family cinema.

---◆---

ISLAND NOTES

LAST PERFORMANCE TONIGHT AT THE "GRAND" NEWPORT — The playing of the National Anthem tonight after the performance of "Nearly a Nasty Accident," will mark the closure of the Grand Cinema, Newport, the oldest of the town's three cinemas. The Grand, which was rebuilt soon after the last war forms one of a chain of nine cinemas operated by Isle of Wight Theatres Ltd. - the tenth being the burned-out Theatre Royal at Ryde. The staff will be absorbed by the Medina, Newport - this cinema and the Commodore at Ryde, having been acquired by the company earlier this month. (May 27)

The tortoise exhibited by Timothy Muncaster in a pet show at a school fete at East Cowes on Wednesday gained a first prize out of 20 entries. It also surprised its owner - for although christened Tommy, the tortoise laid an egg during the show.

IMPROVED AIR SERVICE FOR THE ISLAND — The Island is to be better served with air transport this summer. Next month Airsaf Ltd., are to open up a series of air services to the Midlands and the North ... Every Saturday from June 3 to September 30, a de Havilland Heron airliner will leave Birmingham at 10 a.m., 1.30 p.m. and 4.30 p.m., and land at Sandown an hour later ... The return fare will be £6. (May 27)

———————————◆———————————

Harvest time was here and 'Vectensis' had been watching a combine harvester at work. The sight brought back memories of the days of horsepower ...

September 2nd, 1961

AN ISLANDER'S NOTES
[By VECTENSIS]

Last week I made my first close acquaintance with a combine-harvester when I watched Mr. Scott Blake and his men cutting a fine field of barley at Blackwater. Under skilful handling, this amazing machine was making a tidier job of cutting the corn than one so often sees these days in ragged stubbles, and the combine was supported by other appliances typical of present-day mechanical farming — a straw baler, a "shovel" loader, a motor-tractor, and a motor-lorry to take away the sacks of grain and the bales of straw. As I watched this modern harvesting scene my mind went back to the days of my boyhood and the contrasting work and sounds of those times. The combine rattled and roared, the tractor spluttered, and the other machinery added a background hum and clatter. How different to those far-off days, when I was thrilled to lead the "trace-hoss" while the straw-bound sheaves were loaded on the waggon; or when the staggered line of mowers, wielding their scythes with a regular swish, laid the cut corn in neat swaths, and at intervals stopped on the cry of "whet," to draw their whetstones from the frogs at the back of their belts and strike a sweet-ringing note as they put a keener edge on their blades.

There were other sounds, too, which I recalled, now regrettably absent — the 'hoot' and " bither" cries of the carter as he directed his horses right or left, the 'whoa!" to stop, and the "holvast!" warning to the loaders before the waggon moved on to the next pitching-point. "Progress there must be," I pondered, "and the farmers have not been slow to adopt labour-saving machinery. The harvest-month money may not perhaps, be so desperately needed as when I was a boy." But the realisation of the striking changes which have come to the rural scene left me with a feeling of nostalgia for the more peaceful, more musical harvesting of yore.

———————————◆———————————

The Royalty cinema at Cowes was about to close its doors for the last time. The last film be shown was "On the Double" starring Danny Kaye, the poster advertising the film coming a minor Cowes landmark by remaining on the front of the derelict building until ll into the late 1960s ...

September 9th, 1961
COWES AND EAST COWES WITHOUT A CINEMA
THE ROYALTY TO CLOSE

After this week Cowes and East Cowes will be without a cinema. The decision to close The Royalty at Cowes was announced in the following statement by Mr. P. J. Milsom, manager of I.W. Theatres, Ltd., on Wednesday: "The directors of I.W. Theatres, Ltd., have reluctantly decided to close the Royalty Cinema, Cowes, at the end of this week owing to lack of support." The Royalty, Cowes, was the oldest of the remaining Island cinemas and the only existing cinema in the Cowes area since the Kings Cinema at East Cowes was closed some years ago and later purchased by Saunders-Roe for an extension to their premises. The Royalty was built just after the first world war and I.W. Theatres, Ltd., purchased it from Cowes Cinema, Ltd., in 1924.

THE WEEK'S NEWS

FOUND £1000 - £2 REWARD — A Cowes schoolboy, Roger Gallagher, aged 10, a pupil of Denmark Road School, who found a black handbag containing cash and securities worth £1000 in the street received a reward for his honesty from the grateful owner of £2! He took the bag to show his mother who looked inside and found a considerable sum of money. With Roger, she immediately went to Cowes Police Station and while the contents were being checked the owner, a middle-aged woman visitor, from Chiswick, came in. After the bag had been handed to her, with its contents intact, she gave the boy £2 reward.

A BBC television programme on Wednesday, entitled "Divided Island," presented the question which will be discussed by the County Council next week. Should there be a bridge or tunnel between the Island and the mainland?

FIREARMS AMNESTY — There are only four more days before the Home Office firearms' amnesty ends. The Government have asked that all persons possessing firearms or ammunition without licences should hand them in by October 31st. In the Island 152 weapons and 5900 rounds of ammunition have been surrendered. The weapons include 18 rifles, 130 pistols and automatic hand guns, two shotguns and two Verey pistols.

COWES BROADCASTER ORDERED TO REST — Cliff Michelmore, the Cowes born television broadcaster has been ordered to rest and is temporarily to leave the popular BBC "Tonight" feature because of exhaustion caused by the strain of too much television work. Viewers have missed his cheerful smile since Monday, and on Wednesday he stated that he could not say when he would return to the programme. The doctor had told him he would have to slow up and had given him sedatives.

Fifty-three years after the original thatching with Norfolk reeds, St Agnes Church, Freshwater Bay is to be re-thatched with reeds from abroad, as they can no longer be obtained from Norfolk.

COUNTY COUNCIL BUY FORMER RAILWAY TRACKS — With only the voice of Mr. F.W. Long raised against the proposal, the Council on Wednesday agreed to buy the former railway tracks from Newport to Freshwater and Newport to Sandown for £2925, plus fees of £58 16s. Mr. Long asked what use would the land be to the council as it was overgrown. The ditches were filling in, and before long he thought there would be trouble over flooding neighbouring land.

Alderman Russell, a Newport shopkeeper, entertained the Newport Rotary Club with childhood memories of the town ...

December 30th, 1961

REMINISCENCES OF NEWPORT

Alderman G. C. Russell, J.P., a past president of Newport Rotary Club, amused members at a recent luncheon when he talked about the Newport he could remember from his boyhood days. The town was quite a different place, with gravel roads and crossings; rates at 2s. 3d. in the pound and no County Council! He recalled the four-horse coaches thundering down Snooks Hill into the town, and the post horn being sounded as they broke into a gallop past his shop on the return journey. There were no buses, the mail was carried by mail cart, and Queen Victoria, when in residence in the summer, frequently drove into town as far as St. James's Square. Boys at King James I school wore Eton Jackets and mortar boards; the river then was a pleasant place, the quay only extending as far as Messrs. Sharpe's on the town side, with nothing on the Little London side. The business hub of the town was then at the Coppins Bridge end of the High Street. There were many taverns which no longer exist - the Salisbury Arms on the site of Messrs. Duke's; the Globe where the ice factory now stands — the Coopers' Arms, Victoria Inn, White Lion, Valiant Soldier, Green Dragon, and the King Charles.

Beer was then 2d. a pint; one tavern had a room as a barber's shop where a shave was a penny and a hair cut 2d. The farm people came into town on the cheap services run by the railways and did their shopping. He could remember no shoes being sold, but plenty of heavily studded boots hung from boards in the shop doorways, with cards of corn cures in between! The sailing vessels which plied between Newport and Southampton gave a fine service. He could give an order for supplies for his shop on the Monday to the skipper of a vessel, and the goods would be there on the Wednesday. It was a better service than could be had from British Transport to-day.

The bridge at the bottom of the town was tested every Monday. It was a wooden structure and two engines coupled together were driven on to it. Men with a long pole measured how much the bridge gave. Everyone was up and about at 6 a.m. The mills were working at Blackwater, Shide, Pan, Home, and Westminster. They were colourful days, with teams of heavy horses with their jingling harness coming into town. He had seen horses go over the quay into the Medina, and some charge into shop windows. People were more religious. He recalled a local preacher and a farmer talking. "If it weren't Sunday I'd have asked you what the price of hay was in Newport yesterday," and the local preacher's reply, "If it wasn't Sunday I'd have told you it was £3 10s. a ton."

TOWN AND COUNTY NOTES

At Freshwater a two-year-old cat killed and carried home a 10-inch stoat — one of the fiercest wild animals in this country.

While on holiday at Lynmouth last week, Mr. P. Oakley (Yarmouth piermaster) was delighted to hear a party of strangers in the hotel talking about the amenities of the Isle of Wight, and speaking with particular appreciation of the fact that all public car parks in the Island are free.

PAID FOR ITS KEEP ! — The staff of Messrs. S. Guy, Ltd., of Newport, are trying to trace the owner of a pullet which was found wandering in the street outside their shop in Pyle Street on Saturday. They have been feeding and housing the bird, a Light Sussex, and each morning it has laid an egg.

AVERAGE FIVE-YEAR-OLD HAS SIX BAD TEETH — A recent survey carried out on children in Island schools,shows that the average five-year-old has six bad teeth; the average 13-year-old has eight permanent teeth either decayed, extracted or flled.

Peter Groves (17), of Cowes Youth Club was selected to play for England against Wales in a National Assoclation of Boys' Clubs football match at Cardiff.

Vectensis writes, "I recently spent a most interesting afternoon with Mr. A. F. Spencer at his residence, Westover, Ward Avenue, Cowes, looking at a remarkable collection of Victorian treasures which he possesses. Mr. Spencer's father (Mr. J. H. Spencer) was for many years employed as the estate carpenter and joiner at Osborne, and, in fact, was the last to look at the dead Queen's face when he performed the sad duty of screwing down the lid of the coffin."

1962

Two Island castles disappeared in the first years of the 1960s. By the end of the decade attitudes had changed and it may well be that the demolition would not have been allowed if they had survived just a few years longer. The first to go was East Cowes Castle. It had passed through various hands since the Vereker family had sold the estate in 1933, and it was now owned by Arthur Guy, a local businessman. He wrote to tell County Press readers how he had submitted what he thought were imaginative plans for the sensitive redevelopment of the estate, only to have the necessary planning permission refused. It was the end for the castle ...

January 6th, 1962
East Cowes Castle
As I was the last private person to own it I was very pleased to see the photograph of East Cowes Castle in the last issue of the County Press.* East Cowes Castle was built to the instruction of John Nash, the designer of Regent Street and Buckingham Palace, and of local interest, Newport Guildhall, completed in 1796. He resided there until his death in 1835, when he was buried at St James's churchyard East Cowes. The Castle then passed through the hands of the Earl of Shannon, R. Harwell, R.C.J. Sawder, Geo Tudor and finally Lady Gort, who died there in 1935. It was then purchased by a syndicate of business men in Cowes and just before the war I believe it was opened for inspection by visitors. During the war it was occupied by troops of various types and that started its period of destruction which has finally brought it to its present pitiable state. After the war the owners sold all the lead, copper, valuable wood partitions, etc, and then, in the late 50s the magnificent cedars were cut down from the hillside facing Cowes, and so the castle came into full view of York Avenue and provided a background to East Cowes from the harbour. Originally, the place combined the features of a mansion with that of a baronial-type fortress of a much earlier date and some of the rooms were fitted out in magnificent style, the library and the picture gallery especially. The conservatory was one of the largest in the south, being about 250 feet in length and the gardens and lawns were really beautiful, the whole place full of character. I purchased the place in 1958 with the intention of tidying it up, grouting the cracked and broken walls to make them safe, restoring the gardens to something like order and generally making it into a place of beauty and interest to visitors to the town. The coach proprietors were very interested. There was also to be an 18-hole pitch and putt golf course, a bathing and paddling pool, all to be open to the public, but I also wanted to build some self-contained red cedarwood bungalows for summer letting but the scheme did not meet with the approval of the powers that be, so I sold the place.

East Cowes will now lose the castle and will acquire a housing estate.
ARTHUR GUY. Barton Manor, East Cowes.

◆

Readers of previous volumes in this series will know that in every age, Victorian included, the Island has always suffered from anti-social behaviour. In the 1890s, cattle were mutilated at night in the fields where they stood, and concrete slabs were placed on railway tracks in the path of oncoming trains. During the 1920s, no bench on any of the Island's piers was safe from vandals, with many of them ending up in the sea, and in the 1930s, beach hut owners were constantly counting the cost of damage to their property.

Vandalism, in all its shapes and forms, was not just a product of the 1960s ...

Feb 24th, 1962
WANTON DAMAGE COSTS RYDE HUNDREDS OF POUNDS
SERIOUS PROBLEM FOR COUNCIL AND POLICE
Vandalism is a national problem and the Island has not escaped. In Ryde and the eastern end of the Island, where I work for the "County Press," vandalism

---

* See photograph, page 53.

(hooliganism) has been widespread and is on the increase. Particularly in the summer months when presumably the local offenders are joined by fellow-thinkers from the mainland, hardly a day goes by without some incident finding its way into Ryde Police Station's occurrence book.

COST TO RATEPAYERS

From a purely financial point of view, Ryde Town Council, and therefore the ratepayers, are out of pocket by several hundreds of pounds each year because of the attacks on public property. Shelters, seats, shrubs, lavatories, lawns, livestock; they have all come in for some kind of "attention" by the people whose hobby is destruction. One frightening aspect of the whole horrid business is that these outbreaks of violence are not done on the spur of the moment. It is not a question of a group of light-hearted young people suddenly deciding on a "jape" to round off a happy day. The outbreaks are planned with the cold, calculating mind of a criminal. Heavy iron seats from Ryde Esplanade have been found in the sea with concrete bases still intact. A crow-bar or some other heavy instrument would have to have been used to have carried out that little piece of engineering.

SPECIAL INSTRUMENT

Mr W. Rowbotham (Ryde's borough surveyor) startled even the most vandal-conscious councillor at one meeting last summer when he announced that a special instrument had been created by one gang of thugs to operate one of their favourite lavatory tricks. This instrument, several feet long, and specially hooked at the end, was used to force paper, rags, and on occasions locks from lavatory doors into the U bends of water closets. That was one of the popular pastimes last summer, but to break the monotony of making water closets useless, they also amused themselves by unscrewing the coin-in-the-slot machines from doors and wrenching paper towel machines from the walls.

On very few occasions do the police receive reports of money having been stolen from lavatory machines. Apparently it is satisfaction enough to see a piece of metal hanging by one screw from splintered woodwork.

Red road lamps left by council workmen at night are another target. If by any chance the gangs are lucky enough to find road lamps near the sea front these are immediately hurled out to sea. But inland they have been content in the past just to smash them or blow out the flame, expecting, presumably, what must be to them the encouraging spectacle of a motor-cyclist or motorist crashing unsuspectingly into a hole in the road.

ANIMALS ALSO SUFFER

At Puckpool Park last summer it was the turn of the animals to suffer. Birds who had become so friendly that they would eat out of a person's hand were pulled from their cages. A beautiful golden pheasant was missing from its pen one morning. It was found a few yards away smashed to a pulp. It had been beaten to death by someone who found entertainment by dashing the bird's brains out on a brick wall. It is natural for people to ask "What are the police doing about it?" The answer is as much as they possibly can. Inspector F. L. Allan said: "The results so far, compared with what has been done, are trifling. We have prosecuted in the case of a person smashing an electric light bulb, and two juveniles were brought to court for causing damage to a beach hut ...

It was still possible to find locally made lobster pots in the early 1960s ...

February 10th, 1962

AN ISLANDER'S NOTES
[By VECTENSIS]

One of the few remaining experts in the craft of lobster and crab-pot making is Mr. William Eldridge, of Puckwell Cottage, Niton, who at 75, still turns out 20-25 pots during the winter.* He has been making pots for 30 years from withy, grown by himself at the bottom of his back garden, firstly as a spare-time occupation - he is a gardener - and since his retirement, as a winter pastime. There is a greater demand for his pots than he can meet and he has regular customers. His particular kind of pot is well-known as he weaves the withy "against the sun," instead of the more popular left-to-right method and says that this gives the baskets added strength. For a man of his years and occupation he has wonderfully flexible hands and strong wrists and, even more remarkable, he has never suffered from rheumatism. Sitting outside his back door in the sun, busily engaged in his craft, Mr. Eldridge said, "I started doing this when I was earning half-a-crown a week and I had to turn my hand to something to help towards raising our family of five. Now I do it to help out the pension. I would rather do it as long as I can use my hands than ask for National Assistance." In these days of dying crafts Mr. Eldridge has commendably taught one of his sons to make pots, so the family tradition and skill will continue.

———————————◆———————————

A full history of the forts and barracks scattered across the Island is yet to be written. For the most part, the buildings which at one time housed thousands of soldiers, have disappeared without a trace and only the closure of Albany Barracks and Fort Victoria appear to have been reported by the County Press. Luckily, the departure of the last soldiers from the Island was reported ...

February 24th, 1962.

ARMY SAYS FAREWELL TO THE ISLAND
R. A. S. C. LEAVING THE WEST WIGHT

The Waterborne Training Company of the R.A.S.C., which has been stationed at Golden Hill Fort, Freshwater, and Fort Victoria, Yarmouth, for the last 16 years, said goodbye to the West Wight with a ceremonial parade on Thursday. When the last troops depart next month, the Island will be left without a regular military garrison for the first time in nearly 300 years ... The proceedings were filmed by BBC and Southern Television cameramen and the effect of the departure of the troops on the Island in general was also discussed in the BBC programme "Round up," ... Since coming to the Island in 1946, the vessels of the R.A.S.C. Fleet have operated from Yarmouth Harbour and from the jetty at Fort Victoria, where the old gun casements have been used as classrooms for training in marine engineering, seamanship and navigation. These "classrooms" still contain the fitted ring bolts for muzzle-loading gun tackles!

The closure of the two forts is a matter of deep concern to some members of the civilian staff although all have been offered alternative employment on the mainland. Eight of them have been retained to keep a day and night watch on the

* See photograph, page 53.

forts to prevent any recurrence of the wanton damage which followed the closure of nearby Cliff End Fort, where every pane of glass has been shattered, and doors, window frames, and flooring have been taken away. The spending power of the troops during the off-season periods will also be missed by tradespeople ... The last of the troops in the Island will leave next month ...

NEWS IN BRIEF

COWES YOUTH RECEIVES CALL-UP PAPERS — Robert Pieton, of Oak Trees, Egypt Hill, Cowes, received a registered letter on Monday. Inside was a note in French asking him to fill in the enclosed forms for call-up in the French army! Robert who is 18 in three weeks time, was born in Cowes and works as a spot welder operator at Messrs. Readers factory at Somerton. His father is of French origin but came to live in this country in 1940 and obtained British naturalisation in 1957 ... His father said the mistake must have occurred because when his son was born he had not then changed his nationality and Robert's birth was registered at the French Consulate.

A prisoner at Parkhurst won a £5 prize on ITV's "Take a Letter" programme on Wednesday. A spokesman at the prison said afterwards "Prisoners are allowed to go in for competitions with small prizes and they are allowed to keep up to £10. Naturally, they cannot go in for competitions where the prize is a short tour of Italy, or something like that."

"JOBS FOR ALL IF SOME ARE PREPARED TO CHANGE" — Alderman Mark Woodnutt, MP, speaking last Friday said, "Since last December at Messrs. J. Samuel White and Co., 636 men had been made redundant. This meant over a quarter of £1 million of spending power suddenly removed ... White's did not obtain the recent order for a frigate because they were not the lowest tender ... It was up to trade unions and managements to sort out their various problems - to have one union instead of 23, and to stop demarcation and restrictive practices.

Some of the idle lads of Wroxall have devised a new way of creating a nuisance. Piling bicycles together at the curb, one or two lie on the bank and another stands in the road flagging down any unsuspecting motorist. When a motorist stops, thinking there has been an accident, they take to their heels and leave him wondering "How stupid can the youths of today become?"

Former editor, Walter Sibbick, repository of Island miscellany, wrote of Pyle Street traders over the last 200 years ...

May 5th, 1962

AN ISLANDER'S NOTES
[By VECTENSIS]

Two of the oldest businesses in the Island - one the oldest in England - face each other across central Pyle Street, Newport. On the south side stands the imposing imitation Tudor facade of the offices of Messrs. Upward and Rich, Ltd., whose wholesale grocery business was founded by one of the Upward family in 1658. Opposite, at No. 114, are the premises of Arthur Wood, Ltd., ironmongers and agricultural and horticultural implement dealers, whose history goes back for over 200 years, although they do not claim establishment until 1792. It is known that an ironmongery business was operated there in 1760 and that one of its proprietors before the late Messrs. J. and H. Wood acquired it early in the 19th century, was Robert Bird Wilkins, who also conducted a banking business, and whose name is perpetuated in one of the best known Isle of Wight token coins. I have a well-preserved specimen of this token dated 1792, which bears the issuer's profile, the Vectis ship arms, and the words "Isle of Wight Half-penny." These tokens (used for small change) were minted at various dates until Wilkins' death in 1815. The business has since been carried on under the titles of Wood and Sons (one of the sons being the late Arthur Wood, a well-known Newportonian and sportsman who managed it for many years), Wood and Horspool, Wood and Tame, and its present title. In recent years the business has been conducted by the late Mr. Arthur Wood, Jr., and Mr. Eustace Wood (the present managing director). It has kept abreast of the times in all its phases and holds an estimable position among the many old-established concerns in the Island capital.

TOWN AND COUNTY NOTES

ISLE OF WIGHT RADIO — In an improvised studio in Newport, "Radio Wight" will go on the air next week.* From Thursday to Saturday, from early morning until late at night, programmes of news and information, discussions, and music will be broadcast, but only those in the studio will hear them; this is the latest of the B.B.C.'s experiments in public service local broadcasting on closed circuit. Programmes giving the latest news and information of many kinds, weather, shipping movements, tides, roads, employment prospects - will be followed by magazine programmes in which many Islanders will take part. (March 31st)

LAST TROOPS LEAVE FRESHWATER — The last troops left Golden Hill and Victoria forts, Freshwater, on Saturday, and teams of civilian employees are maintaining a 24-hour guard over the properties to prevent any repetition of the wanton damage caused immediately the nearby Cliff End Fort was vacated. (April 7th)

The motor taxation department have commenced the issue of the registration letters YDL. (May 5th)

RYDE FIRST WITH S.T.D — The new Mayor of Ryde (Mr. W.G.F. Sutton) will make the first call on May 28th at a special ceremony to mark the official opening t Ryde telephone exchange of the subscriber trunk dialling system. Of the 66

---

* Not to be confused with today's Isle of Wight Radio, who took to the air in 1990.

exchanges in the Portsmouth telephone manager's area, Ryde is the first to go over to the new system, which it is hoped to introduce at Newport early next year. The changeover at Ryde takes place at 9 a.m. on May 27th, and from then on, subscribers will be able to dial numbers in London and many cities and towns throughout Britain. (May 5th)

SWALLOWS RE-HOUSED — A swallow's nest, containing four fledglings, collapsed and fell from the roof of the home of Mr. S. Pullen, at 34 Mill Hill Road, Cowes. He collected the remains of the battered nest and placed them inside a flower pot. After putting the fledglings into their new home he erected the pot near the site of the old nest. The following day Mr. Pullen was delighted to see that the parent birds had returned to their young.

———————————◆———————————

On a foggy Sunday afternoon in May, a Dakota airliner with 14 passengers on board was travelling from Guernsey to Portsmouth in near zero visibility. As it approached the Island, the pilot radioed that he was descending from 3000 to 1000 feet, but for reasons which remain unclear to this day, he descended to nearer 700 feet and as a direct result, crashed head-on into St Boniface Down. The pilot appears to have seen the danger at the last moment and had put the Dakota into an upwards climb, but it was too late. The plane struck the down at 160 miles an hour and the upwards momentum was so great that the plane careered on up the slope for 250 yards, eventually coming to rest 74 feet higher than the original point of impact ...

May 12th, 1962
HOLIDAY AIRLINER CRASHES ON ST BONIFACE DOWN
TEN KILLED IN INFERNO
WROXALL MAN'S HEROISM

A Dakota carrying 14 passengers and a crew of three crashed in thick fog on the 785 feet high St Boniface Down, Ventnor, on Sunday and was completely destroyed. Two of the crew and eight passengers were killed and the remainder sustained serious injuries. Prompt action by a Wroxall farm worker, Mr. Edward Price, and the efficiency of all the emergency services saved some of those on the aircraft, but little could be done for those trapped in the inferno.

CRASHED IN RAF COMPOUND

The plane, a Dakota DC 3, was on a scheduled flight from Guernsey and Jersey to Portsmouth and Southend and left Jersey airport at 2.55 p.m. After calling at Guernsey it commenced the journey to Portsmouth. As far as can be ascertained the crash occurred about three quarters of an hour later. The last radio message from the aircraft stated that the pilot, in preparation for landing, was descending from 3000 to 1000 feet. In actual fact he was considerably lower in the fog and struck the down above Combe Bottom immediately above Ventnor railway station, crashed through the mesh wire fencing on the southern boundary of the RAF compound, tearing an eight feet wide gap, bounced forward about 200 yards and then tore a swathe of about the same distance through the gorse and

CASTLE SITE FOR HOMES

This is all that remains of East Cowes Castle, which being demolished to make way for a modern housing estate of 250 houses and bungalows." eptember 29) [IWCP]

"Mr. William Eldridge, (75) of Puckwell Cottage, Niton, who has made lobster and crab pots for 50 years. He grows the withies in his back garden and makes about 25 pots each winter." [IWCP]

STEEPHILL CASTLE - "QUEEN OF THE UNDERCLIFF."

development of the estate for residential purposes will be welcomed as a solution to the em of a rapidly deteriorating area at the western end of the town." (Nov 10) [IWCP]

undergrowth, leaving a scorched trail of debris. The plane came to rest about 100 yards from the northern perimeter of the compound. Only the tailplane and parts of the wings remained intact. Wreckage, including the burning engines, was scattered over a wide area. Strewn boxes of Channel Island flowers, mainly blue and white irises, together with personal belongings, bore a poignant testimony to the disaster. Four Ventnor doctors answered the distress call and supplies of morphia and other emergency aids were hastily made available. As the ambulancemen and their helpers went about their grim task, police and others scoured the vicinity for further victims following information that there were at least 21 people in the aircraft. The firemen concentrated on extinguishing smouldering parts of the plane as they helped in the search and stood by until all bodies were removed.

ALL NIGHT WATCH

Ironically, the weather cleared in the evening and motorists poured into the area from all parts of the Island. At one time there were over 50 cars parked near the compound fencing and a constant stream of pedestrians toiled up the downs all the evening. It was only as darkness fell that the stream of sightseers dwindled.

First on the scene and the hero of the rescue operations was Mr. Edward Price, a farm worker, of 2 Castle Road, Wroxall, who was on the downs with his dog cutting bean sticks. As he entered the RAF compound two men staggered towards him out of the mist, badly burned, and muttering "air crash, air crash." Mr. Price raced towards the blazing inferno and regardless of his own safety helped passengers who had been thrown clear from the wreckage.

"It was pretty terrible and I duly did what I could. I pulled two girls from the wreckage and the others were all staggering nearby, terribly injured. I found an elderly lady sitting on the grass with a leg injury, moaning for her husband. I put her with the others and told her not to worry, everything would be all right. I also got the stewardess out and helped another man nearby." Realising the urgent need for all possible help Mr. Price ran down the lane. He found members of the Northampton Shortwave Radio Club taking part in a communications exercise with a Civil Defence signals unit. They put out a distress call for emergency services and in a few moments, five ambulances, fire officers and police were on their way from all parts of the Island ... and within minutes the first two injured men were on their way to hospital at Ryde.

EFFICIENT ORGANISATION

The grim task of recovering the dead from the charred and smouldering wreckage was carried out by police, firemen, and ambulancemen. The bodies were covered with tarpaulins until they were removed by Messrs. H. Ingram and Sons to the South Street Mission Hall, at Newport. Some of the irises were placed in the hall. The pilot was captain Philip Diesbach-Belleroche (36), of Essex and the first officer was Eric Fitzackerley (37), of Thorpe Bay, Essex. Both were killed. The other member of the crew, Stewardess Pamela Groves (21), of Leigh on Sea, Essex, staggered from the wreckage terribly injured and died from severe burns late on Thursday night.

DEAD AND INJURED

Of the 14 passengers, eight were killed, Mr. Frederick Marks (59), of Southsea Mrs Susan Gardner (25), of Camberley, Surrey, and her two children, Peter (two and David (eight months); John Vernall (21), of Lee on Solent, returning from honeymoon in Jersey with his wife, Wendy, who was among the survivors; and Leading Seaman George Boucher (25), of Portsmouth and his 18-month-old son Lee. (His wife, Brenda, was seriously injured and is desperately ill at Odstock Hospital). Also killed was Miss Marilyn Drew, aged 17, of Gosport.

Police officers completed their search of the wreckage for personal belongings on Thursday. The investigation by Ministry of Aviation and company officials which began on Monday was nearing completion yesterday. Relatives and friends of the victims and the injured have been visiting Mr. Price at his Wroxall home to thank him, and have also visited the scene of the crash.

◆

Islanders had recently learned to their relief that a nuclear power station would not be built at Hamstead. Now, two years on, a scheme was afoot to locate a huge marina at the equally remote King's Quay. The developers insisted the marina would be discreetly screened, but as one reader pointed out in a letter to the County Press, quite how a yachtsmen's village of over 200 acres could be hidden away, was a mystery ...

July 14th, 1962

PROPOSED MARINA FOR KING'S QUAY
FACILITIES FOR HELICOPTERS, HOVERCRAFT AND WATER TAXIS

A proposal to construct a marina and yachtsmen's village at Kings Quay, Whippingham, has been submitted to the County Planning Committee for outline approval. The proposal is to enclose 40 acres of tidal water at Kings Quay to create a yacht haven for up to 500 yachts and cabin cruisers with "plug" amenities for lighting, fuel, watering, telephone, and modern drainage. Hidden behind the trees would be a yachtsmen's village of some 204 acres with community and shopping centres, club and recreation facilities. In addition, to foster the development of modern transport - helicopters, hovercraft and water taxis - facilities would be discreetly provided so that the whole site would be barely visible from the sea from a distance of three-quarters of a mile ... The site suggested comprises an area of grazing land bounded by a sea frontage of nearly 2000 feet adjoining Kings Quay to the north, and Brocks Copse Road to the south, enclosed to the east by Woodhouse Copse, and to the west by land attached to Barton Manor. The area could be extended to include additional frontage and land attached to Barton Manor, in cooperation with the new owner Mr. A. G. Figgins, if the demand was there ... Kings Quay is in the sheltered waters of Osborne Bay on the north-east coast of the Island. It stands at the mouth of a miniature estuary once known as King's Creek but now known as Palmer's Brook. Kings Quay was the eastern extremity of the estate created by Queen Victoria and was once the termination of the Royal coastal carriage drive from Osborne, through Barton Manor, and the developers plan to reopen this access road along the foreshore, retaining the Cliff Copse screen of trees ... The development is aimed at preserving the natural beauty of the area. There are no public rights of way over the estate so the scheme would allow yachtsmen to share the peace and tranquillity of the area ...

NEWS IN BRIEF

HOVERCRAFT SERVICE STARTS AT RYDE — The world's second hovercraft service began at Ryde on Monday, when the Westland SRN 2 made three round trips between Ryde and Southsea with paying passengers ... They were given souvenir tickets and illustrated brochures of the hovercraft. The craft has been fully booked for the three round trips each day this week. (August 18)

FUTURE OF THE OLD MILL AT WOOTTON — The development of the old mill at Wootton Bridge has caused a lot of speculation in the village, with rumours ranging from a botel to a nightclub. But the mill, which was sold recently, will be pulled down and if planning permission is given, developed as a terrace of eight yachtsmen's houses. (September 1.)

A single tomato plant standing 6' 6" high, grown by Mr. A. E. Brown of Binstead Nurseries, yielded 83 lb. of tomatoes.

FOUR CINEMAS CLOSING — Four Cinemas will close next Saturday after the evening performances. They are the Regent, Freshwater; the Rex, Ventnor; the Queens, Sandown; and the Scala, Ryde, all owned by I. W. Theatres, Ltd. The cinemas which remain open are the Commodore, Ryde, and the Medina and Savoy, Newport. In addition there are two privately-owned cinemas - the Regal, Shanklin, and Rivoli, Sandown. (September 22.)

A bulge the size of a cricket ball which developed in the two-inch thick surface of tarmacadam in Weston Road, Totland Bay, on Friday week was caused by a growing mushroom which finally forced its way through on Monday.

———————————◆———————————

The inquest into the St Boniface Down air crash had taken place. The findings were inconclusive beyond the fact that for some unknown reason the pilot had descended far below the 1000 feet he had intended, putting the plane on a direct collision course with the down. Inevitably, pilot error was mentioned by some of those giving evidence, something still denied to this day on websites devoted to the event * ...

September 29th, 1962

ST BONIFACE DOWN AIR CRASH
MISADVENTURE VERDICT AT INQUEST

A verdict of death by misadventure was recorded by the jury at the resumed inquest at the Guild Hall, Newport, on Wednesday, on the two members of the crew and eight passengers who were killed when the Dakota aircraft in which they were travelling from Jersey to Portsmouth, crashed in thick mist on St Boniface Down, Ventnor, on May 6 ... The coroner sat with Mr. R. H. Garnons-Williams, senior inspector of accidents, Ministry of Aviation, as assessor ... Mr. Garnons-Williams said the plane took off from Jersey Airport at 2.54 p.m ... a number of messages were passed between the plane and London Air Traffic Control. Permission was given for the aircraft to let down from 3000 feet to 1000 feet and after the pilot had acknowledged the message nothing was heard until a few

---

* See www.farvis.com/ventnor2

minutes later when the plane was reported to have crashed at Ventnor, 16 miles from Portsmouth, where it was due to land. Replying to the Coroner, Mr. Garnons-Williams said he was satisfied that the machine was in airworthy condition ... The pilot was experienced and qualified to take the flight and the first officer was qualified to act as co-pilot ... The weather during the first part of the journey was quite clear, but near the south coast it was thick down to the sea with visibility occasionally less than 100 yards. There were no radio or navigation facilities at Portsmouth ... If the aircraft had remained at 1000 feet it would have cleared St Boniface Down, which is just under 800 feet.

James Herbert Lett, a senior investigating officer of the accident staff, said the aircraft was in a slightly nose-up attitude and had been travelling at 158 mph. After striking the down, it slid a further 250 yards and came to rest some 74 feet higher than the point of impact. It was severely damaged. Both engines were torn off, the fuselage was broken open and it was destroyed by fire ... Sydney Walsh DSO, DFC, chief pilot of Channel Airways, asked by the coroner what he thought might have happened said, "I am the chief pilot and also a practising pilot and it is with considerable diffidence that I express an opinion. It is my opinion, and I'm fairly convinced that it is the right one," ... Capt Walsh then stated that in reducing height, the aircraft would drop at about 500 feet a minute and in approximately 4 minutes would have covered 12 miles. There would seem to be some error of judgement as far as the pilot was concerned but he had known Capt Diesbach-Belleroche since he had been with the company and the whole thing was out of character. He was a meticulous pilot. His own investigation led him in no way to find any fault with the first officer and whatever happened must be attributed to the pilot ... His company would like navigational aids at Portsmouth. Whatever the position at Portsmouth on that day, it would not have had any effect on the accident. Answering questions, Capt Walsh said there was not the slightest danger in flying over the Island. They had done it hundreds of times and no danger existed providing one realised that St Boniface Down was 780 feet high. Once the pilot decided to let down from 3000 feet to 1000 feet, he had started a course which showed that he did not intend to use the instrument let down procedure ... In continuing to let down, the pilot did about the most dangerous thing he could have done. "My opinion is that he saw the ground looming up and banged on power and started to turn - all in a matter of seconds. I can find no explanation why the accident happened."

SURVIVOR'S HARROWING EXPERIENCE

Henry Delamere Davin of Jersey said that although take-off at Jersey was delayed there was nothing unusual about the plane. The weather was bright and sunny at take-off. When they were in the plane the hostess said they hoped to land at Portsmouth, but if not, they would land at Southend.

"I was reading a newspaper the whole time, but later I detected that the engine note had changed as if the pilot had increased speed. I looked out and there was thick cloud. I had an idea that the plane was on a slight decline and it was only a minute or two before the impact. I thought it was strange to be going down at that speed. Suddenly there was an almighty crash. I stood up and held the seat in front as rocks underneath were tearing out the fuselage. There was a big explosion as we careered up the hill and I was pitched forward. When everything had stopped, and

I might have been out for a moment or two, I came round and found both feet through the floor of the plane. I looked around and could not hear or see anyone. It was quiet apart from the fire burning. A few flames were behind me and I fell down a couple of times before lying on my side and pulled myself out and up the small incline....

JURY'S RIDER

After nearly an hour's deliberation, the jury returned a verdict of death by misadventure in respect of all the victims. They added a rider that radio communication facilities should be installed at Portsmouth without delay.*

TOWN AND COUNTY NOTES

MYSTERY MISSILE AT COWES — Cowes police are investigating a flying object which smashed through the roof and ceiling of a Southern Gas Board store room in Arctic Road, Cowes, on Monday. It was discovered deeply embedded in the wooden floor ... The body was about 20 inches in length and 3 inches in diameter. Three fins had been spot-welded onto the tail end which appeared to have been subjected to intense heat, indicating that it had possibly reached a high speed and height and could have travelled for about a mile. The object, which was home made, was taken away by the Salisbury bomb disposal unit for examination.

Despite the heavy rain storms which followed the November 5 celebrations on Monday, the remains of the giant bonfire built on the Common at Yarmouth continued to smoulder into the early hours of the following Thursday.

There has been no trace of 23 black-faced ewes and lambs found to be missing over a week ago from a flock at Hebberdens Land, near Shalfleet, owned by Mr. W.E. Maddocks, of New Farm, Nunwell.

Two naval ratings who found 6s. 3d. on the coin box in the telephone kiosk near the Freemasons Hotel, Ventnor, left the money with the licensee (Mr. G. Burton) to be claimed.

Steephill Castle, the second of two castles to be demolished on the Island in the Sixties, was about to disappear. Times and attitudes were different and the demolition attracted just a few token protests. As the County Press had noted, "The development of the castle site into a housing estate was to be welcomed" ...

November 10th, 1962

STEEPHILL CASTLE - "QUEEN OF THE UNDERCLIFF."
DEMOLITION APPROVED FOR BUILDING DEVELOPMENT

News that Ventnor Council have no objection to the demolition of Steephill Castle for residential development marks the end of an important era in the history of the growth of the town from a tiny hamlet to the flourishing community it is today. The building of Steephill Castle 127 years ago coincided with the

---

* The Ministry of Aviation report into the crash was published in October 1963. It found the crash was caused by "an error of airmanship."

commencement of widespread development in Ventnor, starting with St Catherine's Parish Church. The Hambrough and Morgan Richards families especially, brought wealth and distinction to Steephill and Ventnor and the fortunes of the town prospered under their leadership. Although it is many years since Ventnorians looked to the castle to give the lead in local matters, many will have cause to remember with gratitude the influence those families had on the Island. The development of the estate for residential purposes will be welcomed as a solution to the problem of a rapidly deteriorating area at the western end of the town. This should enhance the building which has already been carried out on the site of the old Ventnor West railway station and at Steephill ... Mr. Hambrough commenced the building of the castle in 1833, but he lost his sight before it was finished in 1835 and never saw the final form of the beauty he created. The total cost of the castle and its furnishings, with the improvements effected on the estate, amounted to £250,000.

The accommodation included a grand hall with polished oak gallery staircase; a billiard room with ribbed oak ceiling; library and study, dining room with black marble chimney piece; drawing rooms with panelled oak ceilings and all the offices on the ground floor, including servants' hall, kitchens and pantries. To the south east of the entrance drive, on the opposite side of the road, were the extensive stabling and carriage houses with coachman's and gardener's half-timbered residences. The extensive grounds and gardens were one of the greatest pleasures of Steephill in Victorian and Edwardian times. Copper beech, white and pink chestnuts, cedars, yews, magnolia, myrtles and rhododendrons abounded. A feature of the west front, on the edge of the lawn, was the scallop shell basin filled from a natural spring. The walks within the grounds extended over three miles. There were fields where cricket, football and golf could be played and in one clump of trees a rookery existed for many years. Other features included a spacious conservatory and indoor swimming baths.

The Morgan Richards family purchased the estate in 1903 ... Mrs. Morgan Richards died in August, 1914, and her husband in August, 1918. They were the last private family owners of Steephill Castle. After being empty for several years the castle was bought as a holiday home by the Friendship Holidays Association and over the succeeding years many hundreds of holidaymakers have enjoyed its splendour and surroundings. It was last used by the FHA three years ago. During the early part of the last war the castle was occupied for a time by the Ventnor Council (Leeson Road) School. Now it is rapidly becoming derelict - a decaying monument to a past era.*

———————————◆———————————

In the early days of the telephone, most Island towns and villages had their own manual telephone exchange. Switchboards were installed in the home of someone in the locality willing to take on the task of manning the switchboard virtually day and night to connect every call by hand. They were now rapidly being replaced by automatic ones, the last manual exchange to go being Ventnor in 1969. In Wootton, telephone customers had been faithfully served by Mr and Mrs Smith who had shared their High Street sitting room with a GPO switchboard since the late 1920s but their days of asking, "number please," had finally come to an end ...

---

* See photograph page 53.

November 10th, 1962
AUTOMATIC TELEPHONE EXCHANGE FOR WOOTTON

The Mayor of Newport (Ald. H. E. Harvey) was present on Thursday when Wootton's telephone service was switched to automatic. Serving 386 subscribers, the new system has cost £30,000. For 34 years the manual telephone exchange has been housed in what should have been the sitting-room of Mr. and Mrs. L. C. Smith, caretaker-operators, at 20 High Street.*

THE SWITCH-OVER

At 11 a.m. the busy scene became strangely quiet as Mr. K. A. Dubois (of the telephone manager's traffic staff), in telephonic touch with the new automatic exchange building about 100 yards further up the High Street, gave the order to cease taking manual calls and the switchover was accomplished.

The Mayor thanked Mr. and Mrs. Smith for their public service on behalf of all the subscribers who had enjoyed the very friendly way in which calls had been handled by the staff and recalled how on occasions a caller would be told "It's no use ringing that number yet, we have just seen Mrs. So-and-so going up the High Street. Give her 20 minutes and she will be home!" All that was very nice and friendly and they would miss it now that automation had taken over ... As the Mayor finished his speech Mrs. Clifford Matthews, of Fishbourne, walked into the exchange room and handed gifts to Mr. and Mrs. Smith, saying "This is a little thank you from just one of your many satisfied customers." ... Wootton subscribers will now be able to dial 61 other exchanges. They will now also have the 999 facility, plus access to the speaking clock, weather forecast, and, during the season, test cricket results from Southampton - all local calls ... A "County Press" reporter talked to Mr. and Mrs. Smith in their home at the rear of the exchange room. Mrs. Smith said that she could not imagine what life would be like with a sitting-room once again. When they first moved in the switchboard, with about 20 lines, it was installed in the kitchen. Then it was moved to a small room facing the High Street, across the passage from the sitting-room, where the manual switchboards have increased over the years as the traffic grew.

In their retirement they will not be linked to the outside world by telephone. "No, definitely not; we don't want to see one," said Mrs. Smith.

◆

Back in October, a home-made rocket had crashed through the roof of the Southern Gas Board building at Arctic Road, Cowes, narrowly missing the adjacent gas holder. Two months later the amateur scientists involved dropped in to Newport Magistrates' Court ...

December 1st, 1962
HOME-MADE ROCKET DAMAGED WAREHOUSE

Bryan T— (24), lathe operator of Cowes; Austin K— (20), crane driver, of Cowes; and Peter H— (21), unemployed fitter of Cowes were fined £5 each at the Magistrates' Court at Newport yesterday. They pleaded guilty to manufacturing a chlorate mixture at an unauthorised place. They pleaded not guilty to wilfully damaging a Southern Gas Board store to the extent of £20. A yellow and red metal rocket, about 20 inches long, was exhibited in the court. Detective Sgt Brown said that on October 1st a missile had buried itself in the floor of the Gas Board's

---

* Mr Smith died after only 18 days of retirement. In 2011, the cottage is home to the 'Wister Gallery.'

Well flown? Well sailed? NO – well hovered, the SRN 2

New as it is, the SRN 2 already has a brilliant past behind it. Currently, it's skimming over the Solent with even more success than the SRN 1. Designed to hover well—with 850 gallons of Shell aviation fuel in the tanks. Not to mention a double-decker busload of passengers. And the future? A whole science fiction galaxy of successors, sliding over rivers, swamps, seas or ice the world over. Shell will be there, too, ready to fuel the SRN 2's descendants—with as much efficiency as their forefather met. Both SRN 1 and SRN 2 are coated with paints based on Shell 'Epikote' resin for complete protection.

SRN 2. Up to 76 passengers or 8 tons of freight □ Over 80 m.p.h. □ All up weight 27 tons □ Turn-round time on beach with full load of passengers is as low as 3 minutes.

The SRN 2 was built by the Saunders-Roe Division of Westland Aircraft Ltd., in association with Hovercraft Development Ltd.

HOVER WELL — HOVER SHELL

warehouse after going through the roof and the first floor. When witness spoke to H— he admitted who were responsible. He said, "It was fired from the dump at the back of the cemetery. It went out of sight into the sky towards Cowes. We used a mixture of weedkiller and charcoal set off with a model aircraft jet fuse. We were all worried when we heard where it landed. We did not know whether to go to the police or wait to see if it blew over. We do not intend to experiment further." The missile missed a gas holder by 30 foot. T— said, "I am sorry. I must take the consequences. We got the idea from when we were at school."

1963

Some modern-day accounts of smuggling in bygone days are perhaps a little fanciful on occasion, so a first, or even second-hand account of smuggling from someone actually involved, makes a welcome change. This account from a member of the Buckett family, a name still well known in Brighstone, appears in full ...

January 5th, 1963

BRIGHSTONE SMUGGLERS
EARLY 19TH CENTURY EXPLOITS OF ISLAND FISHERMEN
(BY J.R. (Bob) BUCKETT)

For many years, up to the first half of the 19th century, smuggling of brandy from France was rife along the Channel coast of the Island. In spite of being outpaced by revenue cutters, and the constant watch of coastguards ashore, intrepid fishermen and farm workers, many of whom, be it remembered to their credit, afterwards became gallant lifeboatmen, risked life and liberty to bring spirits across from France for illicit disposal. In this way they added much-needed money to the meagre returns they got in those days for their legal labours. Generally speaking, their smuggling operations were carried out not so much to cheat the Revenue as to give their families a more comfortable existence. My grandfather, James Buckett, was one of the Brighstone band of smugglers and below I recount some of the stories of his activities which have come down to me in family records and otherwise.

BORN IN TRAFALGAR YEAR

My grandfather was born in April of Trafalgar year (1805). His father, Thomas, was caretaker of the barracks which formerly stood at Grange Chine, just to the westward of the old lifeboat house.

Soldiers were stationed there during the Napoleonic wars and before that one of my ancestors, Capt. Buckett, was in charge of the civilian coast watchers, local men who did duty to give warning of invasion by the French. Although his father was not a seafaring man, my grandfather took a great liking to the sea as a lad and spent his life until he was 82 fishing from Sudmore, about half-way between Chilton and Brook. Fishing then was not a very lucrative calling, so in his 'teens he decided to "Have a go at the tubs" — as the local smugglers referred to their bootlegging business.

With a mate he started making trips across the Channel to Barfleur, on the eas side of the Cherbourg Peninsula. They used a 20 foot wherry with a lugsail. When not used for smuggling she was tucked away in Newtown River. The wherry, named The Bet, could be rowed with long oars when there was no wind, and often on their cross-Channel trips the two men had to slog it out at the oars to make a safe landing.

This is how the "trade" was operated. A local resident, businessman or farmer would supply the capital — say £50 — which would buy 100 tubs of brandy. If the smugglers safely delivered the spirit to a pre-arranged hiding place they usually got 10s. a tub from the person who supplied the cash for the deal. In those days such money was riches indeed, and it is not surprising that poorly paid men took the risk.

IN "THE DARKS"

The tubs, each containing about three gallons of brandy, were already tied in pairs by the Frenchmen, with, a short rope between to go over the shoulder so that they could be more easily carried. It was in this way that they were handled after landing. The trips to France were arranged in "the darks," the period three days before and three days after a new moon. Sometimes the men were held up by the weather on the other side of the Channel and, missing "the darks," had to wait until the moonless nights came round again. On one occasion my grandfather was away so long for this reason that he was given up for lost and the good people of Brighstone made a collection for his wife and children. The donations had to be returned as he eventually turned up safe and sound!

BEATING THE REVENUE MEN

These smuggling trips were always an adventure. The perils and discomforts of making the voyage in a small, open boat can be imagined. The smugglers' only shelter was a piece of canvas from the stern to the mast, and when the crossing had been almost accomplished there was always the menace of the revenue cutters, constantly sailing up and down the Channel to intercept liquor-runners. If the returning smugglers saw a suspicious vessel in the distance they fixed a rope, called a girdle, round the gunwhale and the tubs were lashed to this. Then, if the other craft proved to be a revenue cutter they cut the girdle, which was weighted with stones, and the tubs sank. If they were unlucky enough to be in deep water at the time, the smugglers' trip was in vain, as the cargo was irretrievably lost. But usually they were near enough home before the danger of interception came, and were able to recover their sunken treasure by the use of grapnels. More often than not they came home undetected and with the aid of shore gangs the tubs were carried in the darkness to the hiding place. One such secret cache was the cottage and garden of William ("Bung") Russell, at Moortown, where the house known as Buddlebrook now stands.

CAUGHT AND CLEARED

When the coastguards were making things pretty hot for the smugglers, my grandfather thought discretion the better part of valour and decided to give up smuggling. It was not long, however, before some of his customers persuaded him to have another go. As their wherry had come under suspicion, he and his confederate went to France by the packet-boat from Southampton. They purchased the cargo and hired two Frenchmen to bring the tubs across in their three-masted lugger. It was an ill-starred venture however, as a revenue cutter challenged about five miles off St Catherine's. The girdle was cut and a chase followed to Chale Bay before the revenue men overhauled and boarded the French vessel. No visible evidence of smuggling remained, but the explanation that the Englishmen had lost their boat off the French coast and had hired the French craft to bring them home, was not accepted and the four men were taken to Winchester and tried on suspicion of smuggling. My grandfather and his mate were on tenterhooks that the Frenchmen would get flustered and let the cat out of the bag, but they stuck to the agreed explanation and the charge was dismissed.

NOT LUCKY AGAIN

A few years later grandfather was not so lucky. He had reluctantly agreed to take the place of another man on a trip across to France. The coastguards were waiting for them on their return and they were caught landing the tubs. When tried at Winchester he was sentenced to serve five years in the Navy - heavy punishment in those days when life in the warships was very hard ... Forced to leave his wife and two young children, he was away for four years and eight months, the last four months of his sentence being remitted for good conduct. He returned to his fishing and was never again tempted to take part in smuggling.

◆

In the last week of December 1962, the Island was struck by a blizzard. It was to be the forerunner of over two months of snow and ice, and temperatures which at one point plummeted to 15 degrees below freezing ...

January 5th, 1963

BLIZZARD BRINGS ISLAND TO A TRANSPORT STANDSTILL
MANY CARS ABANDONED IN SNOWDRIFTS

A blizzard - one of the worst within living memory - struck the Island on Saturday night and for a time paralysed transport. Deep snowdrifts isolated towns and villages, in some cases for several days. Many workers who normally travel by bus or their own cars had reason to be grateful to railwaymen who worked throughout Sunday to maintain services. Several instances have been quoted of devotion to duty by young and old, several making long journeys on foot in an attempt to reach their place of employment. At the Central Electricity Board's generating station several of the staff slept on the premises.

The steadily worsening conditions on Saturday made it obvious that bus services were to be seriously affected and officials made emergency plans to ensure that as many people as possible reached home. By teatime, buses were running late on many country routes and the going was particularly difficult in the Godshill and Rookley district where snowstorms reduced visibility almost to nil and giant drifts developed. Shortly before 8 p.m. it was decided that all bus services should be suspended. Notices were flashed on the screens of Newport cinemas and some buses left Newport in an attempt to take passengers to their homes. Some were successful, although many buses had to turn back before completing their journeys. On Sunday morning it was decided that all services should be suspended and on Monday morning an attempt was made to restore normal services but by 11 a.m. very few buses were on the roads ... The blizzard which struck the West Wight on Saturday evening left almost every road blocked

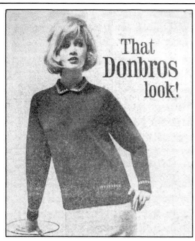

by fantastic snowdrifts, one of the worst extending almost from Brighstone to Shorwell and burying the road to a depth of 10 feet!

Four children from Parklands Children's Home, Cowes, accompanied by Miss Pamela Jenkins, assistant house mother, made the 5 mile journey from Newport to Cowes on foot on Sunday. On Saturday after a visit to a Newport cinema, the bus on which they were returning to Cowes was stopped at Hunnyhill by ice. After consulting with the matron, Mrs. A. B. McLean, Miss Jenkins made arrangements for the children to stay at Newport where one of the children has an aunt. On Sunday morning they decided to make the journey on foot. The party, including three boys, all aged 12, and a 13-year-old girl, took just over two hours to make the journey. The greatest obstacle was the giant snowdrift at Northwood and the journey there was made across country. The party arrived at home in time for a hot lunch and were none the worse for their experience. They were among the first people to reach Cowes after Saturday's blizzard. The matron said that the children were thrilled with their experiences ...

———————————◆———————————

The freezing temperatures, over such a long period, led to some unusual incidents ...
February 2nd, 1963

COWES NEIGHBOURLY ACT

The prompt action of neighbours of Mrs. M. Gunton, of Savernake, Wyatts Lane, minimised damage caused to her unoccupied house in the recent thaw. On Sunday, Mrs. O.J. Ballard saw water pouring out over the front doorstep, and with her husband tried to locate the trouble. Through the letterbox they saw that ice five inches thick covered the entire hallway and water was dripping from the ceiling. Through the police they contacted Mrs. Gunton who had been staying at Watford and obtained permission to break in. Another neighbour climbed through the landing window. He found the lower half of the stairs covered in icicles. Ice more than one inch thick completely covered one wall and had broken the hat rack. A bowl of artificial flowers was entirely encased and letters were also frozen into the thick ice. The neighbours worked for about three hours breaking the ice and clearing the carpets, so preventing water from running into other rooms. Mrs. Gunton returned home on Monday.

———————————◆———————————

TOWN AND COUNTY NOTES

NEWPORT WATER DELAY SOLVED — During the recent freezing conditions a Newport man and his family were without water for two weeks. Concerned that the water supply had not returned following the thaw, he investigated and found the stopcock turned off. Only then did he remember that he himself had turned it off a fortnight before, to protect the pipes when the freezing conditions began.

COWES BOY INJURED BY HOME-MADE BOMB — When a home-made bomb exploded on Friday week a 13-year-old Cowes schoolboy received severe burn and injuries to his right hand. The boy, Nicholas Etches, and his friend aged 14, both of Cowes, were playing in Northwood Park when the accident occurred. It is understood that they were packing a mixture of sodium chlorate weedkiller and sugar into a metal tube when it exploded. Etches was treated at St Mary's Hospital and later admitted to the Royal I.W. Hospital. His friend was uninjured.

AN ISLAND LANDMARK DISAPPEARS — The main gates of Parkhurst prison, thought to have been erected in 1838-9 are being replaced. A prison official said it is a pity that this Island landmark has to come down. The pillars were of Island stone. The reason is that the prison is going over to oil-fired central heating and the gates are not wide enough to allow the entry of large oil tankers. (April 20)

LICENSEE FOUND DEAD - HUSBAND HELPING POLICE ENQUIRIES — Newport police were called to the Blacksmith's Arms, on the Carisbrooke-Calbourne Road at 7 a.m. after Mr. William Roach had called at Newport Police Station to report that his wife, the licensee of the inn, was dead. The police found Mrs Evelyn Roach, aged about 48, dead in bed. She had died from head injuries. They stated that Mr. Roach was helping them in their enquiries. The Blacksmith's Arms is one of the loneliest inns in the Island. (April 18)

------------------◆------------------

The March 30th edition of the County Press had little room for its customary features. That week, two major proposals were announced that would radically change the face of the Island. The proposals took up two whole pages, prompting the inclusion of a notice stating, "Owing to pressure on space, several reports and letters have been held over."

The first news item to claim so much space was the complete redevelopment of the East Street area of Newport, including the demolition of Ford Mill. The work would enable the widening of the river to ensure no repetition of the floods of 1960 and would become the first part of the construction of today's Coppins Bridge traffic system.

The second full-page article was devoted to the news that the Island looked set to lose its remaining railway lines. In an attempt to reduce the running costs of Britain's railway network, Doctor Richard Beeching had been asked by the government to put forward a series of cost-cutting measures. His recommendations were fairly drastic; he proposed the eventual closure of 25%, or 4000 miles, of Britain's railway routes, including the entire Isle of Wight railway system ...

March 30th, 1963

DR. BEECHING PROPOSES END OF ISLAND RAILWAYS

ALD. MR WOODNUTT, MP, PROMISES A FIGHT TO THE BITTER END

Doctor Beeching's long awaited plan for British Railways, published on Wednesday, proposes the closing of the Island's remaining lines. Alderman Mark Woodnutt, MP, promised a fight to the last ditch and said he would resign the whip if a Conservative Government let the Island down.

The reference in the report to the Island was contained in five words. On page 107, under "Passenger service, line and station closures," were the words "Ryde Pier Head - Ventnor/Cowes." Dr. Beeching stated that there would be a debate on his plan in Parliament next month; he explained that if it was approved he expected that 70 per cent of the closures would be effected within a year.

MEMBER'S REACTION

Ald. Woodnutt was asked whether a Government decision to support the Beeching plan could affect the seat. He replied, "Yes, it could. I could not blame Islanders for being up in arms with a Government which was going to cut their life-line ... If a Conservative government let the Island down, I feel so strongly that I would resign the whip." He said it was absolute nonsense to imagine that the Island could get two and a half million holidaymakers back and forth from Ryde to Sandown, Shanklin and Ventnor without a train service. He was prepared to use every Parliamentary device to see the Island kept its railway ...

CONSULTATIONS WITH THE BUS COMPANY

Mr. David McKenna, controller of Southern Regional Railways, in an interview, denied the allegations that the Island's shock news was the most drastic proposal in the whole Beeching plan. It was doubtful whether the stations being closed handled 10 per cent of the transport in the area they served. For many years the remnants of the Island railway system had been run at a very heavy loss. Having consulted with the Southern Vectis Omnibus Company they had been satisfied that the traffic could be handled by road transport just as efficiently.

JOBS IN JEOPARDY

In the summer of 1962 there were 355 men and 11 women employed by the railways in the Island. The figure exceeds 400 if the staff at the Pier head, Fishbourne and Yarmouth are included, but these would not be affected by railway closures ...

HOTELIERS' CHAIRMAN OPTIMISTIC

Mr. J. D. Troughton (chairman of the I. W Hoteliers' Association) told the "County Press" that he was convinced that the Island railways would not be closed ... "I am optimistic," he said, "and I am speaking on good authority."

━━━━━━━━━━━━━━━◆━━━━━━━━━━━━━━━

Protest, in one form or another, was becoming a part of the British way of life and it eventually fed into domestic issues, particularly environmental ones. Attitudes to wildlife and the natural world began to change and the words 'ecology' and 'environment' entered everyday language for the first time. In the post-war years chemicals were seen as one of the wonders of the age, particularly by farmers. Fertilisers and pesticides soon became an important part of farming life but the uncritical acceptance of science and technology slowly gave way to scepticism and chemicals, once seen as part of the solution, were now beginning to be seen as part of the problem. The chemicals certainly delivered dramatic and impressive results but questions were being asked about their toxic nature and their effect on wildlife and watercourses. A reader wrote to question the wisdom of using weedkillers so powerful that they had to be applied by Council staff wearing gas masks. The letter provoked a wealth of correspondence, almost all expressing reservations about the use of chemicals in the British countryside ...

he Royal National Hospital for Diseases of the Chest at Ventnor, awaiting the execution of the
tence of redundancy already passed upon it, now that its role in the fight against tuberculosis is
led." (February 15)   *[Photograph courtesy of Fay Brown]*

old Castle Road toll gate, Newport, at the junction with Cedars Hill. This picture, bearing the
of Mr. Ernest Kime, photographer, of Lower St James's Street, Newport, is in a wonderful
of preservation. Possessing remarkable detail, it is possible with a magnifying glass to see the
of 1883 on one of the posters displayed on the wall." (July 27)   *[IWCP]*

May 25th, 1963

Effect of weedkiller on wildlife

Sir, last week the roadside verges at Newtown and Shalfleet were sprayed with selective weedkiller by council workmen. Residents have since found dead birds and dead and distressed hedgehogs which have absorbed the poison with the insects of their diet, among the shrivelled violets and primroses in lanes which stink horribly a week later. The damage to nestlings from spraying at this time of year may be imagined ... The wholesale destruction of life in the byways of an Island beauty spot by men in gas masks is, to my mind, a senseless and extravagant outrage. I shall be most grateful if you will allow me space to draw attention to what is happening here now, and to invite all your readers who share my views to write to me and endorse a protest to the council. I hope that in this way public opinion can make itself felt strongly enough to restrain the council permanently, from its spraying programme.

C.C. LUCAS. Noah's Ark, Newtown.

———————————◆———————————

Mr Bound, of Newport, was a man impressively ahead of his time. He suggested a possible use for the soon to be redundant railway lines ...

July 7th, 1963

Track for cyclists?

In these desperate days of traffic chaos, destined to grow worse and rapidly, what about using the disused railway tracks as pedal cycle roads with, say, a footpath incorporated for pedestrians? To convert the tracks to roads for motor traffic would probably present technical and practical difficulties, but so will building new roads for present-day and future demands, something which has to be faced willy nilly. The cost of making the old tracks suitable for cyclists, I imagine, would not be all that expensive, it would take a lot of traffic off the main roads and would set us a cycling boom in the Island. Just imagine a lovely straight and, above all, level road from, say, Freshwater to Bembridge or at least Sandown and St Lawrence. The pedal cyclists' dream. Even the elderly and not so young could get a bit of fun out of it, even I could; in fact I fancy myself on a bicycle in these circumstances.

C. F. BOUND. 69 Whitepit Lane, Newport.

———————————◆———————————

ISLAND NOTES

POSTED! — Mr. P. E. G. Wood, of 36 Bellevue Road, Cowes, had an alarming experience when putting up a boundary fence at the bottom of his garden. He attempted to drive a six-foot post into the ground and twice altered the position after hitting something solid. On placing the post in the fourth position and giving it a blow he was amazed when it disappeared into an old well, partly covered with a thick slab of concrete.

ALDERMAN WOODNUTT ABSTAINS IN THE RAIL DEBATE — Alderman Mark Woodnutt, MP, was one of six Conservative Members who on Tuesday abstained from voting for the Government against an Opposition motion attacking the Beeching plan. Alderman Woodnutt told a reporter that he had abstained because he was not satisfied with the assurance given by the Minister of Transport about adequate alternatives to the railway.

The county taxation department is now issuing the registration letters BDL.

PRISON ACTIVITIES INCLUDE DRESSMAKING — A report from Camp Hill and Parkhurst prisons discloses an amazing variety of recreational activities including the rebuilding of a harmonium, the erection of a greenhouse in the gardens, carpentry, marquetry, basketwork, leather work, and toymaking. Some prisoners are making dresses for their wives and daughters ...

TRADESMEN PRAISE ARAB SAILORS' BEHAVIOUR — The United Arab Republic troopship El Quosier arrived at Cowes last weekend to embark 400 ratings from the two U.A.R. destroyers which are being refitted at J.S. White and Co.'s yard ... Their presence in the town has provided a minor boom for some shopkeepers. The Arab sailors are purchasing, often in quantity, a variety of luxury goods unobtainable in their own country. These include cosmetics, garments, cameras and transistor radios ... From all sources there have been good reports of the courtesy and conduct of the sailors.

KING'S QUAY MARINA - PLANNING COMMITTEE RECOMMEND REFUSAL — The Planning Committee on Monday decided to recommend the County Council to refuse the application to build a yacht marina at King's Quay, and a yachting village for 2000 persons ... The area of 67 acres would have comprised a fully equipped yachting centre and haven for 500 yachts and 571 houses and flats.

———————————◆———————————

There had been many letters of protest to the County Press regarding the Council's chemical spraying programme. County Hall had been forced to investigate whether or not their chemical sprays were having a detrimental effect on the Island's wildlife. They eventually decided that the sprays had no effects on insects, but had nothing to say regarding the effect on birdlife. Mr. Rose, Council Surveyor, confidently claimed "It was nonsense to allege that birds had died as a result of spraying," an opinion he would have to revise as the years went by ...

July 13th, 1963
SPRAYING OF ROADSIDE VERGES TO CONTINUE
CONTROL AIMED AT DOCKS, THISTLES AND DANDELIONS
A report on chemical spraying of roadside verges presented to the Roads Committee on Tuesday stated that no evidence had been found that this was harmful to birds ... and the present policy will therefore be continued.
A committee representing the Nature Conservancy, the Agricultural Research

Council and Road Research Laboratories had tested the type of spray used in the Island and there was no evidence that they were markedly insecticidal ... Farmers were advised to keep their animals away from such areas for two or three weeks after spraying ... Mr. M.F. Chambers asked whether the council was adequately insured against the harmful effects of spray drift. He spoke of a case where a hormone spray used by a farmer had drifted across 700 cauliflowers belonging to a neighbour in the Island, with a consequent loss of 1s. 3d. per cauliflower. Mr. A.S. Westbrook said the report was asked for following the outcry in the Press alleging ill effects on bird and animal life. The report made no comment on the effects of the spraying on birdlife. Mr. Rose (council surveyor and engineer) replied that birds had been found on verges, but it was more likely that these had been struck by passing cars. It was nonsense to allege that these had died as a result of spraying! He had asked for evidence. One man had sent a bird away for a post-mortem examination, but no report had been provided by him. No one had yet produced a bird with proof that it had died as a result of spraying ...

At Steephill Castle, the workmen had moved in to begin demolition and as their hammers slowly reduced the building to rubble, it became apparent that all that glistered had not, after all, been gold ...

July 27th, 1963

STEEPHILL CASTLE DEMOLITION
SURPRISING DISCOVERIES

Demolition work commenced this week on Steephill Castle at Ventnor in preparation for the clearing of the estate for residential development. Planning consent has been issued for 29 dwellings ... The demolition is being carried out by Messrs. D. A. Stotesbury and Son, who are to develop the site. They have already carried out considerable development of the old Ventnor West railway station site with attractive modern properties ...

Workmen demolishing the building, commencing with the servants' quarters to make room for the main accommodation road from the entrance in Park Avenue, have found some surprising features. The "oak" staircase was made from deal to look like oak and the handsome carved wooden ceiling beams and figures are plaster mouldings. A previously boarded-up window contained the remains of stained glass commemorating regimental battles. Much of what was thought to have been ornamental woodwork has been revealed as plaster. So far, men clearing the heavy undergrowth in the grounds have not found the shrub Paliurus aculeatus, known as "Christ's thorn," which was said to have been brought from the East and traditionally declared to have descended from that used by the Roman soldiers to make Christ's crown of thorns.

There has been quite a demand for stone from the castle and for souvenirs. The heating system may go to Chale Methodist Church. The castle and its surrounding grounds present a derelict site as the task of taking down the building is progressing. When a "County Press" reporter was shown around by Mr. John Stotesbury there were many reminders of a bygone era and a realisation that despite sentimental considerations there is no economic future for the building and estate in their present condition. One of the last remaining glories must be the memory of the unrivalled panoramic view from the parapet of the 85 foot tower ... The stone from which the castle was built was quarried on the estate. There were two main floors and other floors in the keep and tower. At one time the extensive grounds took in the cricket field, beach and land now built on to the west. There is also a covered swimming pool which could be heated.

TOWN AND COUNTY NOTES

THE SILLY SEASON IS HERE! — On Friday, August 9th, at 8.30 a.m., my husband was approaching Somerton corner. From a field gateway emerged two girls, one dressed in a white brassiere and panties, the other in jeans and a shirt. They were apparently going to cross the road. What could the explanation have been? We are both intrigued and would like to know the answer.

Do not publish my name and address. (August 17)

Bales of rubber, with a salvage value of £4 each, are still being washed up on beaches along the south-west coast from the wreck of the cargo vessel War Knight, which sank off Watcombe Bay in December, 1918.

FULL ORDER BOOKS FOR DECCA RADAR — Group Capt E. Fennessy, CBE (managing director) of Decca Radar, Ltd., states that there is already more than enough work on their books to keep them busy right through next year ... The new factory and laboratories due to come into operation in a matter of a few weeks would be unsurpassed in Europe. There were already more than 300 people at Somerton and when the new buildings became fully operative the strength would come up to about 600 men and women.

The lady and her husband wondering what the two girls were doing, coming from a gateway on Somerton Corner, can now have their explanation.

It was not a girl in shirt and jeans, it was a boy, a beatnik where I come from, and that boy was me. If she had looked over the gate about five minutes earlier she would not have been so inquisitive.

G. SOMERS. Brighton. (August 24)

NEW RECORD FOR CRAIG DOUGLAS — Craig Douglas had a new record released yesterday, on the Decca-Ritz label, entitled "I'm so glad I've found her." This is his 21st record ... He is booked for a number of radio and TV shows, including an appearance on the popular TV show "Thank Your Lucky Stars" on Saturday, September 14th.*

---

* The Rolling Stones appeared on the same edition. In his 1990 autobiography, 'A Stone Alone,' Wyman wrote, "Craig Douglas had given our debut single a poor review three months previously. Stones never forget anything. We remembered that he'd been a milkman ... so we all went round studios gathering up empty milk bottles and put them outside his dressing-room door with notes saying things like 'Two pints, please' tucked in. Furious, he reported us to the producers, who sternly reprimanded us."

Albany barracks, closed in 1960, were about to be demolished. There was just time to pay a last visit to the derelict site before the bulldozers moved in ...

September 21st, 1963

THE END OF ALBANY BARRACKS

By Cynthia Horsham

Seagulls now squat on the barracks square. Weeds and wildflowers grow knee-high beside the CO's office where heavy boots once clattered down the main drive, roofing slates lie broken, and the sentry box at the main gate has a weary list. Soon the bulldozers and demolition gangs will move in and Albany Barracks will be no more. HM Prison authorities have taken over the site and soon a new prison is to be built. Before this transformation takes place it is interesting to ponder on the story of these old barracks which must have played an important part in the background of England's history. Outside the office block is a tall black noticeboard which faithfully records in stark white lettering, a list of the regiments who have been quartered here from 1881 until the closure in 1960.

From Nelson's Handbook of the Isle Of Wight we learn that the barracks were first established in September 1798. We can presume they were one of the first in the British Isles as before 1790 the militia were always billeted on dwelling houses or pubs. The barracks could accommodate 2000 men and we read that "they occupy an area of about 100 acres and include five officers' houses, eight large and 12 smaller barracks, a house for the commandant, another for the chief accountant, a chapel, necessary offices, and a large parade ground." The hospital portion was converted in 1838 to a reform prison for juvenile offenders. Apparently they were first known as Parkhurst Barracks, but the name was changed to honour the Duke of York and Albany, who was then commander-in-chief.

This summer we were visited by an elderly friend from Birmingham who had been stationed at Parkhurst in 1911. 50 years of living rolled away like a dream when we took him to see the once familiar red brick buildings. He remembered each one and nodded respectfully towards the officers' quarters, discreetly hidden from the square by trees and shrubbery ... I first remember them in the late 50s. They were my young son's first experience of "live" soldiers and he would gaze saucer-eyed through the railings, to the constant amusement of the sentry ... For almost 165 years the garrison must have followed the fortunes of their comrades in many battles and the two world wars and doubtless, in the peace between, they re-fought the battles in the NAAFI or in the Old Horseshoe Inn at Northwood.

Now the story is told, the battle is won, but perhaps memories of Albany Barracks will be like the old soldiers themselves and never die, but simply fade away.

———————◆———————

The 1961 attempt to sell the Princess flying boats had come to nothing. Two years later and nearly 20 years after the placing of the initial order with Saunders-Roe, another attempt was made to recoup some of the losses ...

December 7th, 196

THE SLEEPING PRINCESSES

If some of the proposals for their future use materialise, the "sleeping" Prince

flying boats are in for a rude awakening. The three giant planes, which were never put into use, cost nearly £11 million to build in the early 1950s, and have been in protective cocoons for eight years. The War Office Sales Department has now offered them for sale, and they were open for inspection by prospective purchasers last week. Tenders close on December 12th but the Princesses are only expected to fetch scrap prices. About a dozen interested persons were shown round the plane at Cowes by Mr. T. Fidderman, a Ministry of Aviation official, who was assisting buyers with technical information. Several had plans to scrap the 140-ton giants, which are 147 feet long and have a wingspan of 220 feet. More glamorous suggestions came from some of the prospective bidders. Mr. D. Tailby, a car dealer of Blaby, Leicestershire, said he planned to take one back to his home town, set it in a "sea" of concrete, and convert the plane into a novel restaurant. The Bachelors "pop" singing group were interested in making one into a floating jazz club and coffee bar for teenagers, moored in the sea off Brighton.

1964

Britain was firmly in the grip of Beatlemania, Newport included ...

January 11th, 1964

Unruly cinema audiences

Once again a Saturday evening at a Newport cinema, at which we pay some of the highest seat prices outside of London, has been ruined by the noise of loudmouthed youths and this time the added nuisance of screaming teenage girls.

I refer to Saturday's performance at the Savoy. Included in the programme was a film which has been highly advertised by the I.W. Theatres; this was a special short film of the Beatles. It should have been quite entertaining, especially to the many adults who enjoy this talented group, but it was completely ruined by shouting youths and screaming girls. I certainly hope this stupid habit of screaming, which is killing the entertainment value of some live shows, is not spreading to the cinema. Then, as if not content at ruining one film, there was again noise and disturbance during the main film.

Surely the cinema managements can take more drastic steps to help curb this all too-familiar happening of ruined cinema entertainment.

REGULAR CINEMAGOER.

---◆---

ISLAND NOTES

7 MILLION BRICKS IN NEW PRISON — The building of the new Alban Prison will use seven million bricks ... The principal unit will be a building 700 feet long and four storeys high, housing five wings each with 96 cells and there are t

be 130 houses for the staff ... Mr. L. R. Smith (consultant architect) told the Council on Tuesday that the Island Brick Company should be able to meet their orders without undue delay. The London Brick Company had a waiting list of several months for certain kinds of brick.

INVENTOR'S CONNECTION WITH COWES — An article in this week's "Sunday Times" colour magazine reveals that a man who has been one of Britain's greatest engineers and inventors for the last 50 years is a former apprentice at Messrs. J. S. White's shipyard at Cowes. He is Dr. Barnes Wallis who will probably be best remembered for his famous bouncing bomb which burst the dams supplying electricity to the Ruhr - a story made familiar to millions through the film "The Dam Busters."

COWES FLOATING BRIDGE — A proposed road improvement at Medina Road, Cowes, in the vicinity of the floating bridge was discussed on Monday. Mr. Rose, county surveyor, said he did not think they would see the Medina Bridge for 15 years ... Mr. S. L. Glossop, JP, commenting on the surveyor's estimate of 15 years stated, "If you said 50 years I would agree with you - the way we dither and don't make decisions."

———————————◆———————————

A photograph of one of the first buses on the Island had appeared in the previous week's issue. It prompted a reader's memories of a trip on the very first bus to operate between Seaview and Ryde ...

February 8th, 1964

First buses at Seaview

I was much interested in the photograph of the very early Island motor bus in your last issue. One of the most vivid memories of my childhood is being taken by my mother, the late Mrs Florence Barclay, for a drive on the first motor bus to run between Seaview and Ryde. I think it was its first trip, and my guess is that it was about 1909, but I'm not sure of the date. The chief reason I remember it so well is that the bus tried three times to get up the hill of Old Seaview Lane, but could not make it, and each time slid gently backwards down the hill. After the third attempt we all got out and went sadly home! I should like to remind readers that in those days the only road out of Seaview was Old Seaview Lane. It was not possible to drive by the Duver, as the old ladies who lived in Seafield House would allow no one to go through their estate, and the other exit from Seaview, Steyne Road, had not been constructed. I wonder if any other of your readers were on the bus?

ANGELA WHITCOMBE. 3 Seafield Terrace, Seaview.

———————————◆———————————

Throughout the late 1950s, Island rock and roll fans had been well catered for, with well-known national acts frequently visiting Island venues, particularly in Ryde. The number ?ll for a while during the early 1960s but rapidly picked up again when the Mersey beat boom took off in 1963. The summer months during the 1960s saw an impressive line-up of well-known national pop acts appearing at Ryde every Saturday night. Reading like a Who's Who of 1960s top bands, acts as diverse as The Bonzos, John Lee Hooker and Gene Vincent all made their way there during the Sixties. Now, tickets were about to go on sale for the Rolling Stones appearance at the Ryde Pavilion in just a few week's time ...

February 29th, 1964

GIRLS WAIT ALL NIGHT TO BUY TICKETS

About a dozen teenage girls, armed with blankets, hot drinks and sandwiches, waited all night outside the Esplanade Pavilion, Ryde, on Saturday in order to get front row tickets for the evening performance of "The Rolling Stones" at the Pavilion on March 22nd. With only scant shelter from the rain outside the locked main doors, the girls gathered at about 9 p.m. on Saturday and besieged the box office with many others when the doors opened at 10.30 the next morning. All the reserved seats for the evening performance were quickly sold, and only a few reserved seats were left for the afternoon show. All the girls who waited throughout the night were in their early teens, and they produced written permission from their parents to the show organiser, Mr. David Sparks, a schoolteacher and member of Ryde Town Council. They included Pat Searle, Brenda Hale, Linda Brown, Ann Michelle and Celia Lake, all of Ryde.

◆

TOWN AND COUNTY NOTES

BAHAMAS COMPANY ACQUIRE PRINCESSES — It was announced on Wednesday that the three Princess flying boats have been acquired by Cargo Sales, a Bahamas firm. It is understood the giant craft may be converted at an estimated cost of 3 ½ million pounds each, by Aero Space Lines of California to carry large missile components connected with the Saturn project for the National Aeronautics and Space Administration.

PENGUIN AT BEMBRIDGE — My husband and I were walking along the beach at Bembridge, near the lifeboat station, when we saw, standing to attention, a penguin. This bird allowed us to approach within 2 feet of it then waddled off slowly to the sea, apparently to catch fish. Is it a rare or unusual thing for penguins to visit the island? DOROTHY HARDIMAN (Mrs) Ivyholme Cottage, Newlands, St Helens.*

PIGS IN NEWPORT MARKET — Could you give me a little space to show my disapproval of the way pigs are marked in Newport Market. Two relatives were with me there on March 10th and we were disgusted with the way the pigs were being treated. Although I know pigs squeal a lot, I am sure these were being hurt. The holes in their ears were as big as sixpences and the amount of blood over the pigs and on the ground was terrible. Surely there is a more humane way of marking these creatures. It is not a very pleasant sight for children, who are always in the market. (Mrs.) G. BAILEY. 13 Mitchells Road, Ryde.

* The following week a sceptical correspondent asked if the penguin was a paperback.

TUG LOST IN ISLAND SALVAGE — The Back of the Wight claimed what is probably the most unusual victim in the whole of its wreck-strewn history when a powerful ocean-going tug, the Witte Zee, was holed and sunk in the course of salvage work on Sunday. The tug had gone to the aid of a steamer aground on Brooke Ledge about half a mile offshore, and had just managed to get a line to the stranded vessel when the mishap occurred. Tugs are always considered to be almost unsinkable but the 16 members of the crew had to be taken off by the Yarmouth lifeboat and another tug only a few hours before she foundered.

———————————◆———————————

More and more evidence was beginning to accumulate indicating that some of the pesticides and weedkillers eagerly promoted by the chemical industry were, as some had suspected all along, killing wildlife ...

March 29th, 1964

Dangerous weedkillers

I wrote to the "County Press" last year on the dangers of the weedkillers being used by the County Council. Today's newspapers illustrate by their reports from the British Trust for Ornithology and from scientists and others, that there is alarm over the use of these dangerous weedkillers. It would appear that those of us who first raised the alarm here on the Island were not so far wrong and the County Council were ill advised to continue their weed killer spraying.

HAROLD W. PIKE. Queen's Bower, Upper Hyde, Shanklin.

[Mr. Pike encloses a newspaper cutting stating that the latest report from the British Trust for Ornithology says a sample of 333 dead birds showed that 304 contained chemical residues. - Editor].

———————————◆———————————

The Vectensis column continued to be a treasure house of facts and information about the Island and its ways ...

May 2nd, 1964

AN ISLANDER'S NOTES
[By VECTENSIS]

DOG AND STILE INN — My note last week with reference to a former inn at Newport bearing this title being located at Town Gate at the bottom of Hunnyhill, and asking if anyone could state its exact site, has brought information from Mr. C. B. Leal, of 4 Albany Road, Newport. He writes: "I believe you will find that the inn was on the site at the corner of Crocker Street and Lower St James's Street where Neat Brothers' ironmongers shop now stands. I understand that its sign depicted a top-hatted gentleman with a lame dog which was trying either to get over or through a stile. As Messrs. Neats' business was established in 1885 the inn must have been there well over 80 years ago." Mr. Leal is quite right. Mr. Norman Neat informs me that the inn was certainly on the site and he had previously understood that its name was "The Lame Dog." After the premises ceased to be a public house it was a peas and faggot shop for several years before Neats became the tenants and started their business. Further perusal of the old copper trade card printing plate, shown to me by Mr. W. S. Brading, of Carisbrooke, discloses that the name of the inn derived from the old proverbial lines: "Do the work that's nearest, Though 'tis dull at times; Helping, when you meet them, Lame dogs over stiles." This is supported by the fact that in very small letters below the representation of the sign on the copperplate are the words, "Help me over."

ORIGIN OF "FOLLY" — How did the Folly Inn get its name? Once again, interest and speculation has been revived by discoveries during the conversion of three small rooms at the inn into a large dining room. Floorboards were taken up and underneath was found the keel and timbers of a 30 foot hulk, on which this original part of the inn was built. Although embedded in shingle and seashells, the barnacled timber is still sound. As a novel object of interest to visitors part of the floor of the new dining room incorporates a glass panel, lit from below, through which the hulk can be seen.

Many suggestions have been made as to how the Folly got its strange name. Some claim that it came from a trading vessel which used to ply between Newport and the West Indies and finished its days stranded high and dry in the mud on the riverbank. Others say the foundation was an old smuggling sloop ...

Now a favourite haunt for weekend yachtsmen, the Folly has seen many changes but it has retained much of the peaceful atmosphere and character of another era ... Around the lounge walls are many interesting and valuable old maps and prints collected as a hobby by the licensee, Mr. Murray Dixon, a keen and accomplished yachtsman who on many occasions has crewed in Prince Philip's Flying Fifteen, Coweslip, with his uncle Mr. Uffa Fox.

TOWN AND COUNTY NOTES

Sir, Re rising bus fares. Has anyone else twigged it yet? It is these sly Conservatives! They are out to price the poor working man into buying a car, so reserving the bus for the elite and wealthy, anticipating the day when cars are banned from parking within a mile or two from town.

N. HALL. 162 Carisbrooke Road, Newport.

LONDON-SANDOWN AIR SERVICE — British Westpoint Airlines Ltd have asked for a licence to operate a pioneer all-the-year-round service of 22 flights a week in each direction from London, Heathrow to Sandown. The proposed fares are £3 single and £5/10/- return. Mr. N. Dixon, director, said "A businessman boarding the 11.05 a.m. flight from London arrives in the Island at 11.45 a.m. He could return by the 2.35 p.m. or 5.05 p.m. flights and still be able to deal with business at both ends of the day ... I think there will be a demand for an all-the-year-round service." He contemplated a daily service in the winter.

The aroma that occasionally comes from the foreshore at East Cowes during summer months is not a modern phenomenon. On and off, the County Press has been reporting on the "East Cowes smell" for over 100 years, and will probably continue to do so for the next 100 years. When the smell got too much in the summer of 1964, community spirit prevailed. Free of risk assessment forms and health and safety regulations, over 200 residents of East Cowes took direct action ...

July 18th, 1964

BUSINESSMEN ORGANISE DO-IT-YOURSELF SCHEME

The first part of East Cowes Businessmen's Association's "do-it-yourself" scheme to clear a section of the seafront of rocks and offensive-smelling seaweed, was successfully carried out on Monday evening. More than 200 men, women and children answered the association's call for volunteers, and armed with rakes, garden forks and wheelbarrows were soon swarming over the beach. "Operation seaweed," as it was called, was planned like a military manoeuvre. As willing workers at the water's edge tugged, pulled and tore the seaweed from the rock-strewn beach, it was loaded on to cleverly contrived "stretchers" made from poles and wire netting and was carried up the beach to the sea wall. Here, protruding from the promenade above, were the lowered scoops of two mechanical shovels. The weed was carried across the promenade and piled on a part of the nearby car park, to await collection the following day.

For many years rotting seaweed on the East Cowes beaches has been a controversial subject and the thick deposits have proved unpopular with swimmers ... A delegation from the Businessmen's Association met with Cowes Council and suggested that the immediate clearance of the rocks and seaweed should be treated as a top priority. The council replied that the clearing of rocks and seaweed was "impracticable." The Association pressed for action, however, and were rewarded when the council finally agreed to cart away and dump the seaweed, if the Association would arrange the clearance.

"Help Wanted" posters immediately went up around the town and preparations were made to clear a small section on Tuesday. Work commenced at 6.15 p.m. as the tide went out and finished just before 10 p.m. Mr. Thomas (chairman of the Association) told the 'County Press' "The response from the townspeople and local organisations was beyond my wildest expectations. It shows the council what the people really think about this matter. It is amazing what has been achieved already, and many of the volunteers have offered their services again tomorrow."

━━━━━━━━━━━━━◆━━━━━━━━━━━━━

Just as the work was drying up for the shipyards of J.S. White's, leaving large numbers of men unemployed, in an opportune coincidence hundreds of manufacturing vacancies appeared on the books of Decca Radar, who were still going from strength to strength ...

July 18th, 1964

OFFICIAL OPENING OF DECCA RADAR
BRIGHT EMPLOYMENT PROSPECTS

An event of significance in the Island's industrial field took place yesterday - the official opening of the new factories and laboratories of Decca Radar, Ltd. These premises at the former Somerton Airport, Cowes, comprise one of the best

OPERATION SEAWEED AT EAST COWES
"The scene on East Cowes front as volunteers cleared the seaweed."   *[IWCP]*

...ains waiting for the off at Ryde Pier Head one summer's evening in August 1965, the one on ...t bound for Ventnor, the other heading for Cowes.   *[Photograph by Alan Stroud]*

equipped radar development, production and test establishments in the world ... Group Captain E. Fennessy, (managing director, Decca Radar, Ltd.) said ... they came to the Island because it was one of the sites offered by the Board of Trade and, most important, because they were welcomed here. From the first proposal (and ever since) they had received great assistance from the County Council, Cowes Council and Ald. Mark Woodnutt MP, who at one stage "twisted the arm" of the Board of Trade. Alderman Woodnutt said ... it was remarkable to think that it was less than five years since a single mobile caravan was wheeled on to the site setting up Decca's headquarters, which now had become a vigourous hive of industrial activity ... The company were now providing jobs for 608 people, of whom only a small proportion had been brought in from the mainland. There are now over 600 jobs where five years ago there were none. It was interesting to note that 600 jobs in a little place like the Island represented two per cent of its employed population. It was a great credit to the company that they had stuck to their programme and in the last year increased employment by 380.

------------------------◆------------------------

The Island and some of its odd, even quaint, ways were the subject of a pair of letters in the same issue of the County Press in August ...

August 1st, 1964

Beeching efficiency

Sunday, 8.25 p.m., Ryde Esplanade railway station. On platform 2, about 60 passengers await trains to Ventnor and Cowes. One of them notices a fire spreading on the outside of the wooden screen on the pier end of the platform and hurries to platform 1 and tells an official. The official, who is checking passengers, tells a porter, who is acting as ticket collector. The porter walks the full length of platform 1, crosses the line and inspects the fire. Then he goes to the staff rest room and gets a bucket of water. The bucket has holes in it, but he hurries to the fire and throws the little water left on the flames. As this does not completely subdue the fire he collects a kettle of water from the rest room to finish the job ...

"ONE OF THE TRAVELLERS."

Brading Roman Villa

I would like to draw attention to the Brading Roman Villa, which my wife and I visited while on holiday. We have never been so disappointed at seeing an ancient monument so neglected. After spending almost three hours trying to find it, we eventually came across a collection of rusty tin huts. Of the three outer buildings only two were labelled with any description, and all were overgrown with weeds. At the entrance we were greeted by an attendant who said, "Three shillings," with no please or thank you. What conclusion we were supposed to draw from exhibits labelled "Animal Bones," "Tiles," "Charred Wood," and so forth, we cannot imagine. The whole lot added up to an untidy mess. The cases were thick with dust and the whole place was depressing. My wife and I came away feeling cheated, and this view was shared by several people we met outside ...

D. PRITCHARD. 63 Falcon Road, Battersea, SW 11.

The number of blacksmiths on the Island could be counted on one hand by the 1960s. The County Press featured the business of Mr. Stay, a Sandown blacksmith, who was still carrying on the family firm which had started in 1790* ...

August 22nd, 1964

POPULARITY OF SANDOWN WROUGHT IRON WORK

Hand-wrought iron work is a dying art. One of the few remaining skilled craftsmen is Mr. George Stay, of Messrs. W. Stay and Son, Fort Mews, Sandown, whose ancestors founded the firm of blacksmiths and ornamental iron workers at Brading 174 years ago in 1790. Mr. Stay learned his skill at his father's forge in West Street, Brading, where he did most of the shoeing and agricultural repair work. Starting in the business at the age of 13, he recalls that he often had to walk many miles to jobs in various parts of the East Wight, but would cycle whenever he could, carrying the shoes on the bar of his machine. The family lived in High Street, Brading where Mr. Wilfred Stay, senior, had established an ironmonger's shop. The business is now run by Miss Nancy Stay.

Forty years ago, Mr. Stay, snr., opened a workshop at Wilkes Road, Sandown, where mostly plumbing and acetylene welding work were carried out. He was one of the first to introduce electric welding in the Island. The forge at Brading remained open until 1937, and it is interesting to note that even then, with the growing popularity of the motor car, the firm still had 350 horses for regular shoeing on their books. Mr. Stay, snr., died in 1952 and the business was taken over by his son, George. About a month ago the premises in Wilkes Road were closed, and the firm moved into a new and much larger building at Fort Mews, Sandown. Working with Mr. Stay is his 17-year-old son, Timothy, a former pupil of the Fairway School, who is rapidly acquiring knowledge of his father's skill ... Many fine examples of wrought iron work are displayed at the forge. Modestly, Mr. Stay told a "County Press" reporter that he seldom works from a set plan, and invariably makes up the design as he goes along. He is, however, always pleased to conform to a sketch or picture of any particular item customers may require ... "In fact, I am happy to make anything from a pin to an ornamental elephant," he said ... At the Brading forge, soon after the turn of the century, Mr. Stay's father made the frame for the first motor scooter on the Island - a forerunner of the popular machine of today. One of the most exacting jobs Mr. Stay was called upon to undertake in recent years was the restoration of one of the two large entrance gates at Nunwell Park, Brading ... The new forge at Fort Mews - which was designed by Mr. Brown - is one of the most modern of its kind. Paradoxically, apart from an electric motor driving the bellows at the fire hearth, it employs no modern mechanical aids. Many of the tools used there have been in the family for generations ...

George Stay is a craftsman who obviously takes great pride in the skill he has been proud to inherit. He has little time for imitation and although wrought iron work is again very much in vogue, he states emphatically that he has no intention of sacrificing that skill for mass production methods resulting in an inferior article.

---

* The company is still trading today.

ISLAND NOTES

BRITISH RAILWAYS BUY UNDERGROUND TRAINS — It was announced on Wednesday that British Railways had bought two trains from London Underground for possible use at Ryde. They would be available for a service between Ryde Pier Head and Ryde St John's Road station if Mr. Marples, the Minister of Transport, decides to close the Island's remaining railway lines ... (August 22)

HELICOPTER OVERTURNS AT EAST COWES — A small helicopter, landing to re-fuel on the concrete apron in front of Westland Aircraft Limited's premises at East Cowes on Saturday, overturned and was seriously damaged. A piece of one of the broken blades smashed the window of J. H. Burgess and Son's chemists shop in York Avenue 150 yards away. Capt J. Crewsdon, the owner, was piloting the machine. He said he bought the helicopter recently. The cause of the mishap was "ground resonance," a rare occurrence which can cause a helicopter to vibrate and destroy itself. In this case the machine was a complete write-off. A spectator described the scene as fantastic as the machine toppled over onto its side and the whirling rotor blades shattered against the concrete apron ... (August 22)

TRAFFIC LIGHTS FOR NEWPORT — Newport Town Council adopted recommendations of the Highways Committee for the installation of traffic lights in the town ... at the corner of South Street and Town Lane, Upper St James's Street and South Street, and High Street and St James's Street. The recommendations were adopted without discussion.

————————◆————————

The political leaning of a newspaper is the privilege of the proprietor. The County Press made no secret of the fact that it was a staunch supporter of the Conservative party, a stance it maintained until 1973. Consequently it did all it could to help the Conservative cause. This next confident editorial set out to remind the Island's voters where their devotions lay as the 1964 general election drew near. In the event, Mr Woodnutt went on to take the seat with an 11,000 majority ...

October 10th, 1964

A MOMENTOUS CHOICE

Next Thursday the Island goes to the polls. The electors have the choice between Liberal, Labour and Conservative candidates, all of whom have been actively presenting their parties' cases during the past fortnight.

When the various programmes are considered, the conclusion is clear that the interests of the nation will best be served by the return to power of the Conservatives. Furthermore, when the claims of the respective local candidates to represent the Island are weighed, it is clear that Alderman Mark Woodnutt stands pre-eminent. The "County Press," a Conservative newspaper, is proud to give him its support.

All Islanders of whatever party recognise the enormous amount of work Mark Woodnutt has done for the Island and a large measure of success he has achieved. He has been more than a Member of Parliament, he has been a true leader in all vital spheres .... Alderman Woodnutt comes from an old Island family; he lives among us, is accessible to all, and is certainly the Island's best-known citizen. He possesses an unrivalled knowledge of the Island's affairs and problems. When Islanders rally to him on Thursday they will elect a candidate who will best serve the interests of the country and of the Isle of Wight. We appeal to all electors to record their vote and ensure an increased majority for a former Member who has done so much for our Island.

———————————◆———————————

TOWN AND COUNTY NOTES

ELECTION BRIEFS — Asked whether she would be voting for the Socialists, a Freshwater woman said "Oh no, I always vote Labour."

Among Thursday's voters was Mrs. Bessie Jane Machin, of Elim, Lower Green Road, St. Helens, who was 101 on February 21st.

The three candidates had the unusual experience of addressing an unseen audience at St. Dominic's Priory Convent, Carisbrooke. They were invited to speak at different times by the Mother Superior and did so through a grille which separated the speakers from their audience of about 20 nuns. Question time showed that although technically St. Dominic's is part of a closed order, the nuns have good knowledge of national and local politics.

FRESHWATER OPPOSE YAR BRIDGE PROPOSAL — The Parish Council are to lodge a formal objection to the County Council's proposal to build a fixed span bridge over the River at Yarmouth ... Mr. G. F. Osman : If we are going to look 100 years ahead, the people will not want bridges. They will all be in outer space. Mr. Chandler : There is a little interval in between...

1965

In the days before cars and rural bus services, the inhabitants of the smaller towns and villages relied on the village shop or travelling salesmen for their everyday supplies. For anything else, the 'carrier' would be used. For a small fee the carrier would drive into town, purchase whatever goods were required by the customer and then deliver them to their door. As Vectensis reflected, their days were nearly over ...

January 9th, 1965

AN ISLANDER'S NOTES
[By VECTENSIS]

COUNTRY CARRIERS - The dwindling number of carriers to and from Newport, serving villages and isolated dwellings on their various routes has been further reduced by the recent retirement of Mr. Arthur Sprake, of Chale, who has acted as carrier between Blackgang and Chale and Newport for 52 years, as his father did for about 20 years earlier. Arthur's cheery smile and courteous helpfulness will be much missed by his clients en route, as no order, however small, was too insignificant for his attention. There are still four or five such carriers left, but like most people having to visit Newport, they find great difficulty in parking their vehicles in places convenient for their customers and themselves. Until recently, when the space was reserved for parking private cars, their headquarters were in St Thomas's Square. But that place was not very popular with some people as at times, packages for the carriers to pick up were placed on the steps of the war memorial. This "desecration" led to a strong appeal to prohibit the carriers using the square, but it was never acted upon until the car park provision pushed them out.

———————————◆———————————

A subject which took up many County Press column inches in the early months of 1965 was the future of Priory Farm pond at Carisbrooke, after the Council announced they were proposing to fill it in. Although perhaps not the prettiest in the land, the little pond had been in existence for several centuries and was the subject of many postcards and photographs. It had an undoubted place in the hearts of locals and there was an outcry over its potential destruction. The arguments for and against filling in the pond provide a useful snapshot of 1960s attitudes ...

January 16th, 1965

Priory Pond, Carisbrooke

I have read with interest, followed by alarm and dismay, your recent report regarding Newport Corporation's refusal to preserve Priory Farm Pond. I have been a ratepayer of Carisbrooke since 1919 and I know for certain that very many residents agree with my point of view. The walk past the pond has been our rightful privilege for very many years and it still represents a quiet oasis in these noisy times ... This pond should be retained, and could be, with very little expense ... The majority of the Newport Borough Councillors appear to be without any imagination or to have time for anything which is not strictly utilitarian. I think that their decision is an absolute disgrace.

J. W. BROWN. Landscape House, High Street, Carisbrooke.

So the Priory Farm pond is to disappear, the trees are being slaughtered on Castle Hill and the waterworks pond is allowed to become overgrown.

May I suggest that unless the powers-that-be are fully occupied with spoiling the character of one of England's loveliest villages they at least plant a few trees around the new Carisbrooke pumping station and thus preserve us from what looks like a millionaire's chicken run!

A.N. DAISH   4 Castle Lane, Carisbrooke.

Possibly limbering up for his future role as Council leader, a young Morris Barton joined in the debate the following week. Although for some the duck pond was a picturesque oasis, and a part of rural life worth preserving in the days of concrete and housing estates, Mr. Barton took a decidedly unromantic view. The pond was nothing more, he declared, "than a stagnant murky eyesore" ...

January 23rd, 1965

Priory Pond, Carisbrooke

There is a section of the community who seem to be constantly reminding us of the past in the shape of ancient monuments and relics, which we are told must be preserved for future generations to pore over. Some of these monuments and relics are indeed important as examples of our past cultures.

I do not think that the Priory Pond is in this category. This is nothing more than a stagnant murky eyesore in my opinion, and will show nothing to future generations, except perhaps that in 1965 we were not very interested in public health, and we could not find any more important issues to debate.

M. BARTON.   6 Pan Close, Barton.

As the 1960s progressed, the genie of sexual liberation began to pop out of the bottle. In Shanklin, efforts were made to put the cork back ...

January 30th, 1965

BOOK BANNED AT SANDOWN AND SHANKLIN

Sandown-Shanklin's Public Library Committee decided on Monday to withdraw the book "A Singular Man," by J.P. Donleavy, from the lending libraries in both towns. This decision was taken after a complaint from Mrs. Dorothy L. Longmate, of Heathside, Albert Road, Shanklin. Mr. W. R. Willcox (clerk) read the letter of complaint in which Mrs. Longmate described the book as unsuitable for young people. Mr. H. Holmes (chairman), who had read the book, said if this one was withdrawn the committee should consider taking about 75 per cent of the books off the shelves. Mr. L. A. Barber (vice-chairman) disagreed, describing the book as one which had no story and said it was a series of descriptions of sexual behaviour. Replying to Mr. W. G. Gray, C.C., Miss M. Wright (librarian) said there had been a good demand for the book, mainly from the "young moderns." It was agreed to remove the book.

The potential loss of Priory Farm pond continued to prove an emotive subject ...

February 20th, 1965

Priory Pond, Carisbrooke

It seems we can be grateful after all for the attacks on the Priory Pond at Carisbrooke, because they have at last rallied its defenders and shown how many there still are who appreciate natural beauty and are not impressed by specious arguments. Of course the pond is a hole; of course where earth and water meet there is mud; and of course every healthy pond is full of green algae in spring. It also breeds tadpoles, dragonfly, newts, pondweed, moorhens and almost as many

bacteria as milk. These are no reasons for filling in every piece of water which reflects the heavens on the face of the earth. Those who have such an obsession with hygiene that they condemn any pond as unhealthy would be doing a greater service to the community if they directed their energies to urging some means of lessening the present pollution of our coastal waters by human excrement. Here in the Island, and especially in the Solent, there is need for a public awakening of conscience about this problem, besides which the possibility of a few mosquito bites pales into insignificance.

MARGERY WEARN Shore End, Queen's Road, Cowes

For J.S. White's shipyard it was the end in all but name, as this gloomy financial report makes clear. The last ship ever to be built by the yard, HMS Arethusa,* was just a few months away from launching, and after that, the order books were empty ...

February 27th, 1965

DIFFICULT YEAR FOR J. S. WHITE & CO.

At the annual meeting in London on Wednesday of J. Samuel White and Co., Ltd., of Cowes, Sir James Milne, chairman, said, "The year has not been a very happy one financially. Losses have occurred on the motor coasters and the United Arab Republic contract, the combined effect of which more than absorbed the profits of the parent company's other work and there was an overall loss on the year's operation of £116,000. Our subsidiaries, Henry Bannister and Co., Ltd., and the Island Transport Co., Ltd made profits compatible with their turnover.

J. Arthur Dixon, Ltd., made a net profit of £105,000, the overall result being a group loss of £7980 ... An order has been received for a workboat for service in connection with the North Sea oil drilling rigs. The current major new work in hand is the coastal collier to be completed next month, the workboat due for delivery in May, two sets of turbines due for completion in August and HMS Arethusa due for delivery later in the year. From this it will be observed that when HMS Arethusa is completed there will be no more work in hand in the shipyard."

TOWN AND COUNTY NOTES

ORDER FOR WORK ON 'PROTECTED HOUSE' TO HALT — An 18th century Newport house has received an 11th hour stay of execution. The property, Seymour House, in Sea Street, is listed on the schedule of buildings of architectural or historic interest, but a firm of contractors, acting under instructions from the Ministry of Works, have already stripped the roof and removed part of the interior timber preparatory to demolition. The contractors, Messrs. George Weeks, of Freshwater, have now received instructions from the Ministry to make the building weather-proof ... The Post Office had asked for the site to be demolished for future development and application was now being made to the planning authority for Seymour House to be removed from the schedule and for permission for the house to be demolished. (February 6)

---

* See page 97

Two young anglers who experimented with a trot-line in a landlocked stretch of water adjoining the river at Yarmouth on Sunday, landed 30lb. of flounders.

Bembridge telephone service became automatic on Thursday week with the switchover from the manually operated exchange to the new automatic exchange in Kings Road ... The staff of nine (six during the day and three in the evenings), with one exception, are being transferred to Ryde. (February 20)

PLESSEY'S TAKE OVER DECCA RADAR — As part of a £4 million deal announced this week, Decca Radar is to be taken over at the end of this month by Plessey and Co., the electronics and nuclear components company ... A reassuring statement from a spokesman for the new owners said, "The firm will be taken over without interruption and our intention is to further expand the factory." (March 13)

RAILWAYMEN'S UNUSUAL PET — Willy, a tame rook who has lost all fear of humans, is a constant companion of two leading porters at Mill Hill Station, Cowes, Mr. Horace Cade and Mr. Arthur Darke. To the amusement of passers-by he accompanies them on their duties, either walking along the railway line with them to nearby Smithards Lane crossing, or perching on their shoulders. Three years ago the rook was found with a broken leg by a lady whose home is near the railway line. The rook now lives in fir trees near the station and flies down in answer to a whistle from his two human friends. Each day he comes regularly to the station for a ration of broken biscuits, egg yolks, and other titbits.

SANDERS OF THE SPRINGS By Vectensis — In the early 1880s the inhabitants of Newport had no convenient access to the many wells in the borough and used to be supplied with water from a spring in his garden by James Sanders, of Carisbrooke, who made regular rounds with his watercart and charged a ha'penny a gallon. This spring was in the former market garden he owned on the site now occupied by the new waterworks buildings and the road running by it was appropriately named Spring Lane. The name survives, but the garden, with its watercress beds, has been swallowed up by building developments, as has the large market garden laid out on the opposite side of the road from Newport.

———————————◆———————————

After two months of debate, the fate of Priory Pond was finally announced ...
March 20th, 1965

PRIORY POND, CARISBROOKE

The County Planning Committee decided on Monday to accept Priory Pond as a gift from the owners, Three Mile Estates, and to maintain it as a beauty spot. The pond has been the subject of controversy and a petition signed by 300 residents was received opposing a suggestion that the pond should be filled in. Mr. R.W. Rose (county planning officer and surveyor) said the land was being offered as a gift, and if, as had been suggested, the pupils of Priory Boys School looked after the pond as a school project, its maintenance could be accomplished without an appreciable charge on the rates ...

Mew Langton was the largest Island brewer until its closure in 1970, and their red and brown enamel signs were a common sight, swinging from the posts of many a pub garden. Operating from the Royal Brewery in Holyrood Street, Newport, the company was a very profitable one, generating profits of over £160,000 in 1964. To put that in perspective, J.S. White's, a shipyard employing nearly a thousand workers, made a loss of over £100,000 during that same period.

Mew Langton had just been sold for £1.5 million to the Romsey brewer, Strong and Co., who announced that nothing would change and the Newport brewery would continue to produce the Island's beer. The County Press took the opportunity to produce a potted history of the company ...

April 3rd, 1965

MEW LANGTON TO JOIN STRONG GROUP
£1.5 MILLION OFFER

The boards of Strong and Co. of Romsey, Ltd, and W. B. Mew, Langton and Co. Ltd, of the Royal Brewery, Newport, announce that they have reached an agreement with a view to Mew, Langton joining the Strong group. This will be effected by an offer of three Strong shares of 5s. each and £6. 15s. in cash for every two of the existing 300,000 shares of £1 each of Mew, Langton. The shares of Mew, Langton are not quoted on any stock exchange. Full acceptance of the offer will result in the issue of 450,000 shares of Strong and Co., and the payment of just over £1 million in cash ... It is the intention of Strong that Mew, Langton shall continue to trade under its existing name and management, and Strong have assured the directors of Mew, Langton that the interests of staff and employees generally, will be safeguarded. Lt. Col. F.J.T. Mew, the present chairman, will be invited to join the board of Strong. The profits before tax of Mew, Langton for the year 1964 were £ 162,834 ...

HISTORY OF THE FIRM

In the latter part of the 18th century Benjamin Mew apparently started to collect inns and formed a partnership with his brother under the name of Mew and Co., Brewers of Newport and Lymington, and with the help of his three energetic sons, Tom, William Baron and Joseph, the firm prospered and grew to considerable dimensions, so that at his death, he was able to leave the Lymington Brewery to his eldest son Tom, and the Isle of Wight business to his second son, William Baron. The business expanded and to deal financially with all this expansion it was necessary to obtain more capital and this was achieved by taking in Mr. Walter Langton ... Francis J. Templeman Mew took over the running of the firm in 1960.

The beer cellars were built of cast concrete, at that time quite a novel method of construction, to deal with the export trade. Hogsheads were brewed in March and stored in the cellars to mature ...In 1898 the new malt house was built in Holyrood Street; a very modern method of pneumatic malting was adopted, there being very few similar plants in this country. The advantage was that malting could be carried on throughout the year and not only during the months of September to March as in the usual floor malting, a method which was normal in this country. Its value was more than ever appreciated during the wars. At the same time a new venture was started, the manufacture of mineral waters. A factory was built and equipped with the most modern plant. It was a great success and has continued to grow Luckily, during the last war the Brewery was not hit and at one time the firm was brewing for six other brewers. The branches at both Portsmouth and Southampton were destroyed, but each has subsequently been rebuilt. After the war the last of the brewery horses, "Old Tom," was retired to Ningwood. Altogether 17 members of the Mew family have been engaged in the business and four Langtons.

———————————◆———————————

The Beatles' new single, 'Ticket to Ride' had just been released. Councillors at Ryde discussed whether there was any capital to be made out of what at the time was thought to be nothing more than a happy coincidence of wordplay. Had they known it, the title was, in fact, a direct and deliberate reference to Ryde, Paul McCartney and John Lennon having visited the town more than once in the early 1960s* ...

April 17th, 1965

BEATLES TO PUBLICISE RYDE?

The chart-topping Beatles may unknowingly help to publicise Ryde as a holiday resort this summer with their latest record. "Ticket to Ride" was released on Monday, and in Tuesday morning's charts it appeared as number one. At a meeting of Ryde Town Council on Tuesday Mr. R. V. Bourn drew attention to the title and said there was a first-class opportunity for the publicity department to use a play on the title in their national Press advertising. One of his suggestions for an advertisement in the national Press: "Why not take a ticket to Ryde this summer?"

———————————◆———————————

Brading's historic bullring was on the move ...

May 15th, 1965

ANCIENT LANDMARK MOVED

Brading's famous bull ring, from which the old township takes the name for its principal road junction, was moved on Wednesday. A mechanical shovel was used to dislodge it to make way for road improvements. Dating back to the 14th century, the bull ring, in which bulls were secured by their nose rings while they were baited by a special breed of bulldog, has been the centre of community life in the township throughout its history. At one time it is believed the ring was also used for bearbaiting. The practice was made illegal in 1835.

About a foot of the massive iron ring showed above the level of the ground but when it was lifted out of position the relic was found to be nearly two feet long, weighing about 4 cwt. It is planned to incorporate the ring in a traffic island in the middle of the main Ryde-Sandown Road.

---

* They came to visit Paul McCartney's cousin, Elisabeth, (Bett) and her husband Mike. The details appear in McCartney's 1998 book 'Many Years from Now' co-written with Barry Miles, "Mike and Bett became the publicans of the Bow Bars, on Union Street in Ryde on the Isle of Wight, and Paul and John hitch-hiked down again to stay with them. Paul's brother spent the summer of 1961 working here as a short-order cook. It was a journey which in due course would reappear, punningly, in the single 'Ticket to Ride.'"

The closure of all, or part, of the Island's railway lines had been a foregone conclusion for many years and had been confirmed by the 'Beeching Report' back in 1963. The only question now, was when. A clue came when British Rail announced the withdrawal of all freight services on the Island's railway system, a decision which caused surprisingly little protest. Tellingly, the Island's coal dealers, by far the biggest user of the freight network, were unconcerned at the decision ...

July 10th, 1965

ISLAND FREIGHT TRAINS TO BE WITHDRAWN

Notice of their intention to withdraw freight services from all Island stations in not less than three months has been given by British Rail to traders. Mr. G. H. R. Gardener (Island assistant) told the "County Press" the move was not part of the Beeching plan for rail closures. No date has been fixed for the withdrawal but it would probably be some time in October or November. Consultations had already taken place with staff, and union representatives had been in touch with those employed at Medina Wharf, Cowes - the Island's main distribution centre for domestic coal supplies. Letters giving warning notices of the withdrawal had already been sent to Island traders, most of those concerned being coal merchants. Mr. E. C. Golding - director of Corralls, Ltd., the Island's major coal importers - confirmed that his company had received notice of the intended withdrawal of freight services. Their first concern was the initial distribution of coal from Medina Wharf to points where it was discharged to distributors for delivery to customers. As far as could be seen there would be no problem switching from rail to road.

———————————◆———————————

Another closure which had been waiting in the wings and came as no surprise, was that of the Cowes shipyard of J. S. White. The company still had a few strings to its bow which enabled them to operate for a few years longer before the final end came. They owned Bannister's, a small rope making business,* and on the manufacturing side they branched into producing air conditioning equipment, steam turbines and bow-thruster propulsion units† ...

July 24th, 1965

J.S. WHITE'S SHIPYARD TO CLOSE

The Board of J. Samuel White and Company, Ltd., announce that the board has been closely studying the development and diversification of the engineering activities of the company for some time. They intend to inform shareholders of these plans at the earliest opportunity. As part of the reorganisation, however, it has been decided, with regret, to close the shipyard as soon as H.M.S. Arethusa is handed over, towards the end of this year. This has been a very difficult decision to make, particularly in view of the redundancy of 400 shipyard workers which will result. This will be kept to a minimum by meeting the labour needs of the more productive engineering activities, which over the longer term are confidently expected to be more profitable to the company.

---

* Bannister's ropewalk premises, which ran from Mill Hill Road through to Pelham Road, were sold the following year, the little work remaining being transferred to the main works.

† Bow thrusters allow 'sideways' movements of craft during docking

Launched in 1963 and commissioned in 1965, HMS Arethusa was the last ship to come from the yards of J.S. White & Co. (See page 92.)

In 1991, the Arethusa was decommissioned, not to be scrapped, but to be used for target practice. She was taken out into the Atlantic, in the Western Approaches, and sunk by repeated attacks from missiles, guns, torpedoes, bombs and depth charges.
Both photos by kind permission of Martin Mitchell. See website www.hms-arethusa.co.uk,

ISLAND NOTES

COMPUTER ARRIVES — The County Council's computer arrived on Thursday. The "robot-age" machine, weighing one ton, and its data printing equipment, weighing half-a-ton, were cautiously manoeuvred from a transporter into the former office of the motor taxation department. The overall cost of the installation is approximately £44,000. It is estimated that the computer will eventually achieve savings of £15,000 a year.

Annoyed at the damage caused to one side of his lawn by a burrowing mole, a Totland Bay resident set a trap. He caught a vole, so tiny that it is a wonder that the trap even touched it, and then a full-grown weasel. The mole has now reached the other side of the lawn.

ISLAND WELCOME FOR THE QUEEN — Her Majesty the Queen, accompanied by His Royal Highness Prince Philip, Duke of Edinburgh, visited the Isle of Wight on Monday and Tuesday. (July 31)

Visitors to the country fair at Shalfleet on Thursday disposed of two whole roasted sheep, 500 sausages, 500 rolls and 32 loaves of bread in two-and-a-half hours!

◆

The Queen was about to visit the Island and after a trip up the Medina she would be landing at the Old Quay in Newport Harbour. The County Press took the opportunity to explore a little of the area's history ...

July 24th, 1965

NEWPORT HARBOUR - WHERE THE QUEEN WILL LAND
INTERESTING SIDELIGHTS ON COMMERCIAL CENTRE

One of the least known but most fascinating centres of commerce in the Island is Newport Harbour where Her Majesty will land at the old Town Quay when she pays her first official visit on Monday. Most of the necessities of life are carried here but only a very small proportion of the residents appreciate the vitally important part it plays in the economy of the Island; or that it is a bustling hive of industry handling 2000 vessels a year. All imported soft woods from the Baltic and Scandinavia are brought into the Medina at Cowes and then transhipped to the Vectis Shipping Company's barges for their final journey upstream. In 1951 the timber amounted to 5600 tons but by 1964 this had grown to 9000 tons and it is confidently expected that it will exceed 10,000 tons this year. General cargoes of cattle food, fertilisers, foodstuffs, bricks and cement arriving in the harbour have also increased, from 107,000 to 132,000 tons in 1964 ... Exports have dropped owing to the reduction in the acreage given over to sugar beet in the Island but the amount of grain - mainly barley - which has been shipped out has more than doubled in the last 13 years, increasing from 3000 tons to 6800 tons. The harbour has 700 yards of quay space on either side and is navigable for 10 hours out of the 24 under normal conditions. It is in use day and night, seven days a week, and is used by some 2000 vessels each year. There are never any labour troubles in the

WHERE THE QUEEN WILL LAND

One of the least known, but most fascinating centres of commerce in the Island is Newport Harbour, where Her Majesty will land at the old Town Quay when she pays her first official visit on Monday. Only a very small proportion of the residents appreciate the vitally important part it plays the economy of the Island." (July 24).   *[Photograph by Reg Davies]*

...nor station in August 1965, the last summer of steam operation on the Island. Soon the Cowes ...de line would close and the Ryde to Ventnor line would in future only run as far as Shanklin. ...er London Transport tube trains, dating from 1938, were introduced to operate the only ...ce to remain, the Ryde to Shanklin line.   *[Photograph by Alan Stroud]*

harbour and ships are turned round quickly and efficiently.

Like every other tidal river the Medina has siltation problems but these are now dealt with by the Ballaster, a steam dredger ... Since its purchase in 1959, the Ballaster has dredged up 34,000 cubic yards of mud from the river. Of that total, the straightening of Five Trees Bend to the north of the harbour, to allow easier access for shipping, accounted for 3400 yards. The mud is loaded into a lorry and tipped at the Seaclose recreation ground, where it is planned to reclaim two acres of land. It is essential to have flat mud berths in the harbour and for hundreds of years the level was maintained by men using shovels, but a few months ago the corporation acquired a second-hand fire pump for £45 and by using the powerful jet the harbour staff can move more mud in an hour than they could in a month by the old method. What is more, the mud now finds its own level ... The schedule of rates, tolls and duties for the harbour makes fascinating and sometimes mysterious reading. What, for instance, are ufers? These are listed at 1s. 6d. for 120 pieces above 24 foot. The answer after considerable research, turned out to be lengths of wood. The charge for almonds, anchovies, anchors or billiards tables is the same - a penny a cwt. But bog ore - whatever that may be - is threepence a ton. Other items which had the writer guessing include culms, cones, dari and felloes.

———————◆———————

In some quarters there was concern and dismay at the news that the Island's railways might disappear, and some organisations put forward ambitious, but ultimately unviable plans to retain the lines. However, in a repeat of the line closures of the 1950s, the truth is that most Islanders were largely unmoved by the imminent closure. Plentiful buses and the advent of the car had rendered the Island's trains an 'also ran,' and when Ernest Marples, the Minister of Transport, announced the closure of most of the Island network, it was largely greeted with an unconcerned air of resignation ...

July 31st, 1965

RYDE-SHANKLIN RAILWAY TO CONTINUE
COWES LINE TO CLOSE

British Rail announced on Wednesday that the Minister of Transport had refused his consent to the withdrawal of passenger services between Ryde (Pier Head) and Shanklin. He has agreed to the withdrawal of passenger services between Ryde (Pier Head) and Cowes, and between Shanklin and Ventnor. The decision means the following stations and halts will close: Ashey, Havenstreet, Newport, Cement Mills, Medina, Mill Hill, Cowes, Wroxall and Ventnor. The Minister has decided that money must be spent on the modernisation of the Ryde-Shanklin line which is to remain open ... The Minister's consent to the closures is subject to the provision of additional bus services, and until all necessary arrangements have been made to ensure that these services are available to the public the closures cannot be implemented. A Southern Region spokesman said "Provided these arrangements are completed in time, the closures will take effect from Monday, October 4th, after the end of the summer holiday season ..."

NEWS IN BRIEF

Two schoolboys who noticed a couple of large fish stranded in shallow water at low tide in Newport Harbour on Thursday week waded through the mud and returned clutching specimen bass weighing 6lb. and 5½ lb. respectively.

Nikita and Valentina, two six-month-old Russian bears, escaped from Ryde Children's Zoo at Appley Park on Saturday. They were chased along the beach by police and holidaymakers for an hour until they ran into an enclosure made of deckchairs erected by Mrs Barton, manageress of the Appley Park Cafe.

POP STARS VISIT RYDE — More than 20 pop stars bought "tickets to Ryde" at Southsea on Tuesday and travelled by hovercraft on a day trip to the Island. The party, which included the Hollies, the Zombies, the Walker Brothers and the Small Faces were accompanied by staff of the "Fabulous" magazine who had organised the trip. A coach was at the stars' disposal and they drove to Brading Downs for a chicken and salad picnic, before ending the afternoon with a visit to the go-kart track near Ryde. (September 11)

EAST COWES MAN SWALLOWS DOMINO — Mr. Michael Dennis, a 28-year-old ship's plater, was the victim of an unusual mishap in the Victoria Tavern, East Cowes, on Saturday. He knew that the 6-1 domino had dropped into his pint of mild ale but when he drank up, he inadvertently swallowed the domino as well. He was taken to St Mary's Hospital where an X-ray revealed the location of the domino, which was retrieved by a surgeon who inserted a tube down the victim's throat.

———————————————◆———————————————

The end had finally come for shipbuilding at J.S. White's yard. Naval contracts were a thing of the past and the yard was finding it increasingly difficult to remain competitive in the shipbuilding market. Japan's steel industry could import coal and iron ore (Japan had none of their own), turn it into steel, build a ship, deliver it to the customer in this country and still undercut British yards. White's fortunes were not helped by the fact that the yard did not enjoy the best industrial relations in the world (there were over 20 unions to deal with) and they found themselves increasingly unable to compete ...

December 19, 1965

300 YEARS OF SHIPBUILDING AT COWES
CLOSING OF J.S. WHITE'S YARD

The last sad chapter in a fascinating story of Island shipbuilding achievement over the centuries concluded last week, when J. Samuel White and Co., Ltd., closed the shipyard section of their works at Cowes. It was appropriate that the last vessel to be built by J. S. White's, the oldest private firm on the Admiralty list, was one for the Royal Navy. The commissioning of HMS Arethusa on Wednesday week ended an era in shipbuilding probably unparalleled throughout the world ...

GRIM FORECAST

A grim forecast of changes to come in the firm was first given in the annual report early in 1963. It was announced that their efforts were being directed t developing the engineering and other interests which, if successful would enable White's to ride out the shipbuilding storm. The matter was enlarged on in the 1964 report when the reason for the shrinking market was explained as being due to the modern complicated warship being so expensive that most of the world's smaller navies could not afford new ships. Wage awards, coupled with shortened working weeks, were added handicaps in competing for contracts in the international market. The eventual news that the shipyard was to close down was not unexpected, despite strenuous efforts by the local MP, trade unions and other organisations.

To the town, whose history has been so closely linked with the local yard for many years (and the craftsmen from many parts of the Island), it was a cruel blow. Some workers found employment elsewhere, but many who had devoted their working lives to J. S. White's were now too old to change their trade or to move to the mainland. The gradual running down process speeded up a fortnight ago when about 120 workers completed their month's notice and ended finally on Friday week with the dismissal of a final 140.

The shipyard machinery is silent, and the chattering of riveting equipment and the clatter of heavy hammers on sheets of metal has gone. The stocks and slipways at East Cowes, from which so many of the world's finest vessels have been launched, stand gaunt and deserted, a silent memorial to the Island craftsmanship and past glories.

Meanwhile orders pour in to the busy engineering department for gas and steam turbines, boilers, oil burning equipment, filtration plant and general metalwork. At Somerton works, light engineering continues with refrigeration equipment, frozen food cabinets and display counters. Another subsidiary, J. Samuel White and Co, (Scotland) Ltd., at Cockenzie, is engaged in building fishing boats and other small craft in wood, aluminium, steel and glass fibre. Three other firms complete the Samuel White group - Henry Bannister and Co., Limited., of Cowes (rope makers); J. Arthur Dixon, Ltd, (colour printers and manufacturers of greetings cards and tourist publications) and the Island Transport Co., Ltd.

1966

THE WEEK'S NEWS

FAREWELL 1965 — For the Island 1965 will be remembered chiefly as the year of the most successful royal visit and, with one notable exception, prosperity in the industrial field. For the "County Press" it has been a year of considerable expansion. 12 years ago the paper consisted of 10 or 12 pages weekly; now 20 and 24 pages are the rule, a 16-page being insufficient to accommodate the mass of news and advertising that collects each week. This growth is largely due to the perspicacity of advertisers, who are quick to take advantage of the circulation, now in excess of 31,000 copies weekly.

RAIL CLOSURE - "A MATTER OF WEEKS" — The death knell of the Shanklin-Ventnor portion of the railway, with the Ryde-Cowes line, was sounded in more pronounced tones on Tuesday. A "County Press" representative asked Mr. David McKenna, general manager, Southern Region, to explain the closure position. Asked if he could give a closure date, Mr. McKenna said "It will be a matter of weeks, rather than months." (January 15)

RADAR ORDERS POUR IN FOR PLESSEY — Plessey Radar have received a further contract from the Ministry of Aviation for 12 radars for RAF air traffic control. This brings the total installations ordered to 30, for use at stations at home and overseas. In addition to substantial contracts for the armed forces of a number of countries, Plessey are also executing extensive orders for installations at civil airports at home and abroad. This work will keep the firm's factory at Somerton busy for a long time. (January 22)

BRITISH RAIL ANNOUNCE CLOSURE DATES — British Railways, Southern Region, announced this week that arrangements had been completed to close the line to passenger traffic between Ryde St John's Road and Cowes with effect from Monday, February 21st. Withdrawal of service between Shanklin and Ventnor will take effect as from Monday, April 18th. (January 22)

One of the great strengths of the County Press was its publishing of readers' first-hand accounts of life in bygone days. A former Islander wrote of her early school days at Node Hill School...

February 12th, 1966

'MY FIRST SCHOOL'
ISLANDER'S PRIZE-WINNING ESSAY

Memories of Nodehill Infants' School, Newport, which she entered in May, 1896, at the age of three, gained first prize for Mrs Elsie Evans (72), of Devizes in a local essay competition. A copy was sent to Mr. A. L. Hutchinson, county education officer, who kindly forwarded the cutting to the "County Press" expressing the view that this remarkable essay on education on the Island as it was in the past would be of considerable interest to many. Mrs Evans wrote:

Many years have passed since my first days at school but they are still fresh in my memory. In those far-off days at the end of the last century, children started school at the tender age of three and soon after my third birthday, my big sister, aged five, took me to school. Not unwillingly at first, but full of curiosity. The building had church-like narrow windows which only opened high up at the top. The school was very hot in summer, and cold in the winter (no central heating for us!) The heating was by an iron stove, standing out from the wall, and is surrounded by a high iron guard. In winter the stove was kept burning with coke, and a bowl of water stood on the "hob." The fumes were often unpleasant and caused numerous coughs.

Only those in the immediate area really felt warm. Classes at either end of the hall shivered in winter, while in summer, the heat was almost unbearable owing to insufficient ventilation. The building was on the main road, and the windows on that side were kept closed on account of the noise of traffic.

There were about four classes in the hall and a small room entered through a glazed door for other "babies" class. There I was given a small chair in the front row. I don't remember any lessons that day, but can recall trying to sit up very straight with my hands behind my back so that I could qualify for a ride on the rocking horse. Just as my turn came, the bell went, the long morning ended and it was time to go home for dinner. We were allowed one and a half hours' break and had to be back in our class at 1.30 p.m. The walk home (three-quarters of a mile), dinner and then the return journey proved too much for the "tinies" and before long about 20 sleepyheads nodded and grouped, and as the small bodies were about to fall off respective chairs they were rescued by the teacher and laid in a row on mattresses provided for the purpose.

VIPS FEARED

In those days schools were governed by a board of VIPs (local, hence the name Board Schools) and sometimes these people, men and women, came on a visit. We all had to be on our best behaviour. We were always terrified in case they asked any of us a question, though we feared the school inspectors most. Another fearsome creature was the school attendance officer. He was an uncouth, uncivil person, who stood every morning near the school with a stick and threatened the small latecomers with a beating. As soon as the registers were marked he would enter the school and make a list of absentees, and if a note or message was not forthcoming from the parents, he would set off to call on the mothers to know the reason why. He was often surly and rude when speaking to them. How times have changed!

My home was about four miles from Osborne House, where Queen Victoria spent most of her time during the latter years of her long reign. My mother invariably met us from school in the afternoons and on one occasion she suddenly said, "Look, there's the Queen." My disappointment was intense when I saw, not a regal figure in jewelled crown and royal robes, but a little old lady, dressed entirely in black, widow's cap and veil complete. She was riding in an open black carriage drawn by two horses, and looked neither to the right nor left, but straight in front, as women and children curtsied and men stood with cap in hand. A few years later the Queen died at Osborne and all the schoolchildren of the Island contributed a penny each for a wreath. This was on display in the Guildhall, Newport, and we were all allowed to see it. I went with my big sister in fear and trembling lest I was made to look on the Queen in her coffin, but all I saw was a huge wreath, placed on an easel; the flowers were mostly white, with touches of pale mauve ...

While in the infants' school we had our seats smacked for bad behaviour, in the big school the palms of our hands were caned with the teacher's "pointer," and the sting lasted for hours! Not until I had gained a scholarship to a secondary school did I really enjoy learning. There the masters and mistresses treated us as human beings ...

NEWS IN BRIEF

PARKHURST'S MAXIMUM SECURITY BLOCK WAITING FOR TRAIN ROBBERS — The intense glare of publicity surrounding Parkhurst prison, with press men and cameramen watching for prisoners going in continued all this week. The new maximum security block came into use on Monday and it was learned that child murderer John Thomas Straffen is now imprisoned there. This watch on the prison began 16 days ago, coinciding with reports that members of the Great Train Robbers' gang were to be transferred to Parkhurst. In one 10 day period a photographer from one of the National newspapers did not miss meeting one of the car ferries to arrive at Fishbourne ...

UNPROFITABLE YEAR FOR J. S. WHITE AND CO. — J. Samuel White and Co., Ltd., have had an unprofitable year and the directors are unable to recommend any dividend for shareholders holding ordinary shares.

'CHICKEN IN THE TANK' — Mr. Michael Cunningham of Cowes, a salesman for Messrs. Frank Cheverton, noticed nothing unusual as he drove a car from Read's Farm, Carisbrooke, to his firm's garage at Newport. He had collected the car at the farm after delivering a new one to Mr. Caleb Reed. On the following day Mr. A. Attrill, of Shorwell, was cleaning the part-exchange car when he opened the bonnet and found a hen. It had been there for at least 48 hours but was still contentedly resting on the near side bulkhead by the heater. Apparently none the worse, the hen is now back at the farm and is laying again.

TRAIN ROBBERS ARRIVE — Four members of the Great Train Robbers gang were transferred to the new maximum security wing at Parkhurst on Friday week. Two of the men, Goody and James, came from Durham Prison, and the other two, Cordrey and Hussey, from Leicester Gaol.

JS WHITE'S CLOSING TWO MORE DEPARTMENTS — Two more small departments at J. Samuel White's Yard, Cowes, are to close - the galvanising shop next week and the foundry in March. Although the galvanising shop only employs two men, the closure will be widely felt as no similar service exists on the Island. Since the shipyard was closed there has been insufficient work for the department, whose unusual "outside" jobs have included galvanising dustbins made at Parkhurst Prison. It is believed that about seven men will become redundant when the foundry closes. (See photograph, page 113.)

◆

After 104 years, the last train pulled out of Cowes station ...

February 26th, 1966

PACKED CARRIAGES ON THE LAST TRAIN FROM COWES

SUNDAY'S SENTIMENTAL JOURNEYS

The 14-mile Cowes-Newport-Ryde railway closed down on Sunday. Ironically

crowds packed the last trains of a service which failed for lack of support. Throughout the day booking offices along the line were kept busy and at Cowes where the normal Sunday takings averaged less than £10, enthusiastic travellers paid more than £100 to make their final sentimental journeys. Bridges and vantage points also attracted their full quota of sightseers.

An hour before the last scheduled train from Cowes station was due to leave at 8.31 p.m., the platforms were a hive of activity as television cameramen set up floodlights, and photographers and railway enthusiasts mingled with the crowds. Manned by driver Mr. J. Townshend, of Ryde, and his fireman, Mr. C. Hackett, of Newport, the engine Brading pulled into the station and the carriages rapidly filled. Brading was a former London South Western Railway engine built in 1892 and brought to the island in 1924.

Mr. A. W. G. Smith (Newport and Cowes stationmaster) and Mr. A. G. Smith (Ryde stationmaster) were among those waiting to give it a send off. With a final wave of the guard's flag from Mr. R. Childs of Ryde, the train pulled away, its whistle blowing noisily. Apart from this, the departure was a sober affair and the only incident was a solitary firework thrown out of a carriage window before it disappeared into the tunnel and re-emerged at Mill Hill station to pick up more passengers. At Newport station the mailbags were loaded into the guard's van for the last time. In future, mail will be taken by GPO lorries. As the train whistled its way through the Esplanade tunnel and into the station at Ryde, it was met by waves and cheers from passengers waiting for the last train to Cowes at 9.38 p.m.

It seemed appropriate that the engine pulling this four-carriage train was Fishbourne, built in 1889 and the oldest still operating in the Southern Region. The driver was Mr. K. West, of Ryde, who has had 22 years' service with the Island railways. Mr. J. Farrington, of Carisbrooke, was the fireman, and Mr. S. Wells, of Ryde, the guard. On arrival at Cowes, after an unscheduled stop when the communication cord was pulled, there was an almost festive atmosphere with more fireworks and the usual farewells and handshakes for the railway staff ... Now only 12 ½ out of the original 54 miles of Island railways are still in use, and the Shanklin-Ventnor line is expected to close in April ...

———————————◆———————————

ISLAND NOTES

CRAIG DOUGLAS SUCCESS IN PANTOMIME — The Island singing star Craig Douglas has just completed a successful pantomime season at the Civic Theatre, Barnsley, where he starred as Robin Hood in the production of "Babes in the Wood."

SHANKLIN-VENTNOR RAILWAY PROTEST MEETING — More than 400 people attended a meeting at Ventnor Town Hall on Monday to protest against the closure on April 18th of the Shanklin-Ventnor railway line. A resolution was adopted demanding a public enquiry by the Minister of Transport into the future of the line. The meeting considered that in the meantime the line should remain open. (March 12)

GOODS, NOT GHOST TRAINS! — The Cowes-Ryde railway line is still open for freight. The goods trains do not run to schedule but are put on when required, sometimes daily and sometimes only twice in a week. (March 19)

FRESHWATER ROUNDSMAN'S ORDEAL — Mr. Ernest Hobson, of Granville Road, Totland Bay, was awakened shortly after 5 a.m. on Saturday by a hammering noise. Unable to get to sleep again, he got up to "tear a strip off" the culprit. He found the knocking was coming from inside the cold store in a nearby garage and on opening the door out stumbled Charlie Tiller, Freshwater milk roundsman who had been trapped in the icy container when the wind blew the door shut. Charlie told a "County Press" reporter that he had been trapped for nearly 2 hours. When the chill crept up his legs, and gradually to above his stomach, he began to have thoughts of dying. After a stiff whisky he set out on his round and amongst his customers was Mr. James Callaghan, the Chancellor of the Exchequer, who is spending Easter with his family at his summer cottage at Wellow.

After Strongs' takeover of Mew Langton the previous year, rationalisation had begun almost immediately. One of the first casualties was the cross-Solent shipping of beer ...

April 9, 1966

'FINAL-ROUND' FOR THE XXXX
BREWERY'S BOAT FAREWELL

At the end of this month W. B. Mew, Langton and Co., Ltd., will call 'final-round' for the XXXX — the boat with a name like the end of a love letter. With the exception of the fleet of the Guinness Group, she is the last brewery-owned vessel in Britain. The development arises from the amalgamation last year between Mew-Langton and the Strong Group. In order to achieve the greatest possible efficiency and economy it has been arranged that the company's mainland houses will be administered and supplied from Strongs headquarters at Romsey. Mew, Langton will still send a number of their products, including the award-winning XXXX and nut ales, to the mainland and will continue to administer their free-trade outlets across the Solent. As a result of this re-organisation there will be a reduction in the volume of "exports." Combined with improved ferry services, which compete extremely favourably with the operation of the XXXX, it has been considered prudent to switch transportation to lorries.

The brewery's links with the sea date back for many, many years. Prior to the 1914-18 war it exported large quantities of beer as far afield as China and Australia. This was carried to trans-Continental ports on the mainland in sailing barges owned by partnerships in which the Mew family had interests. The barges were often manually towed down the Medina but earned a reputation at sea for never giving second best to the elements. At the end of the First World War it was decided to ferry the goods in the brewery's own craft and for this purpose the motor vessel Wight was built at Cowes in 1920 by Groves and Gutteridge. Her first skipper was Mr. Ted Foley, who at the age of 82, is now living in retirement at 22 School Lane, Newport ... In 1948, in anticipation of the end of Wight's active life and owing to increasing "exports" to the mainland, the company commissioned a second motor vessel from J. Samuel White and Co., Ltd. Following considerable discussion it was eventually decided to name her XXXX after the brew that was becoming increasingly popular.

———————————◆———————————

The end of the Island's steam train service was approaching. The previous Sunday had seen the departure of the last train ever to leave Ventnor ...

April 23rd, 1966

LAST TRAIN FROM VENTNOR
RAIL LINK ENDS AFTER 99 YEARS

For the first time for 99 years Ventnor is without a rail link with the rest of the Island ... On Sunday night the last passenger train left the town's station to close the four-and-a-half miles of line to Shanklin. Ventnor and Wroxall stations are now both closed and an alternative bus service is being provided.

In spite of cold and wet weather, the occasion attracted large numbers of railway enthusiasts from the mainland. The train spotters were about early, riding up and down the line to Ryde all day and taking pictures at terminal points ... By the time the train arrived at Ventnor from Ryde at 8.10 p.m., there was a large crowd. The train brought in travellers from Shanklin and a large party from Wroxall for the round trip. A large crowd gathered at the end of the platform near the entrance to the tunnel to give a final cheer. Their ironic farewells mingled with the blowing of the engine whistle and the explosion of detonators as the train pulled out and disappeared into the tunnel in a cloud of steam and smoke. There were similar lively scenes at Wroxall, where the local passengers disembarked and cheered the train on its last leg to Shanklin, where, in marked contrast, the scene was remarkably quiet. Driver J. Townson, with Fireman C. Hackett and Guard T. Courtney, were in charge of the last train and they brought Stationmaster B. F. Endicott, from Sandown, to supervise the final trip. Mr. J. Collard, senior booking clerk at Ventnor, who took over the late turn from his colleague, Mr. D. Boynton, dealt with the last-minute rush. More than 320 platform tickets were sold, in addition to train tickets - many collectors bought sets of tickets from Ventnor to all the other stations for 13s. 3d. - but Mr. T. Wye, who came from Ryde for the day to collect tickets recovered only a fraction. The majority were kept as souvenirs ... Three enthusiasts in the last carriage, which was appropriately labelled "The end," carried their sentimental journey to the extent of leaving the train at Wroxall and walking home through the tunnel. The last train to arrive at Ventnor at 10.10 p.m. brought in another large complement of passengers. Residents of houses on either side of the line at Shanklin cheered the train and at Wroxall a large crowd had gathered to say farewell. Between Wroxall Station and the tunnel under St Boniface there was a continual chatter of fog detonators. Some of the passengers had expected to travel back on the train from Ventnor but it was not a scheduled return service and they had to find their own way home.

NEWS IN BRIEF

DISPOSAL OF OLD MOTOR VEHICLES. DUMPING AT SEA BEING CONSIDERED — In the near future the island will be faced with the problem of disposing of about 1000 old cars a year. The solution may be a watery grave. Mr. R. W. Rose (County surveyor and planning officer) told the County Planning Committee on Monday that among proposals he was considering was having old vehicles taken out to sea on dredgers and dumped overboard.

ANONYMOUS LAKE — A complaint that owing to inadequate sign-posting, visitors to the Island often went into shops in Lake and asked to be directed "to Lake," was sympathetically received by Shanklin Business Association at their monthly meeting on Thursday week.

THIRSTY ADDER MEETS ITS DOOM — Patrons are always assured of a friendly welcome at the Sportsman's Rest public house at Porchfield but the exception proves the rule. On Monday Mrs. Jill Tilbury, wife of the licensee, Mr. John Tilbury, had a shock when she saw one of the first customers of the morning — an adder. By way of introduction the visitor flung back its head and hissed. Mrs Tilbury called for her husband, who, armed with a mallet, called a hasty "Time, gentlemen, please" for the adder. With the introductions complete, Mr. Tilbury transferred the adder to a large jar — tangible evidence for any friends who might otherwise have doubted the story.

———————————◆———————————

The unwanted Princess flying boat had been standing on the slipway at Medina Road, Cowes, since 1952. Its future was still undecided, with prospective buyers coming and going. They had ranged from NASA to the Bachelors pop group, but as yet no definite buyer had been found. The only thing that was certain, was that the Princess could no longer stay on the slipway ...

April 23rd, 1966

'SLEEPING PRINCESS'
COWES LANDMARK BEING DISMANTLED

A well-known landmark and attraction for visitors to Cowes — the huge 140 ton Saunders-Roe Princess flying boat — is being dismantled in readiness for its move up river to the former J. S. White's shipyard at East Cowes. The site on which the craft has been standing in its protective cocoon for 12 years is to be used as a landing terminal for British Rail's new cross-Solent hovercraft service, due to commence in the summer. From here a regular service to Southampton and Portsmouth will be operated with SR.N6 hovercraft. The long and troubled story of the three "sleeping Princesses," as they became known, opened in 1946, when the Ministry of Supply ordered them from Saunders-Roe. The first and only one to fly — the one at Cowes — took off from the Solent in August, 1952. Its construction was acclaimed by the world as a triumph for Island craftsmen. The 148 ft., two-deck hull was, at that time, the largest metal structure ever built for an aircraft. In cubic capacity it was equivalent to a suburban train. More than 2½ miles of longitudinal members, 1469 square yards of metal plate, and 3 million rivets went into the plane's construction. It was 56 foot high and had a wing-span of 220 ft. Originally intended to carry 105 passengers in luxury, the Princess was powered by 10 Bristol Proteus engines. With these experimental engines the giant plane flew for a total of 100 hours, in the hands of Mr. Geoffrey Tyson, then the firm's chief test pilot. The first setback came when it became obvious that more powerful engines would be required before the plane went into service, and these would not be available for several years. At this period it was estimated that the total cost of the three craft, if completed, would be in the region of £ 13 million. While waiting for suitable engines to be developed, the three giants were given a protective cocoon, and two were towed over to Calshot. Elaborate precautions were taken to preserve the craft, each of which was sprayed with about nine tons of plastic and sealing compound. A total of eight tons of desiccant was used to dry the air inside and humidity was controlled by a nearby machine ... As the craft remained cocooned, reports and rumours of their fate grew ... In late 1963, the flying boats were put up for sale again. The protective cocooning on the machine at Cowes was opened so that the craft could be inspected by prospective operators, research firms and scrap dealers. Among them was Mr. Hughie Green, the television personality, viewing on behalf of an interested syndicate .... Two months later, in February 1964, it was officially announced that the three Princesses had been sold for an undisclosed sum to Cargo Sales, an American firm who intended to rebuild them to carry large space craft and missile components for NASA ... Now, two years later, mystery still surrounds their future and it is uncertain whether the Princesses will be going to America after all. For several years the nose opening of the flying boat at Cowes has been unfastened, exposing the interior to the weather. Workmen from Westland Aircraft, Ltd., are believed to be removing only the wings of the plane to enable it to be towed by tugs to its new home ...

The County Press published another first-hand account of Island history. This time, an eyewitness account of the rescue of survivors of the collision between HMS Gladiator and the American liner, the St Paul, in 1908 ...

April 30th, 1966

MEMORIES OF THE GLADIATOR DISASTER
FRESHWATER SURVIVOR'S RECOLLECTIONS

On April 25, 1908, the 6000-ton cruiser HMS Gladiator sank off Fort Victoria, near Yarmouth with the loss of 27 lives after being in collision in a blizzard with the American liner, St Paul (12,000 tons). This peace-time disaster to a warship received international publicity and lead to 1908 becoming known throughout the Island as Gladiator year.

Royal Engineers manning Fort Victoria defied the elements and although working in appalling conditions were responsible for preventing the death roll from being doubled or trebled. A first-hand account of the disaster was given exactly 50 years later by Mr. R. Crisp, of Norton Green, Freshwater — one of the very few surviving members of that gallant band of rescuers. Mr. Crisp — in those days he was Lance Cpl Bob Crisp - said "It was a terrible day that Saturday — no

"J. Samuel White's foundry is to close in March. It is believed that about seven men will become redundant." (See page 106.) *[Photograph courtesy of John Groves]*

Cowes to Ryde railway line closed in February 1966. In this photograph, taken the previous ...er, a Newport-bound train pulls in to Mill Hill Station. It has come from Cowes Station, ...d on the site now occupied by the Co-op store, and then through the tunnel which is now ... to the Cowes Rifle and Pistol Club. (See page 106.)   *[Photograph by Marie Coundley]*

fit for a dog to be out. There was a strong wind from the north west, and it was snowing like billy-oh." He explained that because of recent overseas postings the strength of No. 22 Company R.E.s managing the searchlights at the fort was down to about 25 and the men were all sitting round the fires in their Barrack rooms. They were all familiar with the American liners St Louis and St Paul which passed the fort regularly at 2 p.m. on their outward journeys from Southampton, and when the St Paul appeared to be between the fort and Fort Albert they heard another siren from further away in that direction.

HEARD LOUD BANG

They realised that another vessel was travelling in the opposite direction and just as they thought the two would be about to pass one another they heard a loud bang and realised that one of the ships had either struck the rocks or collided with the other. The soldiers rushed down to the beach and were just in time to see the outline of a warship loom out of the murk and come slowly round Sconce Point towards the fort pier. As she approached, the officer in charge dropped anchor to steady the ship and tried to beach her on the sand to the east of the pier.

Mr. Crisp said it was marvellous to hear the calm voice of the officer giving his orders so clearly that despite the howling wind they must have been audible half way to Yarmouth. The vessel came within 15 yards of the pier and those on the shore could see the sailors standing stiffly to attention with the only movement in sight coming from the men handling the chains in response to that solitary clear voice. "It made me proud of the Navy to see the way in which those sailors stood steadfast and made no effort to save themselves until they received the order to do so. Some of them could have got to the pier as she passed but not a man moved. They were marvellous."

By that time everyone could see that the vessel was going to turn over and the men onshore heard the last order from the bridge - still in that calm, clear voice - to abandon ship. The sailors reacted immediately and as the ship toppled over they scrambled up her side. When she took her final plunge her boilers blew up and she was almost hidden in a cloud of steam. Many of those who had reached temporary safety on the hull of the ship remained there, but about 50 dived overboard and made for the shore. Mr. Crisp added that he did not see one of them wearing a lifebelt. One whaler from the ship, loaded mainly with sick-berth men, ready to tend survivors, landed on the west side of the pier from where it could not be relaunched because of the terrific wind and waves but a second whaler landed safely and for the next quarter of an hour about 60 soldiers and sailors struggled desperately to launch her. All their efforts were in vain. Each time she was swung round and carried back broadside onto the beach. "If we could have launched the boat we could have saved all the men in the water" declared Mr. Crisp. "But it was impossible. We were continually being knocked over by the huge waves." ... The soldiers got out their four-oared racing gig but the sailors struggling in the waves grasped the oars and sides of the boat until it sank with the crew waist deep and was washed up on the beach but it carried with it its crew, and some 15 of the sailors, to safety and was launched again immediately after being emptied. Time after time the same thing happened with the sailors grasping at every handhold until the helpless gig went under and was washed ashore again, a most unorthodox but very effective rescue method. The boat made eight trips before all the men between the warship and the fort had been picked up but nothing could be done to help the others who were further out and were being swept towards Yarmouth. Other soldiers stepped forward at once to replace members of the gig's crew as they became exhausted but Mr. Crisp maintained his place in the boat throughout the rescue operation. "We were up to our waists in water most of the time" he recalled. "I have never been so cold in my life." ... Corporal Stenning - a powerful swimmer - adopted the unusual method of jumping from the end of the pier, time after time, to obtain a firm grip on a drowning man as he was being swept past, and swim ashore with him to safety.

The soldiers then went to the beach to care for the rescued seamen who were lying in the snow, and provided them with blankets and scalding mugs of tea prepared by a Mrs. Twaddle, who lived in one of the War Department cottages adjoining the fort. When her husband died she was granted a free tenancy of the cottage for life in recognition of her sterling work on this occasion and she lived there until 1955. The sick and injured were taken to Golden Hill Military Hospital. All this time those members of the crew who had stayed with their ship were still clinging to her hull from where they could not be picked up until the arrival of destroyers from Portsmouth ... All that took place 58 years ago and Mr. Crisp, who retired in 1927 after 25 years' service, is now 81.

CRUISER SALVAGED

The gaping hole torn in the Gladiator's side measured 40ft. by 20ft. and extended 12 ft. inwards into the vessel. To salvage her from where she had toppled presented a problem fraught with difficulties. Huge bollards were built at Fort Victoria and steam winches were anchored to massive concrete bases on the shore; but before the vessel could be moved divers had to cut away her superstructure and remove the guns. A number of steel cylinders, nearly 80 ft. long were allowed to fill and were then attached to the underwater side of the vessel. The water was then pumped out to utilise the enormous lifting power of the buoyant camels. The effect was enhanced by the cables straining from the shore based winches. Once the cruiser was on an even keel she was pumped out and refloated. The salvage operations are said to have cost about £58,000 but the cruiser was sold as scrap for only £7000 but the Admiralty considered that the experience gained was well worth the difference. The massive bollards and winch bases are still to be seen at Fort Victoria and on the beach at Norton.*

◆

ISLAND NOTES

PRINCESS MOVED TO NEW SITE — Part of the mouth of the River Medina at Cowes was closed to shipping for four hours on Tuesday evening, when the 140-ton Saunders-Roe Princess flying boat was moved to a new site on the former J. S. White's shipyard at East Cowes. The difficult operation was completed without mishap and by 11.15p.m. the floating bridge - used as a grandstand by spectators on the East Cowes side - was back in service. (May 7)

RAILWAY MUSEUM FOR THE ISLAND? — The committee of the Isle of Wight Locomotive Society are hoping to "rescue" and restore some items of Island Railways stock before the modernisation proposals come into effect. A fund has

---

* This remains the case in 2011.

been opened for the purpose and it is also hoped to open a museum somewhere on the Island. One locomotive will cost about £800 and the society would like to save some coaches as well. Such a museum would become a valuable tourist attraction. (May 28)

A footnote to a notice outside a Freshwater garden inviting passers by to help themselves to a bunch of cut roses and make a donation to church funds reads, "Collected so far, 30s. Stolen, two collecting boxes and contents."

TRAFFIC LIGHTS COME TO NEWPORT — On Monday a set of traffic signals at St James's Square were switched on. These lights, and another set which came into operation at the same time in South Street, Newport, are the first road junction traffic lights to be installed in the Island. The only others of a similar nature are the signals controlling single-line traffic over the road bridge at Yarmouth - installed some 30 years ago. (July 2)

◆

Until his death in 2009, Harry Spencer, the owner of Spencer Rigging, was a well-known face in Cowes. Hale fellow, well met, and larger than life, Harry was always ready for a brief chat. Here, speaking to the County Press in the early days of the company's operations, he revealed a lesser known side of the company's activities in its early days - the rigging of 'pirate radio' ships* ...

June 25th, 1966

COWES FIRM PROVIDES VERSATILE SERVICE
RIGGING, TOWING INVOLVES WIDESPREAD ACTIVITIES

Pirate radio ships, Scotland Yard's wireless station, yachts, fog signals, hovercraft, the Princess flying boat, ship's models and flagstaffs - all these seemingly unconnected items have one common link. They are just a few of the everyday jobs tackled by the small but versatile firm of H. R. Spencer, of Cowes.

On the harbour side of their premises, hidden behind the archway of Bank Chambers in the High Street near Cowes pontoon, a painted sign modestly describes the firm's work as rigging and towing. This understatement covers a surprising wealth of out of the ordinary jobs ... If a man is seen working up a mast in Cowes Harbour in any kind of weather, the chances are that it is Harry Spencer, or one of his hand-picked team of experts, who include John Alder and Gerald Wildish.

CLOAK AND DAGGER

There are many applications for rigging, in fact, on anything which depends on ropes or wires for support or control. Working in a cloak-and-dagger atmosphere, Mr. Spencer erected the tall masts of several pirate radio ships. Radio Caroline North and South were worked on in Holland and Spain and fitted out in Ireland.

---

* In the mid -1960s, 'pirate' radio stations dotted around the British coast provided all-day pop music for millions of listeners from ships anchored just outside territorial waters. In 1967, Labour Government legislation effectively brought the pirate ships to an end by making it illegal for British subjects to assist or work for them. Radio Caroline defied the law and continued to broadcast until March 1968.

COWES FIRM PROVIDES VERSATILE SERVICE

orking in a cloak-and-dagger atmosphere, Mr. Spencer erected the tall masts of several pirate radio ps. Radio Caroline North and South were worked on in Holland and fitted out in Ireland. The first sel was completed and put on station in the Thames without the secret leaking out."   *[IWCP]*

ell-known landmark and attraction for visitors to Cowes - the huge 140 ton Saunders-Roe ess flying boat, is being dismantled in readiness for its move up river to the former J. S. White's ard at East Cowes. The site on which the craft has been standing in its protective cocoon for ars is to be used as a landing terminal for British Rail's new cross-Solent hovercraft service, commence in the summer" (See page 111)   *[Photograph by Marie Coundley]*

The first vessel was completed and put on station in the Thames without the secret leaking out. On the way from Ireland, Radio Caroline South was on passage round Land's End when a shackle from the mast to the bow broke. Land's End radio refused to accept a message, but it was picked up by a Dutch radio station who telephoned Mr. Spencer at Cowes at 4 a.m. He went straight to Falmouth Harbour to carry out the vital repair - the first time a radio ship had ever dared to enter a British port. He had previously spent seven weeks in Ireland, covering more than 6000 miles, collecting the engine, transmission and aerial equipment for the ship.

He was next called in to supervise the purchase of Radio Scotland - formerly the 360 ton Barrell's lightship, and spent a further five weeks in Ireland checking the vessel's conversion. Mr. Spencer made all the arrangements for the ship to be towed to Guernsey, where the transmitters, generators, mast and aerials were fitted last Christmas. The following day he was the only man aboard - apart from the Hull tug crew - when the vessel was towed to the Firth of Forth and anchored. The mast for Radio 270, the latest "pirate," was erected by the Cowes firm at Guernsey a short while ago. In contrast Mr. Spencer last year rigged the 75 ft. aerial mast on top of the new Scotland Yard building in Theobalds Road for the Metropolitan Police wireless station ...

TOWN AND COUNTY NOTES

ISLAND RAILWAY ELECTRIFICATION — Details of a half million pound scheme to electrify the lines between Ryde and Shanklin were announced by British Rail. In order that the work can be carried out quickly and in time for the 1967 holiday season, the line will be closed completely for about 10 weeks in the New Year. The line will be re-opened with the third rail electric service by Easter, 1967. (July 2)

ZOO FIGHT - PYTHON V. KEEPER — A battle between Cassius the 27 ft., 195lb. Malayan python and Nyoka, head keeper at the Isle of Wight zoo at Sandown was waged on Wednesday. Nyoka has about 40 tooth marks on his forearm, Cassius lost several teeth, still embedded in the keeper's arm. The struggle started when Cassius refused to budge from his bath-house so that it could be cleaned. He lashed out at the keeper ... but he wrenched his arm free ... "There was blood all over the place" said Nyoka. Shortly after the struggle, Nyoka, forearm still bloody, was in the lion's cage with Simba doing the first of his five-times daily shows before holidaymakers.

While prawning in the shallows with a push net, a Yarmouth resident came across a brand-new outboard engine. He had the engine dried out, cleaned and running perfectly within two hours.

DEVASTATION BY HOOLIGANS. — It is six months since British Rail closed the Ryde-Cowes line; in that short time a siding at Newport station has become the

scene of morbid destruction ... About 30 disused carriages stretching for more than a quarter of a mile, which were shunted there in February, have been wrecked. Most of their windows are broken and many even have bullet holes in them ... A British Rail spokesman stated that children would be incapable of removing carriage fittings. That was obviously the work of men with tools. Most of the fittings, including the screws, were brass, and valuable ... (September 10)

LAST STEAM TRAIN ON RYDE PIER — The last steam train to travel down Ryde Pier left the pierhead at 9.35 p.m. on Saturday and another historic moment, with an even greater degree of finality, occurred with the closure of Smallbrook junction. In official language, the junction has been "abolished," the closure being effected on Sunday morning. (September 24)

ISLAND NOTES

LOST BUDGERIGAR FLEW 15 MILES — Benjie the budgerigar and prolific talker, a pet of Miss Pam Triscott of Seaview, escaped last week. Nothing further was heard until the Chale police constable advised his owner that their budgerigar had been picked up at Chale, somewhat exhausted and hungry ... The following day he was his normal talkative self in spite of his flight of about 15 miles. Benjie has played truant once before, when staying at Sevenoaks in Kent, but was restored to his owner because he was able to tell his finder his name and address and telephone number.

GOODBYE, NUBIA. END OF A FAMOUS COWES HOUSE — Nubia House, in Baring Road, Cowes on the wooded rise above Egypt Point, for 84 years the home of the Baring family, a favoured centre of the social and sailing life of Cowes, frequently honoured by visits from British and Continental royalty, will soon disappear. The site and grounds of three acres have been purchased by Mr. Michael Jackson, of Cowes, who is having the residence demolished so that the site can be developed as a housing estate with about a dozen smaller dwellings ... In a few weeks this gracious old Victorian house, one of the best-known of the Marine residences of Cowes, will disappear. Only memories will remain ...

SOFT DRINKS BOOST FOR ISLAND RETAILERS — Earlier this year the share capital of Gould, Hibberd and Randall, Ltd, was acquired by Beecham Group, Ltd. Corona Soft Drinks, with a production and sales branch at Ryde, are part of the group. Corona acquired a small factory at Ryde, previously operated by Brooke and Prudencio, in 1957. New plans involve the ending of the Corona door-to-door service and the handing over of the production and distribution of the Corona products to the Newport factory, as important additions to their well-known Kixse drinks.

1967

Over the last 15 years the Island's railways had suffered death by a thousand cuts. The coup de gras came on New Year's Eve 1966, when the steam trains passed into history ...

January 7th, 1967

STEAM TRAINS GO WITH THE OLD YEAR

AN ERA WHICH LASTED 104 YEARS

For more than a century steam trains have made a significant contribution to the life and development of the Island. On New Year's Eve an era which began in 1862 came to a clanking, hissing halt at St John's Road railway station, where, just an hour before midnight, one of Britain's oldest locomotives arrived with the last passenger train. The Island will be without rail services for about 10 weeks, then electric trains will take up where their steam predecessors left off - over all that remains of the Island network, the eight miles of track between Ryde Pier Head and Shanklin.

Each Island closure has been marked by pilgrimages by rail enthusiasts from the length and breadth of Britain, as well as by sentimental journeys and demonstrations by Islanders. Although Saturday's landmark was quite different - no services were being permanently withdrawn by British Rail - all the trappings of excitement and nostalgia were there in full measure. The sense of local history in the making, even if expressed in carnival atmosphere, was profound... Yet such is the fascination that the steam locomotive holds for so many men and boys that it would be a rash man who would say with complete conviction that the sight and sound of one of the sturdy old engines with its retinue of coaches has gone for ever. Already the Wight Locomotive Society have raised enough money to save one locomotive and least four coaches, and if the Cowes to Ryde line is reopened by Vectrail, the society hope to run special trains.

DWINDLING STOCK

Meanwhile, two of the dwindling stock of the Adams tank engines will be kept in working order by British Rail to haul materials being used in the electrification of the line, now well underway. The fate of the remainder is uncertain, but Mr. R. Streeter (Island railway manager) told the "County Press" that many enquiries had been received concerning them ... Because the steam railways have been running down, not a great many men's livelihood will be affected by the latest event. About a dozen will receive resettlement pay, but the others will take up alternative railway employment on the mainland ... The last train left Ryde Esplanade for Shanklin at 9.53 p.m., some 13 minutes late owing to the ferry from Portsmouth being delayed. At the head, bearing a wreath over the smokebox door, was the oldest of the Island locomotives, W 14 Fishbourne, which was built in 1889 and arrived in the Island in 1936. The crew were Driver P. Harbour, of Brading, Firemen R. Knapp, of Newport, and Guard R. Yule, of Ryde. About 500 travelled, and at each station large crowds turned out to cheer. Along the route at station approaches motorists sounded their horns, and at almost every line side house families stood in the glare of their open doors, waving or flashing torches.

Fireworks added to the din made by exploding detonators as the train pulled away from each station. Not surprisingly, the train drew into St. John's station half an hour late ... On Saturday about 1150 tickets were issued at Island stations, excluding platform tickets, which many bought as souvenirs. The number of passengers was far greater, for many had booked through from the mainland, including hundreds of club and society members, and a lot of enthusiasts had Rover tickets.

When the Island's Workhouse at Parkhurst closed in the late 1940s, the Council found themselves the owners of some George III chairs and a George II mahogany writing table. On the grounds that they did not match the modern decor in County Hall, the Council put them up for auction ...

February 4th, 1967

ANTIQUE CHAIRS FOR SALE

Twelve valuable antique mahogany chairs and a writing table formerly used in the Newport workhouse are being sold at Sotheby's next Friday.* They have been sent for sale by the County Council, who have been using the furniture at County Hall, since it was removed from the Forest House Public Assistance Institution. The removal was sometime between 1930, when the County Council became the Poor Law Authority, and 1948, when the National Health Service was inaugurated. A spokesman said that it was decided to sell the furniture because it was felt it did not fit in with the modern décor at County Hall, which was built in 1938. The chairs are early George III and the writing table George II. Forest House, which is now known as St Mary's Hospital, and is being modernised, was founded as a workhouse in 1774 during the reign of George III.

THE WEEK'S NEWS

COWES ROPE-WALK IS BEING DEMOLISHED — Demolition work started last week on a section of Bannister's rope-walk at Cowes — a 1000 ft. long shed in which the company manufactured ropes for more than 50 years. The firm was established in 1820 when Cowes was the centre of a busy Solent shipbuilding industry, and produced ropes for men-of-war, commercial sailing vessels and yachts. Bannisters made ropes for Nelson's flag-ship Victory, the Royal racing yacht Britannia, and for most of the yachts owned by members of the Royal Yacht Squadron. In 1957, Henry Bannister and Co., became a subsidiary of J. Samuel White and Co., Ltd. With modern compact machines, the old-fashioned rope-walk has become redundant, and Messrs. White have now transferred the business to their main factory. (January 28)

---

* The table sold for £180 at the subsequent auction but the twelve chairs failed to reach their reserve. They were put up for auction again in the early summer but the outcome was not reported.

ELECTRIC TRAINS SHOW THEIR PACES — Proving trials of electric trains on the Island began on Wednesday over all but about a mile of the eight-and-a-half miles of the new electrified railway between Ryde Pier Head and Shanklin. At 1.30 p.m. a four-coach train drew away from St John's towards the Esplanade, and later in the afternoon the train made a round trip from St John's to Shanklin without incident giving an indication of the rapid acceleration familiar to all who have travelled on the London Underground system ... On a nostalgic note, No. 31 Chale, one of the two Adams tank 02 locomotives remaining at St John's Road shed, is still occasionally to be seen in steam, assisting with everyday work* ... (March 4)

COWES-PORTSMOUTH HOVERCRAFT SERVICE OPENED — The Isle of Wight, birthplace of hovercraft, now has the most intensive regular service by this means of transport in the world. British Rail "Seaspeed," which already provides a 20 minute service between Cowes and Southampton, on Thursday opened a new route, again taking 20 minutes, between Cowes and Portsmouth. Hovertravel, Ltd., already provide fast services between Ryde and Gosport and Ryde and Southsea. (March 25)

◆

In the small hours of a dark and windy night in April 1967, the Princess flying boat made its final journey. Its last outing was to be a tow across the Solent to a waiting Southampton scrapyard. The operation, carried out in pitch darkness, was supervised by Harry Spencer, directing affairs in Indiana Jones style, standing on top of the aircraft, 60 foot above the dark stormy waters below ...

April 15th, 1967

FINAL MOVE FOR PRINCESS

A well-known Cowes landmark disappeared on Wednesday when the giant Princess flying boat made its last journey – across the Solent to a Southampton scrapyard. Of the three craft developed by Saunders-Roe, Ltd., at a total cost of £10 million, this was the only one to fly.

On Tuesday the Princess was winched down to the water's edge at the British Hovercraft Corporation's slipway at East Cowes in readiness for floating into the river on high water at 1 a.m. the following morning. Cowes Harbour was closed to shipping from half an hour after midnight until 3 a.m. on Wednesday. Despite careful planning by Mr. Harry Spencer and his team of towing experts, who gained valuable experience when the Princess was moved across the river from Cowes recently, this latest move was not without its dramatic moments. Soon after midnight, final preparations began, but the 140 ton flying boat stubbornly refused to become seaborne until 2 a.m. The difficult task of manoeuvring the unwieldy craft, with its 220 ft. wingspan, through the harbour in pitch darkness was accomplished without incident. In the bitterly cold conditions and heavy rain, Mr. Spencer directed operations throughout, standing on top of the 58ft. high hull,

---

* Full passenger services began on March 20th.

...rs on the wall of the Seagull Ballroom on Ryde pier. The venue was renamed the Big 'L'
...easy in April 1967, when it became associated with Radio London, or Big 'L', one of the most
...ssful pirate radio stations. The alliance was short lived. Within two weeks of this photograph
... taken, most of the pirates, Radio London included, were closed down by Government
...ation. The Pink Floyd concert advertised, was cancelled, the Small Faces stepping in to take
...place. This evocative photograph appears by kind permission of Roger George Clark, and is
...from his book, 'The Island in the Sixties.'

with colleagues at the end of each wing-tip sharing his discomfort. As the thre
towing launches started turning the Princess off the Royal Yacht Squadron, th
huge hull was buffeted by a force 4 north-easterly wind and this, and a stron;
outgoing tide, swept the plane tail-first down the choppy west Solent for nearly
mile, dragging the launches with it. They finally gained control of the runawa·
Princess just beyond Egypt Point, and completed a slow and tedious slog agains
the tide back to the buoy, which was reached at 5 a.m. Later in the mornin;
launches assisted a tug from Newhaven to complete the tow to the flying boat'
final destination on the River Itchen ...

ISLAND NOTES

COLOUR TELEVISION IN NEWPORT — The first colour television set in th
Island is now on show at Radio Rentals, Newport, where BBC2 experimenta
transmissions are received each afternoon. Wednesday's Shell documentary on th
rescue of African wildlife following the Kariba dam construction was an excellen
medium. A black-and-white version shown simultaneously on another se
provided a striking contrast. The BBC will provide colour coverage for the law
tennis championships in June, and plan to launch regular colour programmes i
December. (May 6)

BOMBSHELL FOR THE POLICE – An East Cowes schoolboy walked int·
Cowes Police Station on Saturday and announced that he had found a bomb a
Thorness Bay. The policeman on duty received a shock when the boy pulled a
object from his pocket and placed it on the counter – a rusty, but still live, morta·
bomb. It had been carried from Gurnard, through the crowded High Street a
Cowes, to the police station. It was promptly removed to a safe place to await th
arrival of bomb disposal experts, who took it away to destroy it.

CARGO VESSEL AT YARMOUTH – Believed to be the first cargo vessel to ente·
the harbour for more than 40 years, the old Mew Langton barge XXXX arrived a
Yarmouth from Lymington on Tuesday with 100 tonnes of lignacite buildin;
blocks on board.

WARMINSTER MYSTERY — A large audience at the meeting of the I.W
Unidentified Flying Objects Society were left divided in their opinions afte·
listening to Mr. Arthur Shuttlewood talking about his experiences concerning th
mysterious sights and sounds around the town of Warminster in Wiltshire.* Hi
meeting with what he claimed to be some of the Space People intrigued, amuse·
and perhaps annoyed some of those present. His sincerity was without question .
The question period, which concluded the meeting, revealed great interest in hi
claimed contact with space beings and he described in great detail his first meetin;
with one of these people.

---

* For 10 years Warminster was renowned as the centre for British UFO sightings. The sightings
ended, as mysteriously as they had begun, in the mid 1970s.

TV COLOUR

PLACE YOUR ORDER NOW!

Test colour pictures are already transmitted by Rowridge with regular programmes later. Deliveries from the makers shortly to commence so *consult us now* to enable orders to be placed. Price for a colour set to also give BBC/ITV in black and white, approximately £ 330.

YOUNGS
THE TV-RADIO SPECIALISTS

RYDE · NEWPORT · COWES · SANDOWN · SHANKLIN

Automatic?

Now you can take it or leave it with the AUSTIN MINI!

Revolutionary four-speed automatic/manual gearbox. Front-wheel drive. Transverse engine. Hydrolastic® Suspension. Automatic transmission available on Austin Mini Saloon and Saloon de Luxe – £75.0.0. plus £17.3.9 P.T.

Austin Mini Saloon from £508.10.0 incl. P.T.

BACKED BY BMC SERVICE — EXPRESS, EXPERT, EVERYWHERE

 AUSTIN THE BRITISH MOTOR CORPORATION LTD.

Ask for a free trial run at

WESTRIDGE GARAGE
Telephone — **(RYDE), LTD.** — Ryde 2717 —

ON THE MAIN RYDE TO BRADING ROAD

Another final trip was about to take place. Standing in the disused Newport railway station were nine steam engines awaiting the cutter's blowtorch. They were to be moved so the staff of Jolliffe's scrapyard, Clifton Grade today, could begin dismantling them. For the last time ever, British Rail fired a steam engine on the Isle of Wight ...

April 22nd, 1967

FINAL TRIP FOR STEAM ENGINES

Newport railway station was a scene of great activity on Tuesday when nine steam railway engines made their final trip before being scrapped. The locomotives have been redundant since December 31st, 1966, when steam operated rail services ceased and the Ryde-Shanklin line closed for electrification. They were moved to Newport in February and have since been sold to Messrs. H.B. Jolliffe, of Cowes, for scrap. All previous scrappings of railway vehicles at Newport was undertaken at the yard formerly used by the old Freshwater, Yarmouth and Newport Railway but the engines have been placed in the main station and had therefore to be moved to the yard. The problem arose of how to move them as the Island's diesel shunter, which would normally have done the job, could not run through to Newport from Ryde as the line is severed at Smallbrook Junction. The only alternative was to steam one of the redundant locomotives and this honour fell to locomotive number 27, formerly Merstone. On Tuesday morning, officials assembled at Newport for the operation. A fire appliance from Newport was brought to the station to supply the engine with water and the task of raising steam in the locomotive for the first time for nearly four months began. This process took nearly 3 hours but at 3 p.m. number 27 was ready for her final journey. Members of the Wight Locomotive Society had cleaned the engines, all of the 02 class, and placed a wreath on the smoke-box door of number 27, with suitable slogans chalked underneath. At 3.30, Merstone attempted to pull away five of her sister engines, including the oldest of the class, number 14 Fishbourne. The strain proved too much for the veteran and the last two locomotives had to be uncoupled. Merstone, claiming the distinction of being the last 02 class locomotive to be steamed by British Rail, made three trips before the nine engines were in the yard.

The Wight Locomotive Society have acquired some old steam coaches from British Rail. The society's 02 locomotive, number 24 Calbourne, which is still at Ryde, may soon be brought to Newport by road and it is hoped will be steamed at a future date.

———————————◆———————————

Visitors to Sandown Zoo were not impressed with the conditions that some of the animals were kept in ...

August 19th, 1967

This spoilt a family's holiday

My family and I are spending a very pleasant holiday in the Isle of Wight .. however the holiday has been marred for us by one thing. Yesterday we visited the Zoo at Sandown and were very upset at the poor conditions under which the animals are kept.* The cages in which they are confined are much too small fo them to get any proper exercise, but in particular the lion and the bear are kept i

---

* Readers who visited the zoo as children may well share those opinions, particularly with regar to the conditions the bear was kept in.

such cruel conditions, having hardly any room to move, that something should be done for them as soon as possible. My daughter was so upset on seeing the lion lying apathetically on a wooden stage in a tiny confine that she walked straight out and was unwell all day ...

R. E. ROBERTS. 11 The Knowle, Basildon, Essex.

———————————◆———————————

The following week, two letters appeared in defence of the zoo; one from the owner and the other from the zoo's animal handler. They were both self-serving, and as patronising as they were eccentric. The complaint had struck a nerve with other visitors to the zoo, who wrote to agree with the previous writer ...

August 26th, 1967

Animals in captivity

I read with some amazement the comments made in the letter you published last week. It is quite obvious to me, and to others acquainted with the zoo, that Mr. Roberts is quite ignorant of the behaviour and needs of undomesticated animals ... To state that the bear and the lion have hardly any room to move is quite ridiculous. Their cages have been measured by the RSPCA Chief Inspector and myself, and have been recognised as satisfactory ... I have their authority to quote that they are quite satisfied with the condition, and conditions, of the animals in this zoo ... I feel sure that the Island doctors are thankful that the other 40,000 children who yearly visit the zoo do not contract tummy-ache, lasting a whole day, as easily and ridiculously as does Miss Roberts.

R.G. BATEMAN, Director. Sandown Zoo.

The letter in last week's issue concerns my famous film and TV lion "Simba," at present at Sandown Zoo. Mr. Roberts stated that my lion is confined in a small cage and cannot get any exercise. This little cage measures 36 feet by 15 feet and his separate sleeping quarters are as big as a holiday chalet sleeping four people ... Mr. Roberts states that his daughter saw the lion lying apathetically on a wooden platform. Surely the Roberts family look in the same state when they are asleep in bed? Completely at peace with the world. I do not think the Roberts saw my show that I give five times a day at the zoo, when I go in armed only with my love for the "King of Beasts." Is it cruel to groom a lion as I do in the cage or give him a pint of milk or feed him on 20 pounds of beef a day? Is this cruel, Mr. Roberts? ... Does Mr. Roberts realise that without people like myself who go into the jungles of the world to catch dangerous animals and risk life and limb to train them to appear in films and on TV that millions of children and adults would never see such films as "Where No Vultures Fly" and "Tarzan?" ... I wonder if Mr. Roberts' daughter goes all unwell when she sees dear old Clarence the cross-eyed lion in "Daktari" in a little box when he is travelling.* I have come across animal cranks and have done so all my life. They never speak to the person concerned. They either waste the valuable time of the RSPCA or write a non-factual letter to a newspaper. Please, Mr. Roberts, carry on with your own business and leave the wild animals to the experts.

A. NYOKA. Big Game Hunter. Wild Animal Trainer. Sandown Zoo.

---

* A popular children's drama series of the 1960s, filmed on an African game reserve.

Available in larger American cities since 1953, colour television had just arrived in Britain. Costing over £300, the cost of a colour set represented four or five months' pay for someone on average earnings and for the next few years, colour televisions would remain the province of the wealthy. Such was the attraction of colour television that an open day at the BBC's Rowridge transmitter attracted over 9000 visitors, keen to catch a glimpse of the new arrival ...

September 23rd, 1967

TWO-MILE QUEUE TO SEE COLOUR TV

A two-mile queue of cars stretched from the entrance road to the BBC transmitting station, Rowridge, to the top of Carisbrooke on Saturday, when an open day was held at the station. More than 9000 visitors came to inspect the facilities and particularly to view colour television, and take advantage of the opportunity of seeing themselves on television. This total was 5000 more than at the last open day two years ago. Visiting cars numbered 3000, and there were also five coaches. Many waited an hour in their cars and queued for another half an hour to enter the buildings. Colour television provided the major interest ... Meryl O'Keefe, BBC television interviewer, announcer and commentator conducted interviews among the visitors, who were then able to see themselves on a closed circuit television network ...

Guy's shop in Pyle Street, which has only recently ceased trading, had a long history. The County Press related some of the story on the occasion of the shop's centenary ...

October 28th, 1967

NEWPORT CORN MERCHANTS' CENTENARY

S. Guy, Ltd., corn, seed and agricultural merchants, of 115 Pyle Street, Newport – who over the years have faithfully served Island town and country dwellers alike – celebrate their centenary this year. They still occupy the original historic premises, and the family link remains unbroken. Mr. Ralph Guy Daish, grandson of the founder, is a partner with Mr. John Edwin Heal, whose family have a 36 year connection. Samuel Guy purchased the premises in 1867 and decided to set up as a corn merchant. He went to Newport Quay and trucked a sack of maize – and that was the humble start to what was to become a flourishing concern ...

HOUSE WAS ONCE AN INN

The Pyle Street building is believed to be over 300 years old. An old "County Press" cutting records that as far back as 1768 the house was the Star and Garter Inn, owned by John Brett, brewer ... In 1785 it was owned by John Haddon, brewer. In 1826 it was conveyed to John William Pfiel and it continued to be a public house for some years. Then for some years prior to its purchase by Samuel Guy, the property was occupied by a family named Beard, carrying on the family business. The premises were rebuilt in 1937. Former bedrooms over the shop are now used for storage and the firm have garages and stores in Pyle Street, separate from the shop. Premises in the Mall, where horses were formerly stabled, are still in Messrs Guy's possession, but unoccupied. In the old days, horses and traps used to line up every morning for their round, which would take all day. Transport is now by lorry. Corn and maize formerly came in sacks of more than 2 cwt., and at one time were measured by the gallon. In the old days, too, Guy's used to buy raisins and currants by the ton and supply them to the Swainston Estate for pheasant rearing ... One of the biggest changes is in the growth of the pet food trade. In the old days, two dozen 1lb. packets of cat and dog food represented a week's supply; now 200 cases are required to meet the demand. An ever-growing interest in gardening has rocketed the sales of seeds ...

The County Press endeavoured to shed some light on the day-to-day life of inmates in the Island's prisons ...

November 11th, 1967

CAMP HILL PRISON
TRAINING FOR WORK, STUDY AND PLAY

Nestling in the shadow of Parkhurst Forest, in a sylvan setting secluded from the public gaze, is an establishment which could be mistaken for a hospital or college of early 20th-century vintage. High walls and locked gates, however, reveals the building to be a prison. Camp Hill is perhaps the least publicised of the three Island prisons, due in part to a minimum of sensational occurrences. Its inhabitants are, nevertheless, members of society – and, in the interest of enlightening the rest of the community, the "County Press" were pleased to have the opportunity to go the prison and to meet Mr. D. T. Cross, the new governor ... Camp Hill is classed as Category C; it is a secure prison, but the majority of men, mostly under 30, are serving comparatively short sentences ... The largest of the six prison halls, St George's, built to house 150 has been partitioned into two sections of 75 which facilitates the aim of a better understanding between prisoners and staff ... Each hall possesses a television set, and generous time is allowed for a free association, with the result that the cell is virtually only a bedroom.

TIN AND TEXTILES

The largest workshop is the tinsmith's shop where a wide variety of articles were being produced for Ministry and Defence and other Government departments, including the Post Office and all branches of the Services. They included cake tins, dust pans, coat hangers, oil measures of 1 gallon capacity, large baking and serving trays, funnels of various sizes, petrol cans and several other products ... Another skilful task is to produce stencils, by hand, to facilitate printing on GPO mailbags.

GARDEN AND FARM

Newportonians partial to pumpkins might have, unawares, eaten the produce of Camp Hill. There is an excellent market garden here, where, in addition to the pumpkins is grown a variety of the more normal vegetables, notably some excellent tomatoes, cucumbers and lettuces. Much of this produce is sold to a chain store in Newport ... Outside the prison is a farm owned by Camp Hill, where men who have proved their trustworthiness are allowed to work. It consists of 183 acres of attractive landscape), but housing development demands have made inroads and the farm might be further reduced in the future. About 15 prisoner-farmhands are engaged in tending nearly 100 cattle and 250-300 pigs ... At 5 p.m., when work is finished for the day ... the men return to the prison yard, a count is taken, and, in what seems to be split seconds, the men are away to the halls ... Tea is taken in association, until 5.45 p.m. At six o'clock all the men on evening classes are taken to the classroom block. At 7.20 those not on a study session may come down to watch television, play table tennis or darts, read the papers, or engage in similar pursuits, until 8.45 p.m., when supper is served. Then they are locked in their cells for the night. The evening pattern is varied at weekends, the prisoners remaining in their cells during the evening - as the staff are entitled to their own leisure pursuits!

1968

St Swithin's Approved School, located just outside Yarmouth, where the La Salle private estate now stands, came to the attention of the national Press in late 1967. A school for young offenders, it was run by a group of Roman Catholic priests, one of whom, Brother Cassian, was alleged to have administered over-enthusiastic beatings (there were also other unproven allegations regarding other members of staff). The then Home Secretary, James Callaghan who, coincidentally, had a holiday home at Wellow, set up an enquiry to be held jointly by school managers and Government Inspectors. The enquiry was held in private. The County Press received many letters speaking well of Brother Cassian, but they all came from readers who had no personal experience of the inner workings of the school. One letter came from someone who did - a former teacher at the school. He suggested the allegations were not as fanciful as some were claiming ...

January 27th, 1968

St. Swithin's Enquiry

I was pleased to learn of the interest of the general public regarding a further enquiry into the dismissal of Brother Cassian as headmaster of St Swithin's School. I would like to point out that I myself pressed for a public enquiry right at the beginning of this affair. The Home Office, however, preferred to keep it private. I realise after reading the letters how little the public can know of the facts brought to light during the enquiry that has taken place.

I am not against corporal punishment when deserved, neither am I unduly concerned with "overzealous" legal punishment, but I am very strongly opposed to brutality and illegal punishments.

Mrs. Lewis has said that the boys' own opinions are the best evidence - I would therefore like to quote part of one of many letters I have received.

"Congratulations on bringing to light the brutal way the boys are treated at St Swithin's school. I was one of the first boys at Yarmouth from Basingstoke in 1947. The sort of brutality of which you complain was going on then, and I suffered for it. I do not deny that I occasionally needed to be caned but it was the sadistic way and the amount given, that I can never forgive or forget. Through fear of hard times I have had there I have turned against my religion and will not even send my children to a Roman Catholic School. I and ex-boys of St Swithin's will back

you all the way. It is likely that the brutality is going on now, as it was when yo■ were an instructor there, and when I was a pupil. Lots of luck from many of th■ boys who have suffered. No one would believe us. Perhaps now they will. B.F Ryan." *

For obvious reasons, I am asking for the address not to be published.

W. G. WILLIAMS. Barling, Victoria Road, Freshwater Bay.

———————————◆———————————

The last soldier had left Fort Victoria in 1962. The barracks, consisting of many mor■ buildings than can be seen today, had stood empty ever since. The demolition men wer■ about to move in and reduce most of them to rubble ...

March 23rd, 196■

DEMOLITION OF FORT VICTORIA

A full-scale operation has been launched at Fort Victoria, Yarmouth - but not ■ military one! Heavy equipment has been moved in to demolish the former defenc■ stronghold, and the County Council are hoping to create a public open space in i■ place. Destruction of the fortress, with its 45 foot high walls, presents quite ■ problem and is phased over three years. The firm carrying out the work, Messr■ George Weeks and Co., of Freshwater, are under contract to the London financ■ company who purchased the property from the War Department some years ag■ They will retain the existing 14 cottages and store sheds on the site, and the pi■ will remain in the hands of the War Department. The contractors have purchase■ for re-sale the 30,000 cubic yards of hard-core from the demolition. The Counc■ intend to acquire the fort area as a car park and they are negotiating for this an■ the land to the west. Fort Victoria provided the setting for the recent televisio■ serial Les Miserables.†

———————————◆———————————

The Wight Locomotive Society, formed by railway enthusiasts here and on the mainlan■ had, in just a short while, raised enough money to purchase some rolling stock from Britis■ Rail. Unfortunately, their longsighted act of genius was now stymied by the fact that the■ engine was landlocked at Ryde ...

April 20th, 196■

WIGHT LOCOMOTIVE SOCIETY

The Wight Locomotive Society, which has purchased for preservation the la■

---

* The enquiry, which was held in secret, decided that there had been ill treatment of boys by Brother Cassian and others. James Callaghan, the Home Secretary, noting that Brother Cassian had accumulated months of unused leave, insisted that he took it at once, and ruled that he would not be allowed to return to the school. A 2000 signature petition was sent to Callaghan protesting at the outcome. A search online in 2011 revealed that two files detailing the enquiry findings are held in the National Archive. They are marked, "Closed for 75 years and cannot be viewed until January 2044." A request to see them under the Freedom of Information Act (with names redacted) wa■ denied, the reply stating, *"Included are unproven allegations against (other) named teachers at th■ School."* References to ex-staff can be found online.

† A 1967 'mini-series,' made for the new colour service on BBC 2.

surviving Isle of Wight 02 class tank locomotive and five carriages, has launched an appeal for money to remove their engine from Ryde St John's Station to Newport. This move, which it is hoped will take place in May will be with the aid of an ex-Army tank transporter. For this to take place a sum of between £300 and £400 must be raised within the next six weeks. If this amount is not realised the engine might be lost for ever, and the society's aim, which is to set up a railway museum with the train as a working exhibit, will be quashed.

The engine, No. 24, Calbourne, was built by the old London and South Western Railway Company at their Nine Elms Works in 1891. She was brought over to the Island by the Southern Railway in 1925 ... Calbourne was purchased by the society from British Railways at the beginning of 1967 for £900 when the old steam service was replaced by the ex-London Underground Electric trains between Ryde and Shanklin.

Restoration is already in progress on the society's aged carriages at Newport, but the preservation of the locomotive has been beset by ill luck; first, Smallbrook Junction, which was the link between the Ryde and Newport lines, was taken out within a few weeks of the engine's purchase; then a promised method of cheap transport fell through; and a further source of promised equipment came to nothing. Now the future of this historic engine depends upon the ability of the society to raise sufficient finances for the transportation of Calbourne a distance of six miles.

Mr. T. P. Cooper, 63 Mill Hill Road, Cowes, is hon. secretary of the society.

━━━━━━━━━━━◆━━━━━━━━━━━

TOWN AND COUNTY NOTES

Two boys who absconded from the St Swithin's Approved School in the early hours on Saturday reached the mainland in a rowing boat they took from the school. They were seen to catch a train at Brockenhurst and were picked up by the police the following evening at Brixton, London. (January 27)

Charles Wilson (37), one of the train robbers, was moved into Parkhurst Prison under heavy escort on Sunday to join five other members of the gang who are serving sentences in the maximum security block.

"GRASS SNAKE" WAS AN ADDER — Tim Medland, aged 11, of Noke Farm, Parkhurst, will not touch a grass snake in a hurry again. For the one he tried to catch in Parkhurst Forest on Sunday afternoon turned and bit his thumb. It was then he realised the true identity of the snake - an adder. He obtained a lift to St Mary's Hospital where he received seven injections to combat the venom. Tim leaves hospital tomorrow after a week under observation.

UNUSUAL CATCH — Fishing with a line from the bank of the River Medina near White's shipyard on Tuesday, Mr. R. Beasley, of 2 Tennyson Road, caught a lobster weighing 10lb. the huge catch was sold to a local hotel. Last week Mr. Beasley caught a 5lb. lobster in approximately the same place.

A twelve week gun amnesty lead to over 60 firearms being handed in to Newport police station, including an American rifle dating from 1794. Whether it went the way of the other guns handed in was not revealed ...

May 4th, 1968

ISLANDERS HAND IN THEIR GUNS

A bizarre assortment of 61 guns and about 1000 rounds of ammunition comprises a motley miniature arsenal at Newport police headquarters. The lethal days of these weapons are numbered. However, this collection represents the Island response to a three-month firearms amnesty which ended on Tuesday, and it is all earmarked for destruction. Inspector E.T. Hoar, who has charge of the collection, showed the "County Press" a wide range of weapons. They include 22 shot guns, 14 rifles (the majority .22), nine revolvers, seven pistols, three airguns and six other types - including a Verey-light gun and three starting cannon as used for yacht races. The ammunition includes .303 and .22 rifle bullets, .38 and nine-millimetre revolver, and a large number of shotgun cartridges. The most interesting weapon was a .22 rifle made by J. Stevens and stamped "Cherokee Falls, April, 1794." This historic gun - which no doubt could have a fascinating story to tell - was not in particularly good condition, but was still in working order. The type of weapon which Inspector Hoar said the police were most pleased to see handed in was a Browning small-calibre pistol, in very good working order. Compact, efficient and lethal, this was the kind of gun which the hard-core criminal element would like to get hold of. A number of similar weapons were handed in at the last amnesty - from August to October, 1965 - and it would now appear that the police were receiving the last of the old war souvenirs. Generally, the standard of firearms compared with the last amnesty, was not nearly as good, and some of the weapons were described as junk. There was an exception in the case of several shotguns, in really excellent condition. The latest amnesty coincides with the introduction of part five of the Criminal Justice Act, 1967, which came into force on Wednesday ... Previously, a shotgun licence was issued by the Post Office, but now it is necessary to obtain a certificate from the police. Demand has been great and the Newport station alone has received 600 applications, many in the last few days ...

◆

Vectensis printed a reader's query about Island characters of the past ...

July 6th, 1968

HORSE AND CART DAYS

MR. C. F. Bound, of 69 Whitepit Lane, Newport, writes : It would be interesting to know if any of my fellow elderly citizens can recall, in their memories of the horse and cart days, the following:

The dog on a farm near Blackwater, who daily collected and carried home the newspapers thrown to him in the field by the guard on the train as it passed through to Sandown. The famous ice cream parlour in Pyle Street kept by Luge Pesca, (I believe that was his name). The swarms of smelts that used to be caught by longshoremen at Watch House Quay, Cowes - they used big loop nets on poles

'WHOLESALE SLAUGHTER OF NEWPORT' TO BE RESISTED.

nan Harvey said many parts of old Newport were being lost, as a result of which, the town
ng its character. He believed that the old buildings should be preserved so that the character
wn could be retained. Mr. Swan thought that the council should resist the wholesale slaughter
n older parts of the town and maintain some of their character and amenity value."
*the fine words, these warehouses in Sea Street were demolished in 1972 to make way for a
car park. (See page 149.)*   *[Photograph by Colin Fairweather]*

I have seen none of these fish for 50 years or more. The lobster pots all the way along from the R.Y.S. to Egypt Point, again, none for 50 years. My father, long deceased, used to tell me that in the 1880s, as a boy, he and his friends used to catch in the stream at School Green, Freshwater, a small crustacean which they called molejars. They were like small lobsters. Could these have been crayfish? Does anyone recall those old characters "Bread and Butter Bill," "Freddie Manhole," or old "Holy Joe"?

I can answer some of Mr. Bound's queries. The newspaper-collecting dog belonged to Miss Hills, of Birchfield, Blackwater. Lugi Pesca's ice cream parlour in Pyle Street was a very popular establishment, particularly with the young men of Newport. He was affectionately known as "Johnny Ice Cream" and his special ices, made with real cream, were superb. Unfortunately his recipe for these delights died with him. He was a devoted Roman Catholic and there is a memorial to him in the RC Church in Pyle Street ... "Freddie Manhole" was a lamp-lighter in the nights of gas lamps and "Holy Joe" was an itinerant preacher with long locks and beard who used to sleep rough, and with a tattered Bible in his hand, used to deliver sermons in the streets to anyone who cared to listen.

More information arrived the following week ...

July 13th, 1968

"HORSE AND CART DAYS."

Mr. C. F. Bound's memories of Newport and Cowes over 50 years ago have brought more reminiscences from readers.

Mr. E. Ely, of 40 Stephenson Road, Cowes, writes that the lobster fishing along the seashore at Cowes near the R.Y.S. Castle was carried on for many years by Mr. Paskins, of Medina Road, who also carried on the "Newtown River" oyster fishery. "It is quite true," he writes, "that members of the R.Y.S. had to look out on stacks of lobster pots on the beach! Smelt fishing with crushed crab for bait was a popular pastime in the harbour, particularly at the old Saltern Quay where the smelts gathered round the piles."

Mr. Cecil R. Atkey, of Wootton Bridge, writes : There were large shoals of smelts about in the harbour 50 years or so ago. The late Mr. Tom Ratsey always had a spar rigged out over the end of Bellevue Quay at the rear of his sail loft, from which a large loop net was suspended. Children were often invited to use it, and we made substantial catches, using for bait a mixture of ground-up rotten potatoes and whitening, a large quantity of which we bought for tuppence from Scovell's shop nearby. I also remember the lobster pots which were laid along the line of rocks from the R.Y.S. to Egypt Point.

ISLAND NOTES

Unigate and Stainers Dairies advertise on page 15 that as half pint bottles are no longer being made, no half pints will be supplied when present stocks run out.

ISLANDER MEETS BING CROSBY – Mr. and Mrs. Bing Crosby flew into London on Friday week. Mr. Leslie Gaylor, of 114 Medina Avenue, Newport, one of Bing's most ardent fans, met them at their hotel and took tea with them.

BEMBRIDGE HARBOUR SOLD – Negotiations have now been completed for the purchase of Bembridge Harbour from British Rail. The transfer of ownership to the Bembridge Harbour Improvement Co., Ltd., will take place before the end of this month ... The aims are: To develop and improve the harbour for both yachting and commercial purposes ... The "County Press" understand that the County Council desire to take over the toll road from British Rail, as a separate transaction; but as to when, and at what figure - and whether the toll will be removed - are matters yet to be resolved.

The two-tier postal system, introducing first-class and second-class mail, has begun.

———————————————◆———————————————

Although the war had been over for 20 years, the memories were still fresh. A Cowes reader provided a graphic account of the 1942 bombing raid which demolished Cowes Town Hall, then located at the bottom of Market Hill ...

July 20th, 1968

COWES TOWN HALL

Mrs J. Whitcher, of Redworth, Three Gates Road, Cowes, writes: When I was collecting views of "Old Cowes" for a show in connection with the Lifeboat, I discovered the above photo of the Old Town Hall and Cenotaph taken by the well-known photographer, the late Mr. Stevens, who used to live in Cowes.

It revived very poignant memories for me as I was one of the last four to leave the building before it was bombed. The Ladies' Lifeboat Guild were in charge of the canteen in the Town Hall that week ... We had just managed to clear up the piles of dirty plates that remained, when the wail of the siren could be heard and I made ready to go. On opening the door I found it as bright as day with Verey lights everywhere. As I shouted back to those inside, the first bomb fell in the works area and all hope of getting home vanished and we had to find shelter on the spot. But for the Grace of God we should have all been killed. The air raid shelter under the stairs was jammed by old chairs and we could not get in. It was then that someone suggested that there was a shelter nearby and we only just made it in time before the bombs began to fall. We were still scrambling over those inside when the whole shelter seemed to heave and threw us in all directions. The door blew in and we could see strings of incendiaries hanging from the tree above, and the corner of a house in Castle Road was already alight from one. How long we remained there I do not know, but it seemed as if all hell had been let loose and we were the only people left alive. When at last we came out and saw the devastation around, we marvelled at our escape. Hewitts, with its front blown in, had a small fire burning and the crater in the middle of the road was all too near to where we had been seeking shelter.

Then began for me the nightmare journey home. Thanks to the help of an air raid warden, Mr. Saunders, I struggled through the High Street over broken glass and tiles that covered the ground until reaching Marshall's, where I had to be lifted over the piles of rubble and masonry that blocked the road as a result of a bomb that had fallen in Carvel Lane. What a relief it was to find that my parents were safe and my home had been spared, the only damage being an enormous lump of "pug" on the floor of the sitting room. How it got there is a mystery because no windows were broken ...

———————————————◆———————————————

In the 20th century, antibiotics and immunisation brought to an end many common but fatal diseases. Among the last to be beaten was tuberculosis or TB. It was a widespread and highly infectious killer, which was eradicated almost overnight in the early 1950s, by streptomycin, a newly discovered antibiotic. Prior to that, rest and nourishment in a sanatorium had been seen as the only treatment. One of the foremost in Britain during those years was the Royal National Hospital at Ventnor, standing in the grounds now occupied by the Botanic Gardens. The hospital closed its doors for the last time in May 1964 and had stood derelict ever since. Demolition and redevelopment of the grounds was imminent and the County Press took one last look at the building ...

August 24th, 1968

FUTURE PLANS FOR FORMER HOSPITAL

Locked and deserted for four years after its final closure in May 1964, the former Royal National Hospital at Ventnor has deteriorated into a silent shell of its past glory and the grounds have become a veritable jungle. Now that its future has been decided in its purchase by Ventnor Council as an open space and amenities centre, the sound and sight of workmen is once again in evidence within the hospital, as a start has been made in the mammoth task of planning. The council are aiming for a local public weekend in the autumn and for the site to be open to the general public in some form next Easter.

Since the final act of closure took place, the hospital has seriously deteriorated through the ravages of weather, the uncontrolled growth of vegetation and wanton damage. Some parts of the hospital blocks, including upper balconies, have collapsed and have had to be supported by scaffolding as a safety measure. Entrances are overgrown with weeds, some several feet high. The whole area, including the extensive grounds, is now generously covered with 10 foot high undergrowth, presenting a desolate and depressing spectacle.

AIR OF NEGLECT

As one wanders through the empty rooms, wards, corridors, dining rooms and kitchens, the air of neglect and damage fails to dim the appreciation of the vital part the hospital played in the fight against tuberculosis during nearly 100 years of service. Broken windows, torn fitments, debris-littered floors, swinging cupboard doors, smashed light fittings and empty dispensing and instrument chests all tell woeful story of neglect as the future of the hospital was being decided. Efforts by the County and Ventnor councils to ensure the future of the hospital, commenced some four or five years before closure took place, but they came to nought by delays at Whitehall and the property was left to the mercy of the weather and the wreckers ... Items having a potentially high or special value include the stained glass leaded windows throughout all the buildings, the stained glass windows by William Morris and Sir William Reynolds Stephens in the chapel, and the organ.

The area acquired by the council includes 6¼ acres on the north side of the Undercliff Road and 261 acres on the south side, excluding the cricket field, which has been separately purchased for £1150. The total cost of acquisition is £18,400.

OUTLINE SCHEME

The scheme for the basis for discussion is to demolish the buildings at least up to the chapel as a first phase and provide a car park ... to use the large hall in the administration block as a restaurant and clear the greater part of the grounds for public access and provide a putting green, botanical garden and pets' corner ...

1969

J.S.White's had been forced to reinvent itself when its shipbuilding days came to an end. Their efforts were beginning to pay off and the company had moved into profit for the first time in six years ...

March 15th, 1969

ENCOURAGING REPORT FOR J. S. WHITE AND CO., LTD.
FIRST PROFIT FOR SIX YEARS

J. Samuel White and Co., Ltd., engineers, of Cowes, have made a profit for the first time in six years. A dividend is being paid on the 6 per cent cumulative preference shares but there will be no dividend on the ordinary shares.

The company, which employs nearly 1000, was recently taken over by the Foreign and Colonial Trust Group, which has 90 per cent of the preference shares and 78 per cent of the ordinary shares. In his report to shareholders Mr. C. G. G. Wainman, chairman, states that the last financial year was one of great importance... The widening of the range of standard products continued and he looked forward to them playing a more important role in the future. Careful consideration had been given to the boatbuilding yard in Scotland ... and they had decided to dispose of this company. Henry Bannister and Co., Ltd., their rope distribution company, continued to trade from the main works at Cowes. During the year the former rope factory site was sold and the net surplus had been amalgamated into the capital reserve. The greetings and pictorial card subsidiary, J. Arthur Dixon, Ltd., had again increased its turnover .... and they had recently completed negotiations for the purchase of a small company possessing a range of tourist products which it was intended to integrate into the Dixon organisation. The profit for the year after taxation was £19,829. In 1967 there was a loss of £57,080.

NEWS IN BRIEF

SIX HOURS ON TELEVISION MAST — A 32-year-old man spent six-and-a-half hours up the 750 ft. ITV mast at Chillerton on Saturday. He refused to come down until a telephone was fixed up for him so that he could speak to his girlfriend in Manchester ... He was first seen at 9 a.m. on the first stage platform of the mast. He climbed higher whenever anyone approached but was warned that after 600 ft. up, the mast carried a live current, and he would be killed if he went up as far as that ... The man, who had a rope noose around his neck, threatened to throw himself off the mast unless the telephone was arranged ... the police agreed and GPO engineers installed the phone onto the platform ... After talking to his girlfriend for 20 minutes he slowly returned to the ground. He was taken to hospital for treatment.

VINTAGE TRANSPORT GROUP ACQUIRE RYDE TRAM — One of the Ryde Pier trams which lost its job on January 26th will not have to take a trip to the breaker's yard. The tram, number two, which was built in 1927 has been bought by the Island Vintage Transport Group. Mr. D. Hawkins, a member of the group, said that although the tram had cost only £30 from British Rail, it would cost between £100 and £150 to move it without causing damage. British Rail had allowed the group eight weeks to move the tram ... If the money cannot be raised to lift it from the pier by crane, the only other way to move the tram would be slicing it in half, as the entrance to the pier was too small to allow it through in one piece.

DEVELOPMENTS EXPECTED IN VECTRAIL PROPOSAL — A further move in the attempted reopening of the Ryde to Cowes railway was expected yesterday. Mr. C. S. Ashby, managing director of Sadler-Vectrail, Ltd., the company hoping to operate the line with a diesel rail car, was due to meet the County Council to provide firm details of their proposals. Negotiations are at an advanced stage in the County Council's move to purchase the 12-mile line from British Rail ... It is understood that a purchase price for the line has been agreed.

———————————◆———————————

When Dave Dee, of Dozy and Beaky fame, brought his 'TV Pop Stars' to the Island for a football match, the County Press were only too pleased to report the happy event. Ironically, Mr. Dee and friends received more coverage for their modest game against Cowes Sea Cadets than superstar Bob Dylan would for his comeback appearance at Wootton a few months later ...

April 28th, 1969

POP STARS' TEAM AT COWES

A bitterly cold afternoon and a blustery wind did not prevent about 500 turning up at Westwood Park, Cowes, on Sunday to watch Dave Dee's TV Pop Stars play the Pirates, a Cowes Sea Cadet corps team. The cadets scored four goals to the Pop Stars' one but the real winners were Cowes Football Club, for whose funds the match was played. Dave Dee's side had agreed to play in gratitude to Cowes F.C. who have allowed their ground to be used throughout the year for charity football matches. The Pop Stars included Peter Green and Mike Terry, of Fleetwood Mac members of other groups, and disc jockeys. No goals were scored in the first half, although Dave Dee, who was cheered every time he touched the ball, hit the top of the bar with a penalty. The singer did score a minute after the interval but the Pirates gradually got on top and Chiverton, who plays for East Cowes Athletic, scored all their goals. The high standard of some of the Pop Stars, who looked the most unlikely footballers, must have surprised many of the crowd.

Teams: Dave Dee's TV Pop Stars — Dave Dee, Chris Ferguson, Tommy Kaye, Terry Rolfe, Dave Milton, Tim Jopling, Jimmy Warwick, Dave Doling, Bob James, Peter Green, Mike Terry. The Pirates — Revert, Martin, Ward, Blow, Williams, Moore, Godfrey, Chiverton, Bardsall, Beach, Collins.

———————————◆———————————

More and more people had become home owners since the war and were keen to improve and modernise their properties. A whole generation had turned to DIY, and encouraged by television programmes and a whole range of 'Practical Householder' magazines, millions of home interiors disappeared under a layer of formica and hardboard. For many of the older generation, Victorian fashion and design had been seen as a symbol of the past and in a matter of two decades, thousands of fireplaces were ripped out, panelled doors boarded over, and many fine old buildings demolished. It would be the early 1980s before the next generation were in a position to halt the demolition and reopen the fireplaces. Luckily, there were some lone straws in the wind during the 1960s, doing what they could to preserve the occasional building ...

May 10th, 1969

Preservation - an answer

I was intrigued to read the recent letter of Mr. R. B. Rayner of Carisbrooke, in which he greatly regretted the irreparable loss to the community of interesting old buildings and many of their unique architectural features.

Mr. Rayner and many of your readers may be relieved to hear that my company has, for a number of years, sought out and rescued many portions of old buildings with the express purpose of preserving them and giving delight to generations to come. From Hazards House in Newport, we have preserved a number of interesting architectural features, including the old stone mullioned basement window, the fine old lead rainwater head and down-pipe, antique bottle glass window, and various doors. Although the staircase itself, I believe, was destroyed, the front door has been preserved.

During the demolition of the corn mill at Wootton, we saved the majority of the interior machinery, including the large old wooden cog wheels. From Steephill Castle, we rescued the fine pair of main gates, stone arches and steps, gargoyles, balustrading and other features. We have indeed been keeping a watchful eye on the derelict house in South Street mentioned by Mr. Rayner, but we have been hampered by lack of information as to the present owner.

All these domestic architectural features we have rescued are being painstakingly restored, and incorporated in and around the Osborn Smith Wax Museum at Brading in their appropriate settings, all displayed as they stand, and our quest for other Island items to save and preserve continues.

GRAHAM OSBORN SMITH. Wax Museum, Brading.

Mr Osborn Smith wasn't the only person trying to ring-fence a little bit of the past before it disappeared forever. There were others trying to lend a hand before it was too late, but it was an uphill job ...

Hazards House, Newport

I was interested to read a letter from a correspondent recently about Hazards House, Newport. I am sure he will be pleased to learn that the front door and some of the interior fittings were, in fact, saved. I was able to purchase them from the County Council and the door has been restored and is in almost daily use at my offices at Shalfleet Manor. Also restored and in use is the door of a late 17th-century house which was demolished a few years ago in Sea Street.

It is to be hoped that in future, the County Council will follow the advice given in one of the reports on historic towns commissioned by the Minister of Housing, that old materials suitable for re-use in repairs and alterations should be preserved and stored when the building is converted or demolished.

It is a matter of considerable regret that when Messrs. Dukes recently demolished the former Salisbury Arms Inn in the High Street at Newport (opposite County Hall), the attractive early 19th century bow window was not preserved intact. The manager had generously agreed to a request from the Society for the Protection of Ancient Buildings that this important feature should be carefully taken out and stored, but his wishes were not followed. And so another piece of old Newport has gone for ever.

MALCOLM PINHORN. Shalfleet Manor.

◆

ISLAND NEWS

HUMAN BARRIER FACES HOVERCRAFT — About 25 Wootton villagers, including women and children, protested on Saturday against the use of hovercraft at Woodside Bay by blocking the approach to the slipway in an attempt to prevent the first craft from landing its passengers ... Last week the Planning Committee approved the temporary use of the slipway at Woodside Beach to transport holidaymakers from the mainland to Warner's Woodside holiday village on 18 consecutive Saturdays, commencing last Saturday ... A spokesman for Warner's Holiday Camps, Ltd., said ... they were sorry that what they believed to be a minority of villagers were objecting in that way. A Hovertravel spokesman ... warned people that standing in front of a hovercraft was "a very foolish thing to do." Four later runs to the village were made without trouble. (May 31)

FINAL DRINKS IN THE PRINCE REGENT — Patrons of the Prince Regent public house in High Street, Newport, had their final drink on the premises on Friday week. The house is to be demolished in connection with the Coppins Bridge roundabout development. The brewers, W. B. Mew, Langton and Co., Ltd., made sure it was a night to remember by providing free beer and other refreshments. It was a sad occasion for the licensee Mr. A. Lawrence, and his wife. They have moved to the Plough Inn, Nodehill ... Accompanying them will be their parrot Bobby, who sits outside his cage and is an avid television viewer ... (June 7)

"The well known Fighting Cocks Inn at Hale Common, on the Sandown-Newport road, is now, after partial demolition, nothing but a shell. What remains is to be incorporated in a new inn, so that all links with the past will not be broken."
[IWCP]

ey do not grow flowers like this any more! This huge stretcherful of magnificent jonquils e not cut, they were REAPED. The destination was the old London Flower Market at the of the century. Note the five-barred gate and its precautions against intruders."
(*page 149.)   [IWCP]

REGINALD KRAY AT PARKHURST – A Lymington to Yarmouth car ferry was used to bring Reginald Kray (35), one of the Kray twins serving life sentences for murder, to the Island on Thursday. There was strict security during the crossing and on the road to Parkhurst Prison, where some of the Great Train Robbers and members of the Richardson gang are inmates. (July 5)

END OF THE HALFPENNY STAMP – Halfpenny stamps, first issued by the Post Office in 1870, will be withdrawn from sale after the close of business on June 30th. Any already sold will be honoured as valid postage … Withdrawal of the stamps is in preparation for the de-monetisation of the halfpenny, which ceases to be legal tender on August 1st. (June 14)

Readers who grew up on the Island in the 1960s might be familiar with the story of the 'magnetic road' at Shanklin, where cars would roll uphill. 'Vectensis' had the facts...

July 12th, 1969

AN ISLANDER'S NOTES
[By "VECTENSIS"]

WERE WE FOOLED? – I always welcome any subject for a note in lighter vein. One comes from a member of the office staff of the IW Tourist Board at Newport. They received a letter on Monday from a lady living at Ringwood stating that during a motor-coach tour of the Island the driver stopped his coach on a hill between Shanklin and Ventnor and then demonstrated the apparently amazing fact that on releasing the brake the vehicle slowly ran backwards uphill with the engine stopped. He explained that the phenomenon was due to "magnetic attraction in the downs!" "Is it a fact or were we being fooled?" asked the writer. Not exactly fooled, was the answer given, merely a well-known local joke on the part of the driver. As most Island users of the road know, there is a stretch above Luccombe which, owing to the conformation of the roadside land, gives the optical illusion of an ascent when it is a descent. I remember being puzzled by it and I have previously noted the strange illusion in this column …

Developers were seeking permission to demolish the former Eagle Tavern in Newport, at the junction of St Thomas's Square and the High Street. Buildings from a bygone age were not of great interest to the older generation in the 1960s and Newport Alderman, Mr Minns (using language not appropriate today) declared that he could see no architectural interest at all in the building and was happy to see it go. Other counsels prevailed, and in the early 1970s, the Council gave permission for its demolition on the condition that it was then rebuilt, brick for brick ...

September 13th, 1969

COUNCIL SPLIT ON HIGH STREET PRESERVATION
MINISTRY'S WISH TO UPGRADE NEWPORT TAVERN

The "wholesale slaughter" of certain parts of Newport had to be resisted, said one member of Newport Council on Wednesday, while an alderman took the view that the preservation of old buildings was in order provided that there was no hindrance to progress. The council were considering a letter from the Ministry of Housing, stating that representations had been made for the upgrading of the Eagle Tavern and numbers 33-35 High Street … Alderman Harvey referred especially to 33-35 High Street as buildings which were a part of old Newport. It was a matter of great regret to him that the council were not playing their part in trying to make representations to protect them. Many parts of old Newport were being lost, as a result of which, the town was losing its character. He believed that the old buildings should be preserved so that the character of the town could be retained. The motion was seconded by Mr. Swan, who thought that the council should resist the wholesale slaughter of certain older parts of the town and maintain some of their character and amenity value … Alderman Minns said that in this case, he could see no justification for preservation, particularly so far as the Eagle Tavern was concerned. He had stood and looked at the building and could see no architectural interest or beauty and it savoured to him of a "nigger in the woodpile" attitude of trying to preclude progress without reason …

———————◆———————

The previous week, a turn of the century photograph had appeared showing two men sat alongside a large display of flowers which they had just gathered.* Its appearance brought a letter from a relative of one of the men in the photograph …

September 20th, 1969

Jonquils at Apse Heath

I was very interested to see in last week's issue the picture of two men seated by the huge display of jonquils.† The older man in the picture was Mr. Bull – my great grandfather. The younger man was named Smith and he later emigrated to Australia or Canada and died abroad. Both men lived at Apse Heath and the picture was taken at Branstone Cross. The flowers came from nearby Daffodil Farm. An unknown photographer who just happened to be passing asked if they would pose for a picture. An enlarged framed copy was given to my great grandfather and it passed to my father in 1935. In those far-off days the cutting of this type of flower, year after year, in vast quantities was said to affect one's health. People in the work often suffered painful hand complaints. When a stranger was met in the village it was said that the greeting "good morning Mr. Smith" was almost automatic. So many people had the name 'Smith' that it was assumed he must surely be one too!

L.M. WICKENS. 8, Spring Gardens, Shanklin.

---

* See page 147.

† A member of the daffodil family.

The headline says it all. It was a sad day at Newport as the last batch of Mew's beer was produced at their Newport brewery. No more would Mew's IPA or Brown Ale be a part of Island life, and no more would the townspeople of Newport wake to the heady, promising smell of yeast and hops in the air on brewing days ...

October 4th, 1969

LAST BATCH OF MEW'S BEER
SAD DAY AT NEWPORT

A brewing industry which has been in existence for more than 300 years bowed to the needs of economy on Tuesday, when the Royal Brewery, Crocker Street, Newport, produced the last batch of Mew's beers ... In 1965, the firm merged with Strong and Co. Ltd., and last year it was decided that the brewing and bottling of beer at the Royal Brewery should be discontinued.

Bottling at Newport ceased in the early part of this year and Strongs, who have supplied the bottled beer, will now also supply the draught for the Island's 144 Mew's public houses. The supply will include the products of Whitbreads, who took over Strongs in March. Mr. N. Robson (general manager) said that it was ferries which allowed lorries laden with beer to be transported to the Island, dispensing with the need to load and unload, which had closed down the brewery. It was not economical to have one modern and efficient brewery 20 miles away at Romsey and a less efficient one at Newport. The conversion of the Royal Brewery from a production to an administration and distribution centre for Mew's pubs has meant redundancies. Mr. Robson said that the 23 women and 14 men who have lost their jobs would receive redundancy payments from the firm ... The company will still employ 90 at the brewery ... Two members of the staff who obviously regard Tuesday as a particularly sad occasion are Mr. C.D. Seabrooke (head brewer), who has been with the firm for 31 years, and Mr. B. Newbold (64), the tun room foreman, who has seen 51 years service. Mr. Newbold is scheduled for retirement in six months' time and Mr. Seabrooke retires next month ...

For the moment, Mr Woodnutt's name could safely appear in the same paragraph as the word 'Bembridge.' That would soon change ...

December 13th, 1969

ABSURD SITUATION AT BEMBRIDGE

The absurd situation on the Bembridge toll road bridge whereby buses disembark their passengers, then pick them up again on the other side, was referred to by Alderman Woodnutt, MP., at the meeting of the County Council on Monday. "This absurd and ridiculous situation cannot go on for ever," he said. He asked the chairman of the Roads Committee what stage had been reached in the negotiations with British Rail for the purchase of the area. He asked if things could be hurried up, then related how, the previous week, he had seen a little boy with a school satchel alight alone from the bus, cross the bridge, to be followed by the bus carrying two heavy men, the driver and conductor; such a situation was absurd. Replying, Alderman Lawes agreed that the situation was a "proper Fred Karno's outfit." It would not be long before the whole thing was solved.

1970

Following legislation in 1969, the General Election of June 1970 was to be the first in which 18 to 20 year olds were able to vote. Every first-time voter received a letter from Mr Woodnutt, inviting them to meetings to be held across the Island in the coming months ...
Jan 17, 1970.

MEMBER MEETS YOUNG ELECTORS
TALK-IN AT RYDE

A few weeks after coming of age under the new law, voters between 18 and 21 were invited to a free and easy talk-in with Alderman Mark Woodnutt, M.P., at the Royal York Hotel, Ryde, on Thursday. About 150 attended ... Asked his attitude towards pop festivals, Alderman Woodnutt said people should be allowed to do what they wanted so long as they did not restrict the freedom of other people. He did not want to ban an Island pop festival but wanted to see it properly organised, especially the sanitary arrangements. He agreed that the last pop festival could not have been more orderly than it was ... Problems caused by 500,000 pop festivallers would be just the same if 150,000 old boys of 72 came to dance in the fields or shoot duck ... He was worried about large gatherings of people, not just young people. Local authorities had to have the power to be able to say, on the basis of the numbers attending, the minimum standards that should apply.

———————◆———————

TOWN AND COUNTY NOTES

BEMBRIDGE STATION TO BE DEMOLISHED — Demolition work on the derelict Bembridge Railway Station was due to start in the next few days.* The station was opened, along with the branch railway from Brading, in 1882 and train services continued until September, 1953. The station was peculiar in apparently being built the wrong way round, so that all its windows faced over the former railway tracks instead of the harbour. A possible explanation for this is that the line's promoters originally intended to build the railway the other side of the station buildings ... (February 14)

HOPE SPRINGS ETERNAL — If Members of Parliament do not get the increase of £5000 plus, they are seeking, is it too much to hope that they will go on strike? FREDERICK CHARLES TOOGOOD, Holly Farm, Norton, near Yarmouth.

NEW COMPANY TO ACQUIRE HOLIDAY VILLAGES — Solent Riviera Holdings Ltd, has been formed with an initial share capital of £250,000 to acquire control of three holiday villages which are fully owned by the shareholders. These are the Towers Holiday Centre and Pilgrim's Caravan Park, both at Thorness; and Bay View Holiday Park, Gurnard. The directors are Mr. F.G. Sage, Mrs J. Yule, Mr. F. Lawrence and Mr. L. Goodland.

* See page 157.

Multi-millionaire Sir Max Aitken was the owner of the Daily Express, an inheritance from his father, Lord Beaverbrook. He was a keen sailor with a home in Cowes and through his newspaper, in 1961 he had started and sponsored the annual Cowes to Torquay powerboat race. None of this cut any ice with one of his neighbours ...

February 21st, 1970

Birthday bangs

Sir Max Aitken was a popular Cowes resident and yachtsman before he celebrated his 60th birthday on Sunday. But his popularity sank to a low ebb with Cowes folk on his birthday because a celebration of the diamond jubilee at a house party on Saturday night ended in midnight bangs which startled thousands of people from sleep! Someone - I don't suppose for a moment it was Sir Max's idea - arranged for the birthday to be celebrated with a display of fireworks from a barge moored off his residence. It started with a big bang at about 11.40 p.m. and the noisy pyrotechnics continued until 10 minutes past midnight. A motorist can be fined for sounding his hooter after 11 p.m. why, I wonder, should such an intolerable racket around midnight be allowed from the sea? It was very naughty on someone's part to startle the other people into thinking there was another air raid on Cowes - naughty and thoughtless! I suggest that on his 70th birthday Sir Max takes a trip to the moon.

ANGRY OCTOGENARIAN.

The BBC children's programme, 'Watch With Mother,' was home to Andy Pandy, Bill and Ben, and the Woodentops. By 1970 the programme had been showing the same films, twice a day, for nearly twenty years but as popular as they were, the BBC decided the time had come to revamp the programme. A series of real-life films were made, to be shown as part of the new 'Watch With Mother' series. Some were to be made on the Island ...

April 18th, 1970

ISLAND SCENES IN 'WATCH WITH MOTHER'

Several of the scenes in the new BBC1 television "Watch with Mother" series, entitled "Along the River," were shot on the Island. Some were shot at Mill Pond, Wootton Creek,* and others at Newnham Farm pond. The second programme in the series, which was screened on Friday week, also featured two Island families from Fishbourne. Seen in a rowing boat along the river were Mr. Clifford Matthews and his son Marcus, of The Kell, Fishbourne, and Isabel Glenny, of Shoremeade, Fishbourne Lane. Some of the scenes were shot at the top of the Mill Pond at Lakeside and some were of fish in an aquarium at Wootton Bridge. The five-programme series will be followed by a series of two more programmes called, "Along the Sea Shore," giving scenes from Freshwater Bay. This is the first time on a "Watch with Mother" series that humans, instead of puppets, have been featured. The aim is to make the programme more educational.

---

* This was not the first time Wootton Creek had featured in a children's television production. Four series of 'Tales of the Riverbank,' featuring the adventures of Hammy Hamster, were also filmed there, between 1960 and 1963.

The last time anyone had descended to the bottom of the well at Carisbrooke Castle was in 1884. Some local divers sought permission for a new investigation ...

April 18th, 1970

DIVERS DOWN THE WELL
COINS FOUND AT CARISBROOKE

Anything found down the well at Carisbrooke Castle could be of immense interest, Mr. Frank Lilleker, one of the three divers who had been excavating the well, said on Wednesday. Whatever is down there will have to stay there, however, until the Ministry of Public Building and Works send an inspector to supervise the excavations ... So far the divers, Mr. Lilleker, of Hayling Island, who is 42, and Mr. Clive Archer (35), and Mr. Martin Woodward (21), both of Cowes, have recovered £13 worth of coins from the well, which, it is believed, has previously not been explored.* In Mr. Lilleker's opinion there is a layer of coins 8 to 10 feet deep at the bottom of the 161 foot well ... If they are allowed to continue with their dives, through the 40 feet of water in the well, the team hope that they will also be granted permission to use the donkey hoist to lift their finds to the surface. Two men, however, will take the place of the donkey. Mr. Lilleker said, "I shall be very disappointed if we are not allowed to continue," he said.†

THE WEEK'S NEWS

SHALFLEET MILL SOLD – Shalfleet Mill standing in 2 ½ acres of wooded land adjoining Shalfleet Creek (National Trust) has been sold for a sum well in excess of £10,000 ... The property has its own water frontage to a tidal stream, the bed of which, formerly driving the mill wheel, has been diverted, but the wheel remains intact. The property has now been converted to form a private residence. (Aug 8)

DAD'S ARMY AT BEMBRIDGE – More than 500 people visited Steyne Park Recreation Ground, Bembridge, on Thursday week to welcome television's Dad's Army team to the Young Community Centre's second annual fete and donkey derby. The stars – Bill Pertwee, Ian Lavender, James Beck, John Le Mesurier and Hugh Hastings – mingled with the crowd and signed autographs.

DUMPING OF WASTE TO BE DISCONTINUED – The Royal Navy has decided to suspend the dumping of waste material in the sea area under Portsmouth Command, following the discovery on Island beaches of canisters containing ferric chloride. In the last eight days, nearly 200 canisters have been washed ashore ... An enquiry by the Naval Supply Department at Portsmouth has commenced to check how the canisters came ashore after being dumped by the Navy off the Nab Tower at Spithead, and to review the whole policy of dumping at sea. It is thought that the canisters failed to sink because they were not pierced before they were dumped.

---

* The well was cleared of debris in 1884. See Vol 1, page 15.

† Permission does not appear to have been granted, since between 2002 and 2004, divers removed 42,000 coins and thousands of pens and keys from the well.

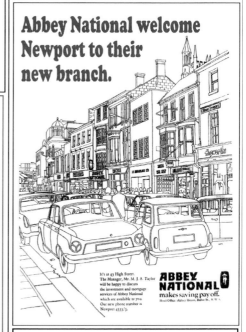

The pirate radio stations operating from ships dotted around Britain's coasts had been closed down by the Labour Government in 1967. Their popularity had demonstrated a clear demand for all-day pop music radio so the BBC were asked by the Government to provide a replacement service, Radio One. It took to the air in September 1967 but for listeners used to the offshore stations it was a poor substitute and within a short while, amateur pirate radio stations had sprung up across the country, providing their own alternative service. Broadcasting on 219 metres medium wave, from their Porchfield studios, Radio Sound City took to the air ...

May 16th, 1970

RADIO SOUND CITY

Richard John Brimson (18), apprentice, of Brookwood Lodge, New Road, Porchfield, pleaded guilty to installing a radio transmitter without a licence and to two offences of using it without a licence.

Mr. R.C. Halse, prosecuting, said that the maximum penalty for this type of offence was a £400 fine or three months imprisonment. No one wanted to stop the amateur enthusiast but to begin broadcasting it was necessary for them to undergo an examination and have a working knowledge of morse code. Then they could be granted a licence. The first reason for this was security. There would be a list of the licence holders and their transmitters could be closed down in an emergency. Another was that the amateurs were kept to a specific band which did not interfere with other broadcasts. The band that Brimson used was very close to a French station, although there was no evidence that it actually interfered with it. Pop music and voices began to be broadcast on the Island, and the identity of the broadcaster was revealed when he gave an interview to a member of the Press and allowed a photograph to be taken at his home.* The photograph showed that his equipment - a transmitter and receiver and a number of record players and tape recorders - made an effective station. On February 7th two Ministry officers heard "Radio Sound City" and went to Brimson's home. As soon as they reached the door the broadcast ceased. Brimson said at first that he had been testing his equipment. Later, in a statement, he said that he had been broadcasting because he believed in free radio and was trying to provide the public with a choice between himself and the BBC monopoly. If he wanted to do this, said Mr. Halse, he would have to go elsewhere than the United Kingdom because it was contrary to the law of the country. The total value of Brimson's equipment was around £100.

Mr. H. Lloyd Bunce, representing Brimson, said that Brimson was extremely interested in the design of electronics and radar. His hobby was the construction of record players, tape recorders and radio receivers. He was an amateur radio enthusiast, of which there were about 60 on the Island. There was no question of his transmission interfering with shipping broadcasts.

Fined £50 for each offence with £15 15s. costs. The radio transmitter was ordered to be forfeited to the Ministry of Posts and Telecommunications.

---

* See opposite

The Last of Bembridge Station

"Disused since the closure of the Brading-Bembridge branch line in 1953, Bembridge Station is now being demolished to make way for yachtsmen's cottages. The site is owned by the Bembridge Harbour Improvement Company." *[IWCP]*

rchfield studios of the Island's very own pirate radio station, Radio Sound City, seen in y 1970. DJ Kevin Lee is at the microphone [Photograph courtesy of The News, Portsmouth]

By the mid-seventies, the informal and intimate obituaries for local characters had all but disappeared. One of the last was for Mr Albert Wade of St Helens; a clever man by all accounts ...

August 8th, 1970

VILLAGE GENIUS
FUNERAL OF MR. W. WADE AT ST HELENS

The Methodist Chapel at St Helens was filled to capacity with relatives and friends at the funeral service on Friday week of Mr. Albert William Wade, aged 81 years, who died the previous Tuesday. He was affectionately known by all as Willie, the man who could make or mend anything ... Anything, from a musical-box to a mangle, was taken to him ... Whatever the challenge, Mr. Wade accepted and overcame it with perseverance and ingenuity which was characteristic of his whole life. In his time, William Wade had been a photographer, picture-framer, electrical engineer, printer, radio and television expert, organ-builder and inventor, excelling in every one of these enterprises. He was making experiments with radio communication at the same time as Marconi ... and was kept busy with the repair and maintenance of receivers in the village and beyond. He charged accumulators and was lovingly bestowed, at that time, with the apt nickname of "Wireless Willie." It followed naturally that Mr. Wade was also first with television, and while experimenting with "low-definition" receivers in the early Thirties, he constructed a mirror-drum type on which programmes transmitted from London were seen clearly on a postage stamp sized screen. Long before that he commenced building a pipe-organ which took in 12 years to complete.

During the whole of his life Mr. Wade received no special training. His only education was from the little school in the village, which he left at an early age to earn his living at various occupations, one of which was the job of caring for hundreds of hens. It may have been this work which inspired him to invent the only machine which he ever patented. This was an automatic chicken feeder, which not only dispensed corn at regular intervals for two weeks without a refill, but made clucking noises which summoned the hens to their grain.

From his early youth Mr Wade was a deeply religious man ... He printed and published a revivalist magazine called "Grace Abounding" which he sent free to all parts of the world. Printed first on an old wooden hand-press, the magazine increased its circulation which led to perhaps his most remarkable invention. This was a typesetting machine of unique design... Unlike the conventional typesetter, which casts a line of type from molten metal, this one selected ready-made type from various slots which were operated from a keyboard constructed from an ancient type writer, parts of a disused gas-stove and an even older harmonium ... Besides all these enterprises Mr. Wade kept up his photography, making picture postcards of the village for summer visitors and recording events. He never failed to help friends and villagers by repairing clocks, radios, musical instruments, toys and household gadgets which were frequently brought to him. At no time did he ever seek monetary gain from his extraordinary genius ... Such was the policy of a man whose memory will live on in the village where he spent all of his life creating, devising, inventing and improving, for the benefit of all who knew and loved him. He will not soon be forgotten in St Helens, the Island and farther afield.

To the dismay of pubgoers, Whitbreads pushed ahead with their closure plans. Over the next few years many quaint but unprofitable pubs on the Island closed their doors for the last time. The closure of the New Inn at Norton Green, and the effect it would have on the residents, was typical of closures right across the Island's smaller towns and villages ...

September 26th, 1970

CLOSING OF THE NEW INN

Norton Green, near Yarmouth, has, since Friday week, been a village without a public house. Mr. and Mrs. T. Rickard, who have been the licensees of the New Inn for nearly 34 years, have put up the closed sign for the last time. Whitbreads have closed several other public houses on the Island and the closure of her premises is accepted by Mrs. Rickard as "a sign of the times." She added that there were other public houses within reach at Yarmouth, Colwell and Freshwater, although many villagers would not go to them ... The closing of the New Inn at Norton Green is only the latest of a long series of "lost amenities" for this charming hamlet, as Mr. Ted Trott, one of its oldest inhabitants, remembers. His memories go back more than 80 years, and in that time he has seen the village lose its two builders, its dairy, its baker, two riding schools and a poultry farm. During the last decade, the end of the military use of Golden Hill Fort and its hospital has taken much of its lively air from the area. A once-thriving chapel has long since been pulled down, the Church Mission Hall is no longer used and the church of St Andrew has only one service a month. Only three new houses have been built in this century. Norton Green has a happy and intimate life of its own; its children play freely everywhere in the village and everybody knows everybody ... Norton Green may be the poorer for a losing its "pub," but it is rich in interest.

ISLAND NEWS

RATS AS BIG AS CATS — A report to Cowes Port Health Authority that "rats – some as big as cats" were infesting a grain elevator which loads grain into ships at J. Samuel White's wharf, was made by a member, Mr. R. Tutton at a meeting at Northwood House on Friday week. He said he had inspected the elevator and had seen two to three inches of rats' droppings in it and rats as big as cats. If the grain going through it was for human consumption he felt something was very wrong.

COWES-RYDE RAILWAY DECISION. VECTRAIL PROPOSALS ABANDONED — The Vectrail Society have abandoned their proposals to reopen the Cowes-Ryde railway as a modern commercial transport system. In a statement the Society allege that throughout the last three years the company has been prevented from having official access to the property to effect repairs, maintenance or reconstruction. (Sept 26)

In 1970, a corn mill was still to be found in Ryde; not perched astride a rural stream or alongside a picturesque river - but tucked away in a shop in the upper High Street ...

October 31st, 1970

WHERE OLD CAN MEAN BEST
CORN MILL IN THE HEART OF RYDE

Mr. F. E. J. Ward, of 38, Pellhurst Road, Ryde, has a maxim, "If it's old and inefficient it goes out. If it's old and inefficient it stays in." As proprietor of Duffett's, High Street, Ryde, he finds on many occasions in his corn merchant's business that machinery of a bygone age can compete on level terms with anything produced today. With careful maintenance it can be more reliable.

Few people realise that behind the High Street store exists a mill, in the very heart of Ryde ... The lofty three-storey mill commands from its top floor a panoramic view of the Solent. It was built in 1933, adjacent to the site of a previous mill and brewery. Mill machinery includes a late 19th-century chaff cutter, in perfect working order but silent because the demand for chaff cutting has disappeared. The grain cleaning plant is modern, but a nearby mixer was brought by Mr. Ward's father from the old Wootton water mill, demolished a few years ago. Against a wall lie old mill-stones from an old mill (now broken up), which was replaced by modern equipment in the 1950s. The stones weigh nearly a ton a piece. Running every day is a general mill machine dating from the turn of the century and rebuilt by Mr. Ward, who claims it to be comparable with any modern mill. Being a plate mill, it turns out a better quality product than a lot of hammer mills, and is more easily controlled. The hopper room hoist was bought in 1872 - secondhand! It has just been recertified for continued use. The grain elevator was recently installed, to be used in conjunction with the general mill machine in a scheme of modernisation. Electric power is used ...

———————————◆———————————

It had been nearly five years since the sound of a railway engine had been heard in Newport, so when the distinctive sound of an engine in steam pierced the air on a Saturday afternoon in November, it did not go unnoticed. The activities at Newport station even interrupted a football match; no mean feat ...

November 14th, 1970

STEAM AGAIN AT NEWPORT STATION

Considerable attention was focused on Newport Station on Sunday on the occasion of the Wight Locomotive Society's 02-type tank engine, Calbourne, being in steam and moved over a short distance. This follows a successful boiler test on the engine and approval being given by the County Council for the engine to be moved under its own power for test purposes within the station limits. This will ensure that all mechanical equipment on both locomotives and carriages is in sound order prior to any further development that would enable the society to move the train to Havenstreet, its proposed site for a railway centre. The engine was put to the test throughout the day and the station echoed with one of the most nostalgic Island engine sounds - the rhythmical beat of the Westinghouse pump ... A football match at Seaclose was momentarily interrupted, however, as players stared in amazement at an engine in steam in the station yard.

TOWN AND COUNTY NOTES

FUTURE OF ST SWITHIN'S SCHOOL — The Children's and Young Persons Act, 1969, becomes effective in January. The new Act provides for schools to be reorganised into a regional plan for community homes and this affects the future status of St Swithin's Boys' School, Yarmouth. At present it is a Roman Catholic boys' school under voluntary management in the De La Salle organisation ... (December 5)

PARROT GIVES FIRE ALARM — "Joey," a 50 year-old African Grey parrot raised a fire alarm by loud and unusual screeching at Messrs. Ralph's newsagents shop in Worsley Road, Gurnard, on Wednesday evening. Damage was confined to the back of the shop ...

YOUTHS INVADE VENTNOR — When about 100 youths from the Newport and Wootton areas invaded Ventnor about 11p.m. on Friday week, police reinforcements were called from various parts of the Island to deal with possible trouble. The youths arrived in cars and on motorcycles and at first congregated near Cascadia, where scuffles and outbreaks of violence occurred before they moved up the High Street ... A shop window in Albert Street and the glass in the telephone kiosk near Cascadia were smashed ... Several youths were injured and one was arrested.

In 1970 Mark Woodnutt became embroiled in a scandal which eventually brought his political career to a dramatic end, when in the general election of 1974 his 17,000 majority evaporated, and he suffered a defeat of nearly 8000 votes.

His downfall was the Bembridge Harbour Affair. Mr Woodnutt had recommended that a syndicate, composed of friends and colleagues of his, be allowed to purchase the harbour from British Railways, only to later climb on board as a director after securing the deal for them. The result was a scandal that became the talk of the Island.

The story begins with the closing of the Bembridge to Brading railway line in 1953, which left British Railways the owners of Bembridge Harbour and 283 acres of surrounding land. In 1958, they approached the Council and tried to persuade them to purchase the entire site. The Council declined as they were only interested in the toll road (which they eventually went on to purchase for £15,000), but asked two Council Committees to recommend a suitable buyer for the surrounding land. Mr Woodnutt chaired one of them, the Finance Committee, and was also the Council's representative on the other one. Their meetings to recommend a suitable buyer were held in private and were not minuted. The Committees eventually recommended that a syndicate should be formed to take over the entire site apart from the toll road. Mr Woodnutt then gathered some friends and colleagues together to form just such a syndicate, which became known as the Bembridge Harbour Improvement Company. In 1962, they were duly granted an option to purchase the harbour. The syndicate comprised Michael Crichton, MP; Captain M. Lowry-Corry, Commodore of the Bembridge Sailing Club, and Major Selwyn, who was Chairman of the Council and owner of the Spithead Hotel at Bembridge. The Duke of Westminster was also a shareholder but played little part in the management of the harbour.

During the negotiations of December 1962, Mr Woodnutt's role was portrayed simply as that of a go-between who would enable the harbour to pass into the hands of a dedicated group, "who have no intention of acquiring the property for their personal benefit," he told the County Press. There was no suggestion at this time that Mr Woodnutt would later become a director of the syndicate. Speaking in 1970 of his role as a local Councillor, he told the Guardian, "I assisted them as I would have done anyone else who wanted to save the harbour. It was obviously in the Island's interest that it should not be allowed silt up completely or pass into the hands of some speculator."

In 1968, negotiations complete, the syndicate purchased the harbour from British Railways for just £24,000, a sum described by the Sunday Times in 1972 as "a bargain for the syndicate - and an expensive deal for the taxpayer." Of the £24,000 purchase price, only £14,000 was payable immediately, the remaining £10,000 being allowed to stand on loan. Eyebrows were raised when just 18 months later, the syndicate recouped all of their initial outlay by selling just the station buildings for £16,500, and they rose even higher when it became public knowledge that in 1966 Mr Woodnutt had quietly become a director of the Company, receiving 200 shares.

The end result was that by 1970 the harbour was effectively run by Mr Woodnutt and Major Selwyn, who in Companies House documents that year, now valued their original £24,000 investment at £150,000. A general unease began to grow regarding Mr Woodnutt's behaviour in promoting the syndicate's case so avidly in 1962, only to join them as a director a short while later, and the affair rapidly became a major talking point on the Island. Eventually, events at Bembridge came to the attention of the BBC's 'Nationwide,' a tea-time news and current affairs programme, watched by millions. The programme was running a series called 'Operation Seashore,' looking at Britain's *coastline, and as part of that, Mr Woodnutt agreed to be interviewed about Bembridge Harbour for a programme to be shown on October 1. The interviewer, Lynn Lewis, was well briefed and armed with information that had obviously come from a well-placed local source. During the interview, filmed in Mr Woodnutt's garden, Lewis asked a series of well-informed questions that Mr Woodnutt found intrusive and impertinent. Eventually, Mr Woodnutt angrily brought the interview to an end by refusing to answer any more questions. Rising from his seat, he threw his microphone to the ground and walked away. It was a fatal error of judgement, and from that moment on, his career began to unravel...*

October 10th, 1970

BEMBRIDGE HARBOUR INTERVIEW

The row which developed between Alderman Mark Woodnutt MP, and BBC Nationwide reporter, Lynn Lewis, over a screened interview regarding the future of Bembridge Harbour on Thursday week, reached the County Council on Monday when Alderman Rowland took the chair to deal with a letter from Alderman Woodnutt.

Alderman Woodnutt stopped the interview in his garden when Mr. Lewis suggested that all the County Council decisions over the harbour had been taken by committees on which Alderman Woodnutt and Alderman S.C. Selwyn, MBE, DL (Chairman of the Council), served. He accused Mr. Lewis of making "unpleasant innuendoes" and threatened legal action. Alderman Woodnutt and Alderman Major Selwyn are both directors of the Bembridge Harbour Improvement Company. In his letter to the vice-chairman of the council, Alderman Woodnutt said the BBC Nationwide programme feature was ostensibly about the future development of Bembridge Harbour, but in reality it amounted to nothing more than an attack on the motives and integrity of both the chairman of the council and himself, with innuendoes reflecting on the good name and reputation of the council itself. "In my view," said Alderman Woodnutt, " it would be wrong for the quarterly meeting of the Council to pass without reference to this deplorable programme. On another occasion and perhaps in another place, I shall be prepared to raise the question of the disgraceful methods employed by the BBC in preparing a slanted programme of this nature, but where the good name of the council and its chairman, quite apart from myself, is involved, some immediate action is called for." Alderman Woodnutt continued that both he and Major Selwyn had been most scrupulous in declaring at all times any interest they might have in matters with which the council were concerned and in refraining from taking part or voting whenever such interest existed. They would both welcome full disclosure of the facts and he suggested that the clerk (Mr. L. H. Baines) should be asked to prepare a full factual statement of the council's and its committees consideration of matters relating to the disposal by British Rail of their interests in Bembridge Harbour ... This course was unanimously agreed.

Mr Woodnutt's subsequent insistence that he had been smeared in the broadcast fell on stony ground. Viewers who felt all along that something underhand had been going on, had their suspicions confirmed, while many of those who had so far given him the benefit of the doubt, now withdrew it. The interview did him great harm and was effectively the beginning of the end of his political career.

Those who wish to seek out the precise details of the charges levelled at Mr Woodnutt during the affair might consider the County Press to be a good starting place. They would be wrong. Nowhere in its pages do any significant details of the allegations appear. They were simply never referred to. Although the County Press did print sizeable articles relating to Bembridge Harbour they manage to reveal little or nothing of any substance. The report of the television interview is a good example of the practice. Readers who had not seen the Nationwide broadcast were left wondering exactly what it was that Lewis said that had caused Mr Woodnutt to stop the interview. The report reveals nothing of the matters raised by Lewis, or what Mr Woodnutt may or may not have done, but instead concentrates on his protests regarding what he described as the 'deplorable' behaviour of the BBC. As Stephen Ross would later note, Mr Woodnutt was indeed a close friend of the County Press.

Consequently, it has not been easy to find precise details of the allegations made against Mr Woodnutt in the 1970 interview. The County Press is of no help in the matter, and while there are references to the affair in the minutes of IW Council meetings and in Hansard, neither reveal anything of any substance. However, a Freedom of Information request to the BBC, by the author in April 2011, was to provide some of the answers. In response to a question about the interview, the BBC revealed that they were in possession of a complete transcript of the entire Nationwide item - interview included. A copy has been obtained. Unfortunately, only a precis of the contents is permissible - the BBC will not allow direct quotes from the transcript due to copyright reasons.

It is a fascinating document, probably the only remaining account of much that lies behind the scandal, and it clearly reveals Mr Woodnutt's anger at what he felt were impudent questions. Michael Barratt, introducing the item, refers to the 'disturbing' story of Bembridge Harbour. The report begins with Mr Woodnutt protesting about unpleasant innuendoes and a lot of mud being stirred up. Lewis tells of swastikas being painted on walls, the harbourmaster resigning from a job he had held for 23 years, and of valuable equipment being vandalised. Mr Woodnutt is confronted with the fact that of the £16,500 received for the station, £10,000 of that was diverted to repay syndicate members' initial costs of buying the harbour, rather than being spent on dredging the harbour as promised. Various locals, including Messrs Thorneycroft, Attrill, Bullen and Bland, together with several unidentified persons, all voice criticism of the company, telling Lewis that no silt has been removed from the harbour so far, only shingle, which has been sold on. They claim the harbour is in a worse state than when the company took over. Mr Woodnutt refuses to disclose the price paid for the harbour, commenting that some people are too damn lazy to find it out themselves from company records. Lewis consults the company records. The figure is not there. He obtains the figure elsewhere. Mr Woodnutt claims there were no other potential purchasers. Lewis reveals that that is not the case and that two serious bids in excess of the syndicate's offer of £24,000 were made for the harbour, one of them being for £35,000, but that for some unexplained reason, neither bid was considered by British Rail. Mr Woodnutt tells Lewis that he is not exactly a philanthropist. Lewis says that rental income from boatyards on the land was not paid into the BHIC account, but into a new company, 'Yarland Properties,' owned by the syndicate. Thorneycroft claims that the existence of two separate companies came as a surprise. Lewis also points out that the County Council never discussed the sale of the harbour in public session but instead, left the decision to the Finance Committee, chaired by Mr Woodnutt, and a second committee on which Mr Woodnutt was also the Council's representative, and it was they who had recommended that a private syndicate take over the harbour. The frustrated bidder of £35,000 is 'speechless' when informed the harbour actually sold for £24,000. Mr Woodnutt expresses his displeasure at the way the interview is going, telling Lewis that he is going to send in a complaint about him. He says that he has been bowled a 'bloody fast ball' and then walks away, throwing his microphone to the ground. He tells Lewis he cannot carry on the interview tomorrow or the next day and then asks if Lewis is 'taking all this down'. There, the item ends.

None of the matters raised in the confrontation found their way into print that week. Puzzled County Press readers who had not seen the Nationwide interview were left to get the information from the Island grapevine.

A year later, when the Council debated whether or not an enquiry should be held into the affair, Stephen Ross, the then Liberal candidate for the Island, said, "To criticise these gentlemen, supported as they are by a powerful weekly newspaper, is a task not undertaken lightly ... Mr Woodnutt took a very active part in Finance Committee meetings and his association with the syndicate was obviously very close ... Was it intended all along that he would join the board in time? I really do wonder if it is in the best interests of this council that its two most influential members should be so deeply involved in planning matters."

Two years later, the Sunday Times revealed that the Bembridge Harbour Improvement Company had not, in fact, purchased the entire harbour, but everything below high water mark, almost exclusively mud and silt, while Yarland Properties on the other hand, had become the owners of everything above high water mark, that is to say, large amounts of land and buildings. This division had important ramifications. One of the terms of sale included the provision that if the harbour were neglected, the Council could compulsorily purchase it, but this division of the property between two companies now meant that if the Council were ever to exercise that right, they would find only the muddy, silted-up harbour available to them, the lucrative real estate being stowed away beyond their reach in Yarland Properties. According to the Sunday Times of April 16, 1972,"the British taxpayer lost thousands, though precisely why is still not clear. British Rail last week declined to comment."

In 1972, Yarland Properties applied for planning permission to build over 120 houses on a nine acre parcel of 'white land' adjacent to the lagoons today managed by the RSPB. The Sunday Times report declared "had they gained planning permission, the site would be worth almost £250,000 to any property developer." Following much controversy and a public enquiry, planning permission was refused.

The affair refused to go away and continued to haunt Mr Woodnutt over the next few years. As late as July 1973, Willie Hamilton, MP, told the Commons, "He (Mr Woodnutt) is deeply involved in the manner in which the land surrounding Bembridge Harbour railway site was sold to a syndicate of which he was a representative. It reeks of corruption and racketeering." The Island's voters agreed, and in the general election of 1974 Mr Woodnutt's 17,000 majority was sensationally overturned. He suffered a crushing and humiliating defeat when Stephen Ross, for the Liberal Party, took the seat, winning by over 7500 votes. The affair was to cast a long political shadow. No more would the Island be seen as one of the safest seats in the country and it would change political colours several times during the next three decades.

Only six months after the shock result, Mark Woodnutt died, aged only 55, his Times obituary reporting, "His friends say he never recovered from his shattering defeat at the general election."

In 1969 and 1970, the Isle of Wight played host to two of the biggest musical events in the world. In 1969, Bob Dylan headlined the Wootton Festival and in 1970, hundreds of thousands came for five days to watch Jimi Hendrix, The Who, The Doors and many more play at East Afton Farm at Freshwater. It was the biggest worldwide audience for a rock concert at the time and it may still be, even now, but it all began on a chilly August night in 1968, when between seven and 10,000 young people gathered in a field of corn stubble at Ford Farm, Godshill. They were there to witness the biggest musical line-up ever seen on the Island, featuring The Crazy World of Arthur Brown, The Move, and from America, Jefferson Airplane. The festival promoters were Ronnie and Ray Foulk, two brothers from Totland, both in their early twenties. For the next three years, they were to enjoy an uneasy relationship with the County Press.

The following pages chart not only the trials and tribulations they faced in putting on the festivals but also the hardening attitude of the County Press towards them as time went by. The 1968 festival had barely registered, but events at Wootton the following year were to put the promoters and the County Press on a collision course. By the time the 1970 festival ended, the paper's scepticism and mistrust had turned into open hostility.

◆

Godshill 1968 - "The Great South Coast Pop Festivity"

Ray Foulk : "In 1968, I was running my own printing business and I was running it when the festival idea emerged. There was quite a team of us, but it was essentially my brother Ronnie's enterprise. I was quickly drawn in, and so too were my brother Bill, and sister Jo. Ronnie, with my support, spearheaded the thing. There was no indoor swimming pool on the Island and there was a campaign to try and raise money to build one, so that's how it really came about. Unfortunately, the Isle of Wight Indoor Swimming Pool Association, or I.W.I.S.P.A., started getting a lot of publicity which they didn't like, and they cut us loose. They said, 'No, we can't continue with this.' They cut off their name from the event. They didn't want to be associated with it ... The County Press did very little to cover it. They were virtually the only news organisation on the Isle of Wight in those days and they were kind of boycotting it. They thought it was a disreputable adventure with connotations of youth culture, drug taking, left wing politics and so on. All that sort of thing was not appreciated by the Isle of Wight establishment."

The County Press lack of enthusiasm for the forthcoming festival may well have been due to the fact that it was being put on by one of their own - Ray Foulk's first employer after leaving school was none other than the County Press itself.

Ray Foulk : "I had worked at the County Press on a five-year apprenticeship and I left there at 21 to set up my own printing business, Solent Graphics, which I set up in competition to them, and when I left I took two of their best printing machine operators with me. I had worked there for five years and instead of them being proud that I was 'one of their own,' it seems it increased their resentment. I'm not aware that it was ever mentioned that this enormous phenomenon for the Island - love it or hate it - was organised by an ex-County Press man."

Festivals and 'happenings,' an integral part of the counterculture movement, were gaining ground across the country, but the fact that a festival was to take place on the Island, featuring top British acts and a major American band, left the County Press completely unmoved. Not a word of the festival appeared in its pages prior to the event, with the exception of the large and striking adverts placed by the promoters themselves in the two editions leading up to the festival. Apart from that, there were just two other mentions. The Isle of Wight Indoor Swimming Pool Association had placed a small advertisement the week prior to the festival, pointing out that it was not the promoter of the event; and the second mention was in a reader's letter. The writer was none other than Jimmy Savile's nephew, an Islander as it happened, who had written to say that despite early posters for the event claiming his uncle would be opening the festival, he was authorised to state that Savile himself had no knowledge of the event, and in any event, was scheduled to appear elsewhere that day. A week later, minus Jimmy Savile, the festival took place ...

Ray Foulk : "We managed to get Jefferson Airplane and we got The Crazy World of Arthur Brown, who were number one just a couple of weeks before .... Steve Ross* introduced us to the farmer that owned 'Hell Field'. It was a very unsuitable location really, because it was quite a trek to get there and it was a stubble field. It wasn't as though it was nice grass to sit on and I think the corn was only cut a few days before we started building the site, so it was a pretty unsuitable kind of set-up really. The stage was on the back of two trucks. My memories of the performers or the atmosphere of the event are very scanty. I can't remember sitting around watching performances. It went smoothly enough. It was a bleak event as I recall. I don't think the weather was very warm and the attendance was not as great as we'd hoped, we only had 10 to 15,000 people attend - it was alright but it was nothing special. Facilities were pretty threadbare. I think the men's toilets were a trench with a bit of fencing in front of it, that sort of thing; very crude. I think the catering was probably restricted to a few hot-dog vans. I really don't have much of a recollection of it and there is very little to look at in the archives. I remember the Jefferson Airplane's amazing light show and circles of colour whizzing around, and in fact we went on the following year to run a thing at the Manor House Ballroom in Lake, it was called the Middle Earth Club, in which we tried to replicate that sort of light show. It was a weekly event with a lot of the acts that were eventually booked to appear in the '69 festival. We had the Who booked, for instance, and the Who were switched from that venue to the '69 Festival."

The following week's County Press carried a factual but businesslike account of the festival. Setting the tone for the festival reporting style over the next two years, the report began not with an account of the music, but instead, of damage to a barley crop and the activities of the St John Ambulance Brigade. The bulk of the crowd are referred to as 'mainland people' while the musical acts are accorded just one paragraph. However, the report was objective and it was almost entirely positive. That was not something that could be said of some of the coverage that was to appear over the next two years ...

* Stephen Ross went on to become Liberal MP for the Island in 1974, winning the seat three more times in a row before eventually standing down in 1987.

September 7th, 1968

POP FESTIVAL WAS ORDERLY
FANS APOLOGISE FOR ACCIDENTAL DAMAGE

Apprehension about the outcome of "The Great South Coast Bank Holiday Pop Festivity" as the organisers styled it, proved unnecessary. The event, held at the singularly named Hell Field, Ford Farm, Godshill, throughout Saturday night, passed off almost without incident.

An estimated 9000 fans from all parts of the country made the journey to Hell Field, chosen because of its remoteness. (The nearest villages of significance, Godshill, Whitwell and Chale, are all approximately two miles away). A shuttle service of buses operated from several points on the Island to the festival but many fans arriving in private vehicles or on foot were confused by the fact that signs originally showing the way to Hell Field had been tampered with and in some cases, removed.

The only damage of note was caused by fans who wandered through a neighbouring field of barley, belonging to Mr. B.A. Corbin, of Holden Farm, Roud. Mr. Corbin told the "County Press" that fencing, hedges and the barley itself had suffered, representing between £30 and £40 worth of damage. He added that the majority of the damage was accidental and the fans he had met had apologised and were most courteous. Fences broken by spectators created a further problem for Mr. Corbin, who spent anxious moments preventing his herd of cattle from wandering through the gaps.

Rest days and leave for Island police were cancelled during the weekend but the absence of trouble meant that the police, together with the security men and their five guard dogs, plus the festival stewards had comparatively little to contend with. Police were on hand, however, when some of those present started using chairs to keep many fires from going out after orthodox fuel had been expanded. In addition, three cars and a motor scooter disappeared during the night but all were recovered later.

For the 30 St. John Ambulance Brigade members on duty, it was one of the busiest nights on record. The complement on duty was the largest number the brigade have used for any single event in one place on the Island. They were drawn from the County staff, the Ventnor, Newport (including Cowes), Ryde and Sandown ambulance divisions and the Ryde and Ventnor nursing divisions, under Dr. F.R.B.H. Kennedy, M.B.E., K.St.J., J.P.(commissioner), and Divisional Superintendent A.H. Worley, in whose area (Ventnor) the festival was held. The 68 cases - 70 per cent of which were mainland people - were treated in a tent well equipped as a medical aid unit with stretcher beds.

Throughout the 14 hour festival they were in direct radio contact with the county ambulance control but the medical facilities available meant that only three people actually needed to be conveyed to the Royal I.W. County Hospital, Ryde - all in the early part of Sunday morning, between 5 a.m. and 7 a.m. These were a severe asthma case, treated with oxygen at the unit, a girl whose foot had been partly run over by a bus who was taken to hospital for X-rays, and a youngster suffering from epilepsy. The main complaints were burns from the fires, collapses of various nature, and cuts, many caused by flying missiles, including beer cans.

One girl received five stitches in a head wound. As the night wore on, the biting wind forced several spectators without sleeping bags to tear plastic sheeting from the arena's perimeter to wrap around themselves and the conditions even proved too much for one youngster who was treated for hypothermia - severe cold.

Dr. Kennedy told the "County Press" that the total of people treated was not excessive when the number of spectators present was taken into consideration. They represented the population of a moderate sized town and the circumstances were unusual, with thousands of people crammed into one field. He added "It shows how necessary it is to have medical facilities at such an event. It would have been a state of chaos if there had been no proper set-up. Without a medical point, about 20 of the patients treated would have had to be taken to hospital."

Three St. John Ambulance Brigade mini-buses were in attendance - the Ventnor Vehicle, the bus presented by the Mayor of Newport (Alderman J. R. Powell) on Friday week for the Newport area, and the one due to be presented to the Ryde division shortly - still in its green Civil Defence coat. The buses are usually employed for transporting the elderly but on this occasion they were used for the transportation of equipment, the bulk of which came from the Ventnor division.

The first of the 14 groups made their appearance shortly before 8 p.m. but there was surprisingly little enthusiasm among the fans - most of whom sat quietly on the stubble - throughout the night. By early morning, the majority had left the field. Many were disappointed by the non-appearance of the Beatles, who were billed as coming to promote their new group, the Smile. Topping the bill were the Californian group, Jefferson Airplane, making their first appearance in this country, and one of the country's currently most popular acts, the Crazy World of Arthur Brown. Island groups, the Cherokees and Halcyon Order, both received good ovations. Compering the festival, which included a "light sound environment" by the Royal College of Art, was Radio One DJ, John Peel.

The whole arena was illuminated by floodlights - bright enough to show fans where they were going without being too brilliant to spoil the atmosphere. Additional lighting was provided on the stage, which was constructed from two road trailers and scaffolding. Long refreshment tents at either side of the field were also well illuminated and patronised. The power for the lighting and the amplification - which at times proved faulty, causing long gaps between acts - was supplied by a generator. Groups occupied large tents behind the stage when not appearing. At the opposite end of the field, marquees were provided for the Police, security guards, the medical aid unit and fans requiring shelter.

The event was held in aid of the I.W. Indoor Swimming Pool Association.*

———————————◆———————————

* The I.W. Indoor Swimming Pool Association, or IWISPA, had appointed Ronnie Foulk as their fund raiser. Following their withdrawal from the event, the Foulk brothers were left to continue independently and their initial £750 investment was repaid to IWISPA after the event.

The Great South Coast Bankholiday Pop Festivity

HELL FIELD, Ford Farm, Nr. Godshill, Isle of Wight

Guest Appearance from the U.S.A.

THE JEFFERSON AIRPLANE

America's No. 1 Group coming over specially for the festival to make their first ever live appearance in this country. The group is bringing over from America 25 Technicians and 4 Van loads of Equipment to make the most Fantastic sound you have ever heard.

and Topping the bill from Brixton

THE CRAZY WORLD OF ARTHUR BROWN

"The God Of Hell Fire at Hell Field !!!" Record "Fire" No. 1 in the charts this week.

(NEXT SATURDAY NIGHT)

Saturday Aug. 31st 6pm to 10 am Next Morning

The complete Festival will be compered by JOHN PEEL, Radio 1 D.J. We regret to announce that due to unforeseen circumstances Jimmy Savile will not be able to open the festival. However, we are pleased to announce that we have added to the bill the latest Beatles' managed group called " Smile "

TICKETS 25/-
(Limited number available to Island residents in advance only at 20/-) Buy Now. From:

ISLE OF WIGHT
INDOOR SWIMMING POOL ASSOCIATION.
177 High Street Ryde, St. Thomas's Square, Newport.

THE MOVE	THE MIRAGE	ORANGE BICYCLE
PLASTIC PENNY	AYNSLEY DUNBAR RETALIATION	BLONDE ON BLONDE
PRETTY THINGS	FAIRPORT CONVENTION	THE CHEROKEES
TYRANNOSAURUS REX	SMILE	HELCYON ORDER

Also

COLOSSAL "LIGHT SOUND ENVIRONMENT BY ROYAL COLLEGE OF ART.
Coaches will be arranged from all parts of the Island and there will be transport from at various times throughout the night for anyone not wishing to stay till the end.
THE HOTEL RYDE CASTLE and THE SEAGULL BALLROOM have CANCELLED THEIR DANCES on AUGUST 31st and will be assisting with the catering at the FESTIVAL to support the I.W.I.S.P.A.

Also Teagues, Ryde and Newport, Youngs, Cowes, Sandown and Shanklin; John Menzies, Ventnor; George T.V. Service, 2 Albert Street, Ventnor; Holdings, Yarmouth, Photo-Wight, Freshwater; Lady Kate Boutique, 7 Union Street, Ryde; Beardsalls, 55 Regent Street, Shanklin; H. W. Bartlett & Son Bembridge; R. H. Gosland, Trinity Road, East Cowes.

Also at HOTEL RYDE CASTLE and THE SEAGULL BALLROOM, RYDE.

Special contracts have been signed for this mammoth event, so all groups will definitely be appearing.

All profits to go to the Isle of Wight Indoor Swimming Pool Association
Extra special security precautions are being taken to avoid gate crashers

"THE GREATEST POP FESTIVAL EVER TO BE HELD IN THIS COUNTRY"

STOP PRESS !!!

It has just been confirmed by the Beatles'' Apple " head quarters that John Lennon, Paul McCartney and George Harrison will be at the Festival especially to see the Jefferson Airplane and to promote their new group " SMILE." Other famous celebrities to be announced next week.

BEATLES COMING TO THE FESTIVAL

THE GREAT SOUTH COAST BANK HOLIDAY POP FESTIVITY

to be held at **GODSHILL**, Isle of Wight, on **AUGUST 31st, 1968**

THE **JEFFERSON AIRPLANE**	**TRYANNOSAURUS REX**
	PRETTY THINGS
(America's No. 1 Group, first live appearance in this country).	**PLASTIC PENNY**
	ORANGE BICYCLE
THE CRAZY WORLD OF ARTHUR BROWN	**THE MIRAGE**
	BLOND ON BLOND
THE MOVE	**AINSLEY DUNBAR RETALIATION**
	FAIRPORT CONVENTION
	Plus Supporting Groups

The complete festival to be compered by Radio 1's top D.J.
JOHN PEEL.

To be opened by JIMMY SAVILLE.

LIGHT SHOW ARRANGED BY ROYAL COLLEGE OF ART.

TICKETS 25/- (20/- to Island Residents),
available from
ISLE OF WIGHT INDOOR SWIMMING POOL ASSOCIATION.

Also Teagues, Ryde and Newport; Youngs, Cowes, Sandown and Shanklin; John Menzies, Ventnor; George T.V. Service; Ventnor; Holdings, Yarmouth; and Photo-Wight, Freshwater.

GENERAL STAFF

REQUIRED FOR

THE ISLE OF WIGHT INTERNATIONAL POP FESTIVAL

Full range of jobs available—some starting AUGUST 4th and finishing SEPTEMBER 5th. Other jobs only available for the WEEK ENDING AUGUST 30th.

Apply in writing, stating age, experience (if any) and type of job required, to the MANAGING DIRECTOR,

FIERY CREATIONS LTD.

TAVISTOCK, WARD ROAD, TOTLAND BAY x

SOUTH COAST POP FESTIVAL

The organisers of the above event, held at Hell Field, Ford Farm, Godshill, Saturday August 31st, wish to extend their thanks to all who helped to make this event successful. Our special thanks are given to Mr. J. Flux, farmer, Ford Farm; Chief Superintendent Paddon, L.o.W. Constabulary; St. John Ambulance Brigade. It is our hope that next year's event will be even more successful than this year.

RON FOULK,
Organiser.

FIRE 69

I.W. International Pop Festival, 69

YOU CHOOSE THE GROUPS

Fill in the form below with the first ten international Groups you would like to see at ipf 69.

Send your choice to the Secretary, ipf, Cornlea, The Broadway, Totland Bay, I.W.

1		6
2		7
3		8
4		9
5		10

Name ....

Address ....

"An Excuse for Dirty People to Behave in a Dirty Manner"

In 1969 Bob Dylan was a counterculture icon with an appeal and mystique like no other performer. He had last been seen in Britain in 1966 when his electrified performances shocked audiences, as a result of which he had been labelled "Judas." The subsequent furore in the music press, and his legendary motorcycle accident, drove him underground to near invisibility for the next three years which left an eager public hungry for their hero to return - Fiery Creations decided he was just the act to headline the 1969 Wootton festival. Getting him to agree to perform took considerable persuasion.

Ray Foulk : "To get Dylan on the Isle of Wight was an international coup.* It was a fantastic thing to happen. He was like the Messiah to a lot of people, a huge name, and I think without getting Dylan we probably wouldn't have had much of an event in '69."

The fervour in which Dylan was held by music fans peaked with his Isle of Wight appearance. The headline performance at Wootton would put the Island at the centre of a musical coup with massive, global appeal. - Except, that is, for the County Press, who had yet to mention it. On the Wednesday before the festival, Dylan agreed to a press conference at the Halland Hotel at Seaview, under pressure from Fiery Creations who wanted to boost ticket sales. It was another coup for Fiery Creations and press and television reporters from around the world descended on the Halland to get their first look at Bob Dylan for three years.

Ray Foulk : "The press conference was slightly bizarre. I'd never been to a press conference in my life before, let alone one like that and there was a whole bank of cameras and microphones and they were asking rather stupid questions. One of the first questions was, "Do you think microphones are like guns?" and Dylan didn't know how to answer that and was looking around for someone else to answer it. Then they started asking about drugs and he didn't want to talk about that - and so on. It was not a great press conference."

Not that County Press readers would have known any of this. While the whole of Fleet Street attended, accompanied by excited television crews from around the world, there was one newspaper conspicuous by its absence - the County Press. In what was an extraordinary decision, the editor, Mr Ash, the man with a world scoop on his doorstep, decided Dylan's return to the music world on an Isle of Wight stage was not a newsworthy event. Not one of their reporters attended.

It is possible that other forces were at work. The fact that Ray Foulk was an ex-employee, possibly seen as a viper in the nest, may well have influenced the County Press attitude to the festival.

Ray Foulk : "The County Press seemed to have it in for me personally where they could. I always felt that they had a problem with the fact that I was, or had been, one of their own - particularly in later years."

---

* The booking of Bob Dylan became the subject of the first of the many festival myths that would be invented over the years. The oft-repeated account of Ray Foulk flying to America and camping outside Dylan's house, using conversations over the door intercom to gain access, is pure fiction Dylan was persuaded to appear at the festival by means of the conventional method of telephone calls between his agent, Albert Grossman, and a persistent Ray Foulk.

So, unheralded and unannounced, at least as far as the County Press was concerned, the festival took place on the weekend of the 29th to 31st of August ...

Ray Foulk : "It was an excellent site at Wootton. The farmer, Ron Phillips, was great. So too was the neighbouring farmer, Albert Thackham, who provided the small area of land for the stage. Ron Phillips was overwhelmed by the event because his farmhouse was literally 50 yards from the stage. I don't think he had any idea of how big it was going to be, but he was all right about it. We got the site in place and there wasn't a lot of local opposition. There were a few people, maybe locally, that wrote letters in and complained but certainly not very many. We didn't have any obligation to talk to local authorities, we didn't need a licence, we just got on with it. We had no interference at all ... I remember arriving on the Friday night. I arrived about six o'clock and I drove through the lanes, with lots of people everywhere, went backstage and I walked up on the stage and got a glimpse of the audience. That was the first time I'd seen the arena full of people and it took my breath away. That was an incredible feeling. Suddenly I felt, 'We've done it. We've pulled it off. We've got this huge audience and they're all here.' It was full, it was just a massive sea of people and there was a group performing and everybody was enjoying themselves. That really was a quite wonderful moment."

◆

The following week's report contained sarcastic digs at festivalgoers, and referred to 'strangely garbed young people,' and 'vagrant-looking individuals,' but like the account of the 1968 festival, it was mostly positive and reasonably objective. It conceded that the police had praised the behaviour of the majority of festival visitors and that the anticipated trouble had not materialised. The report was to be the calm before the storm ...

September 6th, 1969

POP FESTIVAL INVASION

The Island was this week slowly recovering from the hammer blow of pop with its attendant retinue of strangely garbed young people who gave the impression that it was a Hindu prayer meeting on the Ganges rather than a music festival in the Garden Isle. The aftermath left many people debating whether or not the world-wide publicity was good for future tourist trade.

For a week before the event began, vagrant-looking individuals could be seen wandering the streets of Newport, Ryde and Wootton. Some carried tenting equipment on their backs, others just a bedroll or a few blankets. Others who had come unprepared for camping out, went from door-to-door seeking accommodation. A few were lucky, although many found the height of the season was no time to come to the Island and take pot luck.

The police, too, praised the behaviour of the majority of festival visitors. The Island force were stretched to the limit, every available man being on duty throughout the period, plus reinforcements from the mainland. A private house was taken over near the site as temporary headquarters and the drug squad mingled with the festival followers. The "pushing" and use of drugs were not so great as expected, although there were 20 arrests for the possession of drugs, theft and rowdyism. On Monday, a police spokesman said there was not nearly as much trouble as they had anticipated.

THE 1969 FESTIVAL

y Foulk, "I remember arriving on the Friday night and I walked up on the stage and got a glimpse
he audience and it took my breath away. That was an incredible feeling. It was just a massive sea
eople and there was a group performing and everybody was enjoying themselves. That really was
uite wonderful moment."   *[Press Association]*

he view from the crowd on the Friday afternoon. The dots onstage are the Bonzo Dog Band.
[Photograph by Alan Stroud]

This to Island residents, however, was not the only factor about the invasion. For three days, the population was increased by more than twice its size, and for those who could not find accommodation at the camping site, the easiest thing to do, it appeared, was to sleep in the nearest available front garden, with or without the permission of the householder. Another objection by residents was to the sight of hippie-looking individuals squatting on kerbsides in Newport High Street during the day, sleeping or singing "songs of peace," while at Ryde, they stretched out full-length across pavements, forcing pedestrians to walk in single file.

LAST MINUTE EFFORTS

During the week before the event, strenuous efforts were made by some Wootton people, including Mr F. E. Butler, a Newport councillor, to have the festival stopped, mainly on the grounds of hygiene and the unsuitability of the Island for such an influx of people.

Although his fears were eventually proved to be unfounded, Mr Butler said that at one time old people living in the immediate vicinity were greatly troubled by what might happen ... A spokesman for the festival organisers was quoted as saying they hope to make a small profit of something in the region, perhaps, of £10,000." This would be ploughed back into the "next festival."

As for the American star Bob Dylan, who was reputed to have been paid £35,000 for one hour, he was reported to have asked if he could return next year. Then, on Wednesday, on his return to the States, he was reported as saying he had no wish to return to England and had simply used the festival as a "warm-up" for another project.

There have been conflicting views from members of the Island Tourist Board as to the value of the publicity given to the festival. One said it was most welcome, providing there was no trouble. Another said, "I would be the first to agree that the Island needs more national publicity to attract the right kind of tourist here. But I feel that such events as this have a detrimental effect and we could have been set back about ten years with our endeavours. The kind of people who appreciate the natural beauties of the Island are not enamoured with the sight of hippies."

The family-type of holidaymaker would not be impressed by nude dancing and public love-making which some national newspapers reported as having taken place at the festival site. One Sunday newspaper actually published a photograph. A few shops in Wootton reported a flourishing trade and most of them are hoping for a repeat performance next year. Alternatively, some Ryde seafront stallholders said they had been hit by the invasion of Wootton and the fact that many day trippers had not come over from the mainland on Bank Holiday Monday.

The isolated festival site covered 150 acres of Mr Ronald Phillip's Wootton Farm and main points of entry were via Palmers Road or Church Road and a rough farm track. No efforts were spared by the organisers to provide the estimated 150,000 fans with all the necessary facilities for a weekend or longer stay. A large festival village provided shops and services of every kind, including a general store, record shop, boutique, newspaper stall and a shop offering joss sticks for 6d., giving rise to an overbearing smell of incense which mingled none too pleasantly with the odours of cooking hamburgers and hot dogs.

Housed in one of the many marquees - claimed to be the biggest collection ever assembled in Europe - was a refreshment stall manned continuously from five o'clock on Friday evening until nine o'clock on Monday morning by members of Newport Round Table. This enterprise was extremely well patronised - so much so, in fact, that despite stocking up with fresh supplies on Sunday afternoon, the store had only two tins of frankfurters left unsold when it closed on Monday! The Round Table raised a gross profit of over £2000 to be divided between the funds of the Boy Scout Camp at Corfe and the Isle of Wight Indoor Swimming Pool Association.

MASSIVE CAMPING AREA

Near the village was a massive camping area where brightly coloured tents started springing up earlier in the week. For those without their own canvas accommodation, marquees were available for sleeping purposes but in spite of this many fans were forced to sleep in the open. Fortunately for them the festival was blessed with dry weather. Some of the earlier arrivals made use of junk from nearby scrapheaps to build temporary abodes and these were given tags such as "Desolation Row," named after the Dylan record.

The arena - an area of 60 acres - was surrounded during Saturday and Sunday by a large eight-foot wooden fence. Despite announcer Ricki Farr's repeated requests, many fans insisted on sitting on the fence and consequently pulling down electricity cables, causing power cuts.

Those arriving late had a restricted view of the stage - a quarter of a mile away from the back of the arena - but the public address system - when working properly - ensured that nobody, including residents from as far afield as Newport and Northwood, could fail to hear the "beautiful sounds."

Fans not wishing to queue up for pass-out tickets to visit the festival village were almost as well catered for inside the arena with large refreshment tents and extensive toilet facilities. Indeed, the only people not squatting on the ground during the main days were those queuing for either the latrines or one of the several mobile trading fans, all of which experienced trade of fantastic proportions. An absolute necessity for hungry fans was infinite patience as it could take anything up to four hours to purchase a hot dog which had turned into a distinctly "cold dog" by the time it had reached its destination!

MAIN PROGRAMME

The main programme opened on Friday week with a special concert for season ticket holders starring the zany Bonzo Dog Band, the Nice and the Eclection, all of whom received great ovations. Hilarious poetry reading completed a successful curtain raiser.

Saturday's concert started early in the afternoon and continued, with special permission, until the early hours of Sunday. Among the all-star bill were the Who, the Moody Blues, who received their first ever encore, the Pretty Things and Marsha Hunt - star of the hit musical "Hair" - with White Trash. It was the Edgar Broughton Band that provided the day's most memorable moments. They whipped up the huge crowds excitement with their first number "The Psychopath" to such an extent that during their next song a girl, completely naked, walked to the front of the stage and danced for a full five minutes before being led away by a security guard.

Thousands were still pouring into the Island on Sunday for the final day. The concert was underway soon after lunch but the excitement started building up with the appearance on stage of leading American folk singer Tom Paxton. He was followed by Julie Felix with some well-known songs which delighted the fans. Shortly before six o'clock, negro Richie Havens commenced an electrifying two hour performance with his group. It was then that the crowd began to get restless as the advertised time for Dylan's appearance grew near.

Dylan's backing group, The Band, appeared about 10.30 pm. and the air was filled with expectancy until, minutes before 11 pm., the man they had all come to see, appeared — three hours late! Dylan, dressed in a white suit and yellow shirt, sang several of his renowned songs - all to new arrangements - but around midnight he and The Band downed instruments and left the stage. They returned to do a further two numbers in response to an encore but after this they left the ground, much to the disappointment of the crowd who had expected a three-hour performance together with the possibility of a "jam session" to include Dylan and The Beatles.

To quote the organisers Press handout - "To provide the audience with other outlets besides the beautiful sounds at the festival, Fiery Creations have provided an extensive programme of multimedia activities." These included pneumatic plastic "environments" and Krazy Foam happenings, car jousts, film shows in a large marquee housing up to 400, light shows by the Black Sun, local folk singers and a non-stop discotheque.

Assisting the police in providing watertight security arrangements were hired firms, such as Nightguard Security, of Fareham. A total of 18 security men with 18 dogs went to the festival ...

The threat of an influx of festivalgoers being admitted to the Royal IW County Hospital was eliminated by the splendid service of the St John Ambulance Brigade who arranged a full-scale medical centre at the ground and were on duty throughout - from midday on Friday week until Monday evening. Out of the 400 cases dealt with by the Brigade it was necessary to transfer only one patient to the hospital ... The transportation of fans both to and from the Island involved a massive combined operation by bus and ferry operations. In addition to normal ferry and hovercraft services, special boats were run to the Island at frequent intervals and a British Rail spokesman at Portsmouth Harbour said that no fan had to wait more than 45 minutes for a boat to Ryde. Once on the Island, the fans were conveyed to the site by a shuttle service of Southern Vectis buses. These were on hand when the festival closed at midnight on Sunday to convey departing visitors back to ferry terminals.

The main route back to the mainland was via the Ryde-Portsmouth ferry. Removal of the bulk of fans started at 12:30 am. on Monday and continued until 11 am. on Monday when the 20-minute shuttle service was withdrawn. From 7 am., the entire fleet of four passenger ferries was employed.

A British Rail spokesman said, "We would be very happy to carry this crowd again. They were no trouble and we had less complaints about them than we usually receive about a normal Bank Holiday crowd." ...

Mark Woodnutt was given the editorial column in that same issue to set out his thoughts on the event and those who had attended and so, just a few pages away from the previous largely positive report, an altogether different take on the festival was to be found. In a leader entitled 'What Price Pop?,' a blend of prejudice and sensationalism, Mr Woodnutt described "the fields of litter and filth" which remained to be cleared up, (in fact, Mr Phillips's fields were back to normal in a matter of days) and declared, 'However hard the progressive left-wingers may try to wring up a smile in their self idolizing mirrors, the publicity given to the Island could not have been worse.'

Finally, Mr Woodnutt asks about festivals in future years, saying, 'We must decide,' but does not make clear exactly who 'we' are. There appeared to be a blanket assumption on the part of Mark Woodnutt and the County Press that because they were opposed to the festival, everyone else on the Island must be. That, of course, was simply not so.

Mr Woodnutt chose not to put his name to the article, simply signing it 'M.W.' ...

6th Sept, 1969.

WHAT PRICE POP ?

And so the happening came to Wootton Creek in the year of our Lord, 1969. Cloaked in blankets, besandled and worn, the worshippers of throbbing Pop, some 150,000, descended on the Isle of Wight and travelled to their chosen Mecca at Wootton. For most the journey had been long; for many their faith had transported them across seas and continents; but for all, this was the moment of idyllic truth and grandiose twentieth-century style, when their chosen prophets and followers would sing from their own hymnal. Guitar strings twanged, drums beat out, performers gyrated on stage and, with electronic aids unknown in the scriptures, their words rose to the heavens and fell back upon the earth to inspire the believers and mystify the unbelievers for miles around. For three whole days did they sing, dance and make merry, and as night fell they lay themselves down to sleep beneath the stars, sharing tents and bedrolls, one with the other, and lighting fires to keep warm. On the third day they arose and departed, and all was still.

Thus might a benevolent and ancient scribe have written of the Island's August Bank Holiday Festival of Music. A less charitable man, mindful of his responsibility to present an accurate record for posterity would doubtless have delayed his departure to assess the merits of the cause and its effect upon this Island. Like countless others have since, he would have been drawn to the green fields of Wootton and there despaired of human beings who could leave such an indescribable scene of litter and filth behind them. He would, doubtless, have been shocked by the remains of fires on graves in the nearby graveyard, and he would have been understandably concerned by the fears of residents for the safety of their property and the rightful claim that they and their families should be allowed to sleep in peace. It is conceivable, too, that the same scribe would have cogitated on the wisdom of such an enterprise and its possible repercussions on the future well-being of the Island, both privately and commercially.

Side effects

Some may have benefited, some will have suffered. The side effects, which could be long lasting, concern not only the residents of Wootton Creek, particularly if such a festival is held there again, but every man and woman on the Island. The time has now come for questions to be put, and they come readily to hand.

It might be asked if it were fair to impose on the Island, at short notice, a body of people equal in number to nearly double its population? Surely it constituted an intolerable strain on our public services and grave disturbance to those living within the impact of this invasion? Transport to and from the Island was saturated at a peak holiday time so that ordinary regular visitors were debarred from their use. Was this a wise move? Some shopkeepers may have enjoyed an unexpected surge of business, but how far off is the day when they may ruefully contemplate the loss of trade from regular customers and annual visitors? The Island police force, assisted by reinforcements from the mainland, was wholly occupied on permanent duty for some four days. Should this step have been countenanced, what of the cost, and what of the risk to the normal enforcement of the law?

What of the possible dangers to public health in the Island when 150,000 people crowd together in a few fields for four days? "Hygiene," one man is reported to have told a national newspaper, " is the least of our worries."

For almost a week, at the very time when the majority of the British nation lay relaxing at their own favourite holiday resorts reading their papers and watching television, a strong mauve-tinted spotlight focused itself upon the Isle of Wight and made it seem that here was the centre of some modern grotesquerie for which we should be pitied. With 150,000 pop-gospellers out to "do their thing," and having caught wind of other delights in store for them, the Press and television of the world moved in with undisguised relish to again carve up those two old stalwarts who somehow refuse to die — respectability (of habits) and consideration (for others).

Hovering ghouls

Fortunately for all, the giant phallic plastic balloons which were to have risen to a height of 100 feet and ejaculated foam, remained on the ground, and the hovering ghouls of publicity had, perforce, to remain content with one or two rather pathetic exhibitions of nude dancing. However hard the progressive left-wingers may try to wring up a smile in their self idolizing mirrors, the publicity given to the Island could not have been worse.

Uncertainty has been created in the minds of thousands who have been our visitors in the past, and understandable fears have been aroused in the minds of thousands of other ordinary, happy and healthy families who may have been considering staying with us next August. One can almost hear the thankful prayer from the elders of every mainland resort - "There, but for the grace of God" ...

Finally, who is going to clean up the fields of rubbish and filth and restore some semblance of civilisation to the normally pleasant acres?

These are but a few of the important aspects of the matter which should now be discussed and on which every ratepayer should make it his duty to be kept informed. Unless satisfactory answers are forthcoming immediately it can only be assumed that the Island prefers short-term questionable gains to it's wise policy of long-term investment in its tourist programme designed steadily to improve existing facilities for regular visitors, and at the same time setting sufficiently high standards to win new business.

The choice is ours. We must decide here and now and let our decision be known.

M.W.

For Mr Ash and Mr Woodnutt, the festival was clearly an unedifying and unwelcome intrusion into Island life. Over the next few weeks both men used their respective positions to lobby against festivals and their followers whenever they could. Ironically, they need not have bothered. In the event, the most outrageous, the most inaccurate, and indeed the most unpleasant attacks on the festival and those who attended, were to come not from the pen of the editor or from the speeches of the Island's MP, but from the County Press readers themselves. Mr Ash maintained that he printed a fair balance of the letters received, and there is no reason to doubt his word, but even he, an ardent opponent of the festival, must have raised an eyebrow at some of the extraordinary and prejudiced sentiments expressed in them ...

Aftermath of the Festival.

The Isle of Wight pop festival appears to be merely an excuse for dirty people to behave in a dirty manner, to music. The resulting VD, illegitimate births and drug addiction will become obvious. The site is far less attractive than the most sleazy fairground or circus and smells far worse.

The so-called entertainment for the masses of gullible beatniks consists mainly of blaring recorded pop groups, a heap of foam, a few old cars and a dozen shops. Toilets are a mere token and have not coped adequately. Newly arrived citizens have been pestered from dawn to dusk by these creatures who themselves found the standard toilet facilities so disgusting they simply would not use them. Many thousands have roamed this area for a week, using St. Edmunds graveyard (and any other spot, public or not) as a lavatory, changing room and fuel supply, leaving all their muck behind them.

The Inflatable City is bunkum, nothing more than a vast camp site without any of the recognised camping facilities. Thousands of trees and shrubs have been ruined to provide vantage viewing points and fuel for fires. TV coverage (free advertising) has been given to the star and the organisers, but TV have not sought the opinion of the local population.

Local authorities should be ticked off for allowing this frightful upheaval in a village ill-equipped to deal with it. The population of Wootton, indeed the Island, should stand together to prevent this happening again. After this organised irresponsibility ceases, it is hoped the area will be "crop-sprayed" with strong disinfectant to prevent the usual diseases that arise from overcrowded insanitary conditions.

DISGUSTED.

Now that the pop festival is over, and we in this small village are left in peace, the truth can be told. Not the story of "peace" we read about in the national Press, but what really happened in our village. The filth in our highways and lanes; our recreation ground used as a lavatory, refuse dump and sleeping ground; milk stolen from doorsteps; shoplifting; houses on this estate which are partly built, where rooms were filled with excrement and urine; drugs being sold; sex in public and indecent exposure; and the noise which was so intense that we could not hear our television with all the doors and windows closed. Our local shops were asked to open on Sunday. There was fear that if they did not, they would be broken into. To all this, the Police turned a blind eye. They had to, they were so greatly outnumbered ... This so called peaceful crowd did not need to riot. Everything they wanted to do, they did. We had no means to stop them. If they had decided to cause bodily harm or even murder, we in this village would have had no protection whatsoever ...

PEGGY M. HERBERT-GUSTAR. (Mrs.) 4 Glebe Gardens, Wootton Bridge.

Having seen "The Rave" or, I should say, some of it at Wootton, do you not think the ratepayers of this pleasant Island should be consulted before we allow such a revolting exhibition to take place here again. I have talked to many residents and find all feel strongly about this, except, of course, those whose commercial interest is their sole object in life. I have information that a "do" like this weekend is under consideration for 1970 and now is the time to test public majority opinion, so why not see what response you get by printing this letter and then, if the result is as I expect, call a few public meetings - I am quite willing to be of any assistance in an honorary capacity.

H.T. BURDEN. Porchfield

Congratulations, young ones, on your visit to the Island. You were well mannered, courteous and pleasant to have around. You can truly be called The Happy People. You made us smile with you at your hippie gear, remembering when we also wore way out and crazy clothes. You brought a breath of vitality and life to an Island that seems at times to be peopled mainly by the old. After seeing you all I have every confidence in Britain's future. Come back again.

B. WALTER. 67 Newnham Road, Binstead.

I suggest that the cost of clearing up the roads should be included in the expenses of the Dylan Pop Concert. In the short distance from Ryde golf club to Binstead Garage, there were eight empty milk bottles and loads of empty food cartons. Dairies will be wondering where their bottles are, look under the hedges, quite a job for someone to collect. What an example to the children of the estate, "Keep the countryside tidy."

E. A. HAWKYARD (Miss) 48, Arnold Road, Binstead.

Now that all the ballyhoo and adoration for the great pop scene is at last over, perhaps a tired and completely devastated ratepayer of Wootton may tell his side of the story.

Four days ago, the first wave of pop fans started arriving on Wootton Farm, and our property alongside came in for their attention. Our hay crop, which was ready for baling, soon became the ideal bedding for them. Hedges were cut down to make shelters or to be burnt on camp fires, wooden posts holding wire fencing were also removed and burnt. Fires were lit on the hay field and hay was also put on them and burnt. Reason was of no avail, it met with abuse and threats. I then produced a shotgun, and fired several times in the air. This was laughed at and I was told, "Shoot if you dare, there's thousands of us here, we will get you." No police help was apparently available, in spite of two appeals... Then a friend put me in touch with the Ventnor Security Dog Patrol, and although they were working almost impossible hours, they managed to come to our help and saved

MIDDLE EARTH

MANOR HOUSE, LAKE — PRESENTS **TONIGHT** June 7th
THE GROUP THAT CAME NO. 1 IN THE FESTIVAL POLL — PROBABLY THE BIGGEST ACT THAT HAS EVER APPEARED ON THE ISLE OF WIGHT

Ten Years After

ONE OF THEIR LAST U.K. PERFORMANCES BEFORE THEIR 4th BIG U.S. TOUR AND STAR APPEARANCE AT NEWPORT FESTIVAL U.S.A.)
AND
From last year's I.W. Pop Festival

Gary Farr

ADMISSION 12/6   7.30—11.45

INCREDIBLE MIDDLE EARTH LIGHT SHOW

COMING SOON
MARSHA HUNT
Star of the original "Hair" cast,
as seen on **Top of the Pops** recently

FREE RETURN TRANSPORT EVERY WEEK

Cowes—Mill Hill 7.00 p.m. Newport—Bus Station 7.30 p.m. Ryde—Esplanade 7.30 p.m. Totland—War Memorial 7.00 p.m. Freshwater—Post Office 7.05 p.m. Acorn Spring Works—7.10 p.m. Yarmouth—Square 7.15 p.m. Shalfleet—New Inn 7.25 p.m. Ventnor—Braintree Cafe 7.00 p.m.

MIDDLE EARTH

MANOR HOUSE, LAKE — PRESENTS **TONIGHT** June 14th
BY POPULAR REQUEST

THE FREE

LEAVING SOON ON U.S. TOUR WITH BLIND FAITH
AND
A TERRIFIC NEW DISCOVERY FROM POLYDOR

WHISKEY RIVER

ADMISSION 10/-   7.30 11.45

INCREDIBLE MIDDLE EARTH LIGHT SHOW

NEXT WEEK
MARSHA HUNT
Star of the original "Hair" cast,
as seen on **Top of the Pops** recently.

FREE RETURN TRANSPORT EVERY WEEK LEAVING

Totland, War Memorial	7.15
Freshwater, Post Office	7.20
Yarmouth, Square	7.25
Cowes, Mill Hill	7.15
Newport, Bus Station	7.45
Ryde Esplanade	7.45
Ventnor, Braintree Cafe	7.30

MIDDLE EARTH AT THE MANORHOUSE

LAKE — BETWEEN SANDOWN AND SHANKLIN
PRESENTS TONIGHT June 21st
THE STAR OF THE SUCCESSFUL MUSICAL "HAIR," FOLLOWING HER RECENT APPEARANCE ON TOP OF THE POPS

M★A★R★S★H★A ★ H★U★N★T

Her first live appearance in this country with her backing group

WHITE TRASH
AND
FIVE ALIVE

ADMISSION 12/6   7.30—11.45

INCREDIBLE MIDDLE EARTH LIGHT SHOW

COMING SOON
THE NICE

FREE RETURN TRANSPORT EVERY WEEK LEAVING

Totland, War Memorial	7.15
Freshwater, Post Office	7.20
Yarmouth, Square	7.25
Cowes, Mill Hill	7.15
Newport, Bus Station	7.45
Ryde Esplanade	7.45
Ventnor, Braintree Cafe	7.30

our property from complete destruction, giving me a few hours sleep. The disgusting scenes of obscenity which we were unfortunate enough to see from our garden and paddock, we never wish to see again. As a disgusted ratepayer may I suggest we rename Woodside Bay, Bogside Bay, for many more than one reason.

A.J. WHITE. The Sheiling, Woodside Road, Wootton.

A word in praise of the "beautiful people who came to visit us this last weekend." Those that I came into contact with both at the festival and outside might not have conformed to accepted morals and standards of cleanliness and dress, but their level of education and civilised manner and comradeship was a welcome change for me after experiencing other sorts of day trippers on buses and in shops, cinemas etc. this summer.

M.G. BARTON. 6 Pan Close, Newport.*

The following week, Fiery Creations defended their corner ...

September 13th, 1969

WHAT PRICE POP

THE FOLLOWING letter has been received from Mr. P. L. Harrigan and Mr. R. J. Cotton, press officers for the IW Festival of Music, in reply to M.W.'s comments published under this heading last week.

"The organisers of the Isle of Wight Festival of Music are concerned and disturbed at the wave of ill feeling and misunderstanding which the 'County Press' reported in its pages last week. Many of the points brought forward in the letters and reports are, of course, sensibly valid criticism and comment. The fact remains that some of our critics have now obviously succumbed to the temptations, prompted by the festival, to dismiss an increasing number of young people as 'irresponsible freaks,' and this is evident when reading these criticisms, too many of which are couched in scurrilously bigoted and melodramatic language. The disturbing aspect is that the wording of such outright dismissals merely helps to widen the 'generation gap' and perpetuate the unhappy barrier between the age groups.

To despair of 'human beings who could leave such an indescribable scene of litter and filth behind them,' as our semi-anonymous critic has done, is to judge this vast gathering unfairly. We all leave litter, vast gatherings leave more. The site is being cleared and will be returned to its previous state. As Mr. Phillips, the landowner himself, has said 'These fields will be as green as ever in three weeks time.' Perhaps M.W. will now ponder and 'despair' upon the amount of litter evident on public highways in the aftermath of the Island's more established events such as Cowes Week. We accept that the sanitation facilities were inadequate. It was impossible to estimate the demand on facilities as never before in this country has there been an event of this nature catering for such large numbers over three days. At the next festival everyone will benefit from the experience we all gained this year.

---

* Morris Barton, future IW Council Leader.

Should we regard these young people as oddities and discriminate against them as opposed to any other group of visitors to the island? The people who came to the festival injected an estimated £250,000 into the Island's strained economy. 'They had no intention of disturbing the peace,' said The Times, on September 1st, and continued, 'the police have been complimentary about their behaviour.' The phenomenal amount of coverage that the event has drawn from the world's Press and television has resulted in highly favourable comment on the Isle of Wight, its residents and visitors. Nobody can sensibly question the beneficial value of such publicity. Will the same people who condemned the festival out of hand still complain when there is an increase in holiday bookings next year due to the mammoth publicity the Island has gained? Will these same people complain in five years' time when today's 'hippies,' who came and enjoyed the festival, are married with children and return here as regular holidaymakers?

It will be some time yet before the long-term benefits are realised. Since the festival we have been asked by various tourist boards throughout the country, envious of the publicity the Island has had, to run festivals in their areas, financed by their local authorities. The success of any future festival on the Island rests on the continued and improved co-operation of all concerned.

Mr. P. L. HARRIGAN and Mr. R. J. COTTON. Fiery Creations."

Ex-editor, Walter Sibbick, had his say on the festival in his 'Vectensis' column. A man born in 1889 could be excused for not supporting public nudity and drug taking but Sibbick was as philosophical as he was waspish, and spoke well enough of the promoters ...
September 13th, 1969

AN ISLANDER'S NOTES
[By "VECTENSIS"]

THE POP FESTIVAL – After reading the spate of letters in the last issue of the "County Press" about this extraordinary feature of the summer season in the Wight, and anticipating a further deluge of contrast in opinions in this issue, I hesitate, as an old "square", to add to the disputation. Nevertheless, I would like to make a very short comment. I like some pop music – but only some. I acknowledge the right of young people to enjoy what they like, provided they respect the rights and convenience of other people. I suppose it must be taken as a compliment that so many chose to come to the Isle of Wight for their fun, but I should imagine that many of them would have found it more convenient to have had the festival on the mainland, in a more suitable spot, hygienically and otherwise. Apparently, the Island was made the venue because the organisers were Island businessmen. I have heard nothing but praise for the ability with which they performed the task. Therefore, in view of the repercussions aroused by their activities, I suggest that next year they should launch out and cross the Solent to gain even wider notoriety and possibly richer gains.

Finally, I enjoyed "What Price Pop?" for its literary merit but why did the author hide his or her light under a bushel of initials?

September 13th, 1969

Aftermath of the pop festival

In reply to "Disgusted." How dare he suggest that people attending the Pop Festival were "dirty people, behaving in a dirty manner to music." My fiance and I went to the festival merely to hear Bob Dylan singing, something we're not likely to hear again and because of this we are labelled as "dirty." Why? We both hold respectable jobs, have good homes, and dress in a manner which is unlikely to cause anyone harm or embarrassment. Indeed, no one would look twice if we were to walk down any crowded street. We are also exceptionally clean, and may I stress this refers to cleanliness of mind as well as of body. Therefore I think it unfair to label us as "gullible beatniks." ... You are involving a lot of innocent people when you write these ridiculous statements, which is, perhaps why you do not give your name ... Although I hold a responsible position I have nothing to be ashamed of through attending the Festival and nothing to fear from having my name in print as it seems you have. May I therefore sign myself,

DENISE COONEY (Miss). 12, Minerva Road, East Cowes.

... Many of the living dead of my generation are complaining about the invasion of the so-called Hippie people, who came in queer dress with packs and blankets on their backs, excreting in gardens and hedges, laying their women in the fields, and stealing milk and eggs, breaking fences to build fires to keep warm, talking with strange esprit de corps about the future and listening to a thunderous noise at night. I did the same when I was their age, the only difference being that I had a gun in my hand and with all the enthusiasm of youth we killed 3,500,000 and the noise at night was somewhat different, but our elders told us that this was the right thing to do. Thank God this generation has rebelled and are only playing guitars. Youth will never be wasted on the very young this way.

J. ARGLES. 3, Nelson Close, East Cowes.

... I do agree that the noise from the amplifiers at the Pop Festival was unnecessarily loud but this lasted only three days – surely not beyond the limits of toleration. On the whole we feel that the pop festival has brought a breath of fresh air to Wootton, which, judging from some of last week's letters, was sorely needed.

HUGO HAIG-THOMAS, AVRIL LAMB. The Croft, Wootton Bridge.

In the letters about the aftermath of the Pop Festival in last week's issue I was surprised to see that there were none from people who actually attended the event. As I was there all Saturday and Sunday, I would like to express some of my views. Most of the letters were from Wootton residents who were much disgusted with the litter and muck left behind. I would like to point out that I did not see one single litter bin, either on the festival site or in Wootton itself. The other main complaint comes from residents who were shocked to find that festivalgoers had to use the hedgerows and other places as a toilet. All I can say is this, that if Wootton residents had been expected to use the disgusting toilets provided on the festival site then they also would have preferred to use the hedgerow. As for the "County Press" report stating that a few mobile latrines and a single tent enclosing

12 latrine cubicles without a single sanitary towel disposal bin for the girls constituted "extensive toilet facilities" for 150,000 people, words fail me. Also, I noticed in the report that Wootton shopkeepers will welcome another festival. No wonder! It seems that as long as you can line your pockets then the inconveniences experienced by other people are conveniently forgotten …

A 20-YEAR-OLD FEMALE FESTIVAL ATTENDER

September 20th, 1969

EDITOR'S NOTE

A further selection of readers' letters on the recent Pop Festival appear this week. This event, and its repercussions, have brought a record number of letters to the editor on any one topic. He has tried to present a fair balance of opinion in choosing those published, and after this week, no further letters commenting on the festival itself will be published.

(Nineteen letters appeared that week, all but six defending the festival.)

Newport Town Council discussed recent events at Wootton, provoking cries of 'get stuffed,' and comparisons to Auschwitz …

October 18th, 1969

WOOTTON PEOPLE DESCRIBED AS 'INTOLERANT TWITS'
FRAYED TEMPERS IN NEWPORT COUNCIL CHAMBER

Temperatures rose in the Newport Town Council chamber on Wednesday when Mr. P. Jennings told the people of Wootton who disagreed with the pop festival to "get stuffed." When he described them as "intolerant twits," Mr. F. E. Butler, a Wootton resident, leapt to his feet, strode round to where Mr. Jennings was sitting and demanded a withdrawal of the remarks. Later, Mr. Jennings said that his remarks were emotional. It seemed a suitable phrase, he was not sorry that he had used it … Alderman Minns said … it was a pity that some of the younger members never saw Nazi concentration camps like Auschwitz; the smell at the festival site was similar at Wootton on the Monday morning after the festival, even though there might not have been the dead bodies … Referring to the presence at the committee meeting of Mr. R. Foulk (one of the festival organisers), Alderman Harvey said they had faith in whatever he told them and the promises he made for the future. "Quite frankly, I hope they do have another one. I think they are to be congratulated," he concluded.

The last word on festivals that year came not from the Island, but Gloucestershire …

November 15th, 1969

Plans for a two-day pop festival have been rejected by the Parks Committee of Stroud, Gloucestershire Urban Council. One member, Mr. G. Smith, was quoted as saying, "We have not forgotten the Isle of Wight festival. A public park is not the place for orgies."

Afton, 1970

"It is a great worry" - Mark Woodnutt.

No sooner had the new year begun than letters about the next festival began to appear. During the next twelve months, there would hardly be an issue where they did not ...

Jan 17, 1970.

Another Pop Festival

A front page announcement in Saturday's "Melody Maker" states that the second I.W. Pop Festival is definitely on, and this year it will be a five-day event featuring 30 top groups and artists from Britain and America.

The report, under a heading in large type which dominates the page, states that a spokesman for Fiery Creations told '*Melody Maker,*' "The police and authorities are in favour of the festival, we have won their support and the festival will definitely go ahead. It will take place on the Bank Holiday weekend of August 30th ... Ray and Ron Foulk are currently working out the line-up of artists but it is impossible to give names at the moment. We already have a site which is far larger and better than last year's and as it is not near any residential areas we will not have so much trouble with access. This will also give us more time to think about sanitation and catering which were the two main problems last year ... Police Chief Supt P. W. Paddon told the 'County Press' ... "If another festival is to be held in the Island, we will help all we can, mainly to see that there is no trouble. We are neither for nor against a festival, we simply have a job to do if it takes place here."

Jan 24, 1970

Pop festival.

It has been said that the fans' behaviour last year was good, but I submit that this was only so because they met with no opposition. What would happen if everyone did not rally round to meet their demands for food and drink, transport, etc. I suspect that if thwarted, many of these "peaceful people" could prove unpleasant customers. In the event of any kind of riot or mass hysteria, who will control them. We have no army on the Island now, and only the police, who, according to reports, have "no feelings one way or the other on the proposed event," and would be very much in the minority.

M. STEVENS (Miss). 33 Argyll Street, Ryde.

Jan 31, 1970.

Pop festival.

I should like to applaud Mr Austin most heartily for his efforts to prevent this lovely Island being contaminated by a second pop festival. Just who do these promoters think they are and why should this tiny plot be invaded by a quarter of a million weird fanatics. If these people wish to amuse themselves in this way then let them find a more suitable venue, the further away from civilisation the better. They reject our way of life, they are contemptuous of our achievements, our laws and our form of government. Equally I am contemptuous of their non-achievement, their permissiveness and lack of discipline. The youth of this country has been indulged in enough. I do not want them here and neither do the vast majority of Island people, and the holidaymakers on whom the Island, to a large measure, is economically dependent ...

JOAN STAPLEHURST. 71 Great Preston Road, Ryde.

Feb 7, 1970.
Pop festival
I see that the pop man and the tourist board are trying to prove the unprovable and to justify the unjustifiable ... Let us strip away the hypocrisy from this pop thing and see it for what it really is. The pop people enjoy their pastime and are determined to indulge in it whether or not it improves or damages the environment of those who do not want it, but cannot get away from it ... Not having a pop festival would harm no one. Having one will harm many. There can be only one conclusion. If it is held, the festival will be the outcome of sheer selfishness ... Sooner or later there will be serious trouble at a pop festival and that will put a stop to it once and for all. It is a sobering thought however, that people may be injured or might even die in the process. It has already happened elsewhere.

M. G. T. HEWLETT. Brook.

Feb 7, 1970.
Pop festival
Although one is loath to protract this inconclusive correspondence about the ills of the last pop festival and worse in the next, I am finally provoked into having my say. Five years ago I came down from university and now, one husband and two babies later, have become rather enmeshed in domesticity, small talk and the inescapable company of my little children during the daytime. All of this has indescribable compensations so I do not complain, merely assert. However I went to the pop festival of 1969 and the joy of being among one's own age group, among the lively, animated, relaxed and questioning majority who were ready to tolerate, to give and above all, to talk, gave me intense pleasure and nostalgia for my student days ... I for one would welcome the opportunity to repeat this unique experience. Am I alone, among the adults on this Island, in thinking this way?

SHELAGH WARNER (Mrs.) Ager Farm, Long View, Porchfield.

It was important for Fiery Creations to maintain good relations with the Council and as early as March, a meeting was arranged to discuss the site location for the forthcoming festival ...

Ray Foulk : "We learnt a huge amount from 1969. One thing was learning how to deal with the local authority ... I had regular meetings with Woodnutt, at first monthly, and then weekly, at the Mayor's parlour in Newport every Monday morning before he went off to Parliament, and that went on all winter. They were fairly amicable meetings. We got on fine. It was all very cordial ... He did keep piling on conditions, trying to make it more difficult for us, but we were willing to shoulder that. We didn't have a problem with that ... The difficulty we had, of course, was that we didn't have a site!"

March 14th, 1970.

POP FESTIVAL SITE

A special private meeting is to be held on Monday of representatives of the County Council and Fiery Creations, Ltd., to discuss the whereabouts and other aspects of the pop festival this year.

Fiery Creations told the 'County Press', this week that a report of the festival being held within a four-mile radius of Ryde, which appeared in an evening newspaper, was incorrect, and a six-mile radius would be more appropriate.

Later a telephone call was received from Fiery Creations saying that a 12-mile radius would be a better description. The spokesman had said earlier that the festival could still be held anywhere on the Island and added "It is not certain yet where the festival was going to be held, it could be the West Wight or anywhere."

Fiery Creations also denied rumours that the site would be Ryde Airport. He said "We have not been offered Ryde Airport but we might like it if we were."

... Captain Wheeler of British Rail said it was necessary to talk with the organisers of the forthcoming festival and get arrangements on a proper footing ... "If you are going to have, say, a quarter of a million and we are to try and move them all in one day, it is just not on," he said. The ferry service could, however, move 60,000 a day. (Mar 14.)

───────────────◆───────────────

Three weeks later, the location of the festival was now said to be "definitely in the East Wight" ...

Ray Foulk - "We started getting interventions from the Council and the MP. The only thing they had was the threat of an injunction to stop us putting on another festival if we didn't cooperate, so it was almost like a blackmail situation ... They could threaten us in that kind of way, and so we did cooperate. Well, we wanted to cooperate, we weren't cowboys, we were young professionals trying to do a job and I don't think there was anything the Council were making us do that we didn't want to do."

April 4th, 1970

POP FESTIVAL SITE
WEEK OF CONJECTURE

The now familiar cat-and-mouse game of whether the proposed pop festival should be held in the East or West Wight appeared to have been resolved this week when Mr. W. H. Quick, C.C. elicited an assurance from the promoters that the venue would definitely be in the East Wight. This was the latest development in a week of conjecture, during which a spokesman for Fiery Creations had said they had two "hot" sites in the West Wight ... There have been other developments during the week. On Monday, the special committee set up by the County Council and headed by Mr. Mark Woodnutt, M.P., had a further meeting with Fiery Creations. Mr. P. Harrigan, publicity director for Fiery Creations, was reported this week as saying "There is absolutely no question of the festival being squeezed of the Island by reticent landowners."

From the very outset, Douglas Osmond, Chief Constable of Hampshire and the Isle of Wight, had maintained an even-handed attitude towards the festivals, genuinely seeming to be neither for, or against, them. In what must have come as an unwelcome surprise to some, his annual report for 1969 generally spoke well of the Wootton festival, the organisers and those who had attended ...

April 25th, 1970.

CHIEF CONSTABLE AND POP

Any major problems at the 1969 pop festival were caused by failure of some administrative arrangements, such as inadequate toilet facilities and inadequate catering, states Mr. D. Osmond, C.B.E., chief constable of Hampshire, in his annual report.

"If the event is repeated in 1970, it will be necessary to ensure that sleeping, sanitary and catering arrangements receive more attention from the organisers in order to prevent large numbers of patrons leaving the scene of the festival in order to fend for themselves, thus disturbing those who live in the vicinity," he says.

Mr. Osmond estimates that in all, some 200,000 young people came to the Island for the festival. While there was some promiscuity among those attending and more than 20 were arrested in connection with the possession and use of drugs, the police were nevertheless able to cope effectively with the few minor cases of friction which were caused ... It was very necessary for the limited number of police available to ensure that the "temperature was kept down." This was achieved by good humour on the part of those attending and the police who, patrons quickly recognised, were out to help them, particularly with regard to organising additional food supplies.

Mr. Osmond says ... that it was particularly rewarding for the police to have received a number of letters from young patrons paying tribute to the police attitude, which had contributed to their enjoyment. Referring to "magnified Press reports of isolated incidents," Mr. Osmond considers that, on the whole, the festival was a well-conducted and happy affair; this did not suggest, however, that the event passed off without embarrassment, inconvenience and annoyance to some local residents.

Letters to the Editor

April 25th, 1970.

Pop festival problem

As a resident of Wootton with property adjacent to the fields which held the lamentable excuse for music last August I wish to ask why is it that when so many people are against such an event happening again, there are so few grounds for the prevention of such meetings.

Voices have been heard on numerous occasions. Weak, and sometimes strong, but has any group of well informed people considered the possibility of an outbreak of typhoid, cholera or even plague? These diseases, contrary to popular belief, are not confined to "remote countries." We only want one carrier to get through the net for disaster to hit this small, beautiful Island. Then it is too late to legislate.

There are enough people coming from all over the world to make this hazard a real possibility, and if any reader is in doubt about the factors available to spread the disease then let him go to Farmer Phillip's site of last year's festival and he will learn to his dismay, and perhaps horror, there are enough rodents still using the remnants of last year's feast, as their habitat and breeding grounds, to say nothing of other pathogens breeding in the piles of human effluent .... Let us here and now expose the so-called festival for what it is — a commercial bonanza for its promoter, a drug market for the peddlers and for many, an excellent excuse for one of those permissive orgies one so often hears of, which only happen in America, of course. There are grounds enough in public health and nuisance alone, do we need human tragedy before we try to prevent it.

IRATE RESIDENT OF WOOTTON

---◆---

There were many in the 1960s who felt that a great deal of public life on the Island was run by a clique of ex-military men ...

Ray Foulk : "We felt the Isle of Wight was run by retired colonels. My own boss at the County Press was Colonel Brannon. It was that kind of place."

There was some truth in this. The Island's thirty five Councillors at that time included one Admiral, two Vice Admirals, one Major, two Brigadiers and one Commander - and from their distinguished ranks came some of the most vocal critics of the festival. The most visible of the anti-festival campaigners on the County Council was, without doubt, 70 year old Commander William Rees-Millington.* Personable and self-assured, the Commander was firmly convinced that Communism and black power were behind the festivals...

Ray Foulk : "I never had any dealings with Rees-Millington ... I would probably have liked to have had some conversation with him but I think you'd be bashing your head against a wall, really, to talk to people like that, with their views."

Certainly the Commander's views left little room for dissent. This letter to the County Press, co-signed by the Commander, a Major and a Rear-Admiral, all County Councillors, set out their views on the forthcoming festival. The letter states that there was "considerable misuse of drugs" at Wootton, despite the Chief Constable of Hampshire's report, just 8 weeks before, pointing out the opposite - that there were, in fact, just 20 drug arrests and convictions among the 150,000 crowd.

The letter went on to quote passages from a book written by Richard Neville, editor of 'Oz,' one of the leading house magazines of the hippy counter culture movement. His recently published book, 'Play Power,' set out a radical brave new world manifesto for

---

* The Commander's utterances regarding the festival have since become famous. Interviewed i the 1995 film of the festival, "Message To Love," he declared, "If you have a festival with all the stop pulled out - kids running about naked, f—ing in the bushes and doing every damn thing they fee inclined to do - I don't know that's particularly good for the body politic." His words were used by th band Oasis as part of the chorus of the song 'F—ing in the Bushes', on their album 'Standing on th Shoulder of Giants,' released in 2000.

new hippy way of life. A book he would have shunned under normal circumstances, Rees-Millington embraced this most unlikely bedfellow so that he could repeat some of its more extravagant claims. Disingenuously, the Commander quoted from the book as if it were a scholarly study, informing readers that the 'underground' behind the festival were intent on destroying teenage society "by destroying their will to live and work normally, through the use of drugs and sexual promiscuity." ...

June 27th, 1970.

Pop festivals

As County Councillors we recognise that it is not our function to point the morals of the inhabitants of this Island, but as citizens we think it to be our duty at this time to draw attention to an unpalatable aspect of some pop festivals which has so far obtained very little publicity. We are doing this so that Island residents, and in particular the young, who may attend a possible festival, should do so with full knowledge of the risks that may be encountered.

It is common knowledge that the majority of people who attend these gatherings do so simply to hear or see some popular figure and no one would wish to interfere with an apparently innocent form of entertainment. Nevertheless, it is an undeniable fact that some large pop festivals can attract a most disreputable element of the hippie world who come from as far afield as Europe and the U.S.A.

As members of the Select Committee of the County Council appointed to examine all aspects of the impact of large gatherings on the Island we have made a study of this disagreeable aspect of international type of pop festivals and we have had at our disposal the reports of what took place at Wootton last year. We know that there was considerable misuse of drugs and examples of sexual abandon.

Lest there be any doubt about the accuracy of the foregoing statement we have obtained impressive confirmation from a book published early this year and which actually contains an eye-witness account of some of the things that took place at Wootton. After reading the relevant pages one is left in no doubt that drugs were pushed actively and that the behaviour of some of the visitors with relation to sex was deplorable in the extreme.

This book also contains a most disturbing revelation of the aims and objectives of the international underground movement and we believe that it deserves serious study by anyone who has the interests of this country, and in particular its young people, at heart.

In simple terms we are told that the prime objective of the international, underground is to destroy and disrupt the society in which we live and work. This is to be achieved by an attack on the teenager and the even younger by destroying their will to live and work normally, through the use of drugs and sexual promiscuity and by teaching them to live free by dishonest methods.

The foregoing is an attempt at a realistic assessment of a whole book but little imagination is required to visualise the condition of this country if a movement of this sort gains ground. We believe that the movement is directed primarily against the Anglo-Saxon communities and a look at the United States today seems to support this view.

This book makes clear the connection between international pop festivals and the underground movement. The international pop festival is a recognised instrument for catching and contaminating young people and it is this grave risk to which we draw attention.

In conclusion we refer to pronouncements made in a mainland newspaper and on T.V. recently to the effect that there is pressure to turn the Isle of Wight into a world centre for international pop festivals. The demoralised types of people who could be attracted to the Island by such a development are obvious and once here it would be only with the greatest difficulty that they could be removed. Such "communes" have been formed in various parts of the United States and in Europe."

Let us be absolutely clear that such a development on the Island would seriously affect our way of life and our amenities and could lead to demoralisation of our young people.

N. E. H. CLARKE, W. A. HOWLETT, W. O. REES-MILLINGTON, S. C. SELWYN.

County Hall, Newport.

------------------------◆------------------------

When Newport and Wootton residents learned that land off Staplers Road was being considered as a festival site, they collectively applied for a restraining injunction ...

Ray Foulk : "Goshens Farm ran as a main site for some months. I think it was very much a holding operation on our part, I don't think we ever seriously thought we would use it, but we had to have a nominal site that we could talk about as though something was happening somewhere definitely. We were never happy with it."

June 27th, 1970

INJUNCTION SOUGHT OVER POP FESTIVAL

With increasing fears this week that the 1970 pop festival is to be held within the borough of Newport, Wootton and Fairlee Ratepayers' and Residents' Association have instructed counsel to seek an injunction restraining Fiery Creations, the promoters, and certain other defendants from creating, causing or committing acts of nuisance or trespass by holding or permitting a festival of popular music on Goshen land, Staplers Road, Newport.

Goshens is about 60 acres of land in between the roads leading from the top of Staplers to Wootton Common and from the top of Staplers to Havenstreet and bounded on the east by Palmer's Brook and the transformer station ...

------------------------◆------------------------

The letter from Commander Rees-Millington and colleagues drew a response from Fiery Creations. It began by establishing the true nature of the book which Rees-Millington had used to back their case...

July 4th, 1970.

Pop festivals

It was with incredulity and not a little dismay that we read a letter in last week's "County Press," on the subject of pop festivals, which was signed by the chairman and three members of the Isle of Wight County Council.

That our county councillors should base their comments on a book with which, unfortunately, we are familiar, and which was written in a sensational way, aiming at a commercial market, hitting at the Isle of Wight Festival of Music 1969, primarily because it was not an underground festival, is most surprising and illuminating.

Obviously, we would not wish to deny that a small percentage of those visiting the last year's festival did take drugs — but a percentage of holidaymakers who visit our Island each summer take drugs also — but that is no reason to stop our tourist trade. After all, the Isle of Wight Festival of Music takes place for one week in the year — whereas we know that among our resident Island population, drugs are already in plentiful supply.

The general public are aware that drugs are being pushed in dance halls, discotheques, colleges, public houses, youth clubs, on beaches and in the streets — and appalled as we all are, this cannot be stopped by closing down all establishments and areas where people can now meet in groups. The answer is, surely, to strengthen the drug squad — as has been done in Hampshire recently, with the resulting success becoming obvious, judging from the number of cases brought before Island courts for the last few months. We have spoken to the signatories of the letter in question and these gentlemen agreed that in terms of ratio, drug pushing is no more in existence at festivals than elsewhere, and that their letter could have been interpreted as slamming Pop Festivals.

We must agree with the county councillors when they say, and we quote "The majority of young people who attend these gatherings do so simply to hear or see some popular figure, and no one would wish to interfere with an apparently innocent form of entertainment." So let us do just that ... Please remember that we love this Island as much as our opponents. We live here, and we are as anxious as they that the 1970 Isle of Wight Festival of Music should be a success causing as little inconvenience as possible and preferably no distress. We want all our visitors to enjoy this festival — and the Island — and to this end we are working diligently, having learnt from some past mistakes to make this festival really great. We will bring the people here — and the Island's economy can only be strengthened by their visit.

We welcome constructive criticism at all times, and we will always endeavour to learn from it. At the same time, please give credit where credit is due. No man is "wholly bad, nor wholly wrong," even our four County Councillors! or, Fiery Creations Limited.

R. C. CLIFTON. Company Secretary. Fiery Creations.

With the festival now just seven weeks away, Fiery Creations were desperate to find a site ...

> Ray Foulk : "We deemed the Wootton site to be unsuitable for a bigger festival and there was so much hostility from Wootton residents that we couldn't get away with that again. They would have been able to take out an injunction and stop us, and we did have injunction proceedings against us in a couple of locations, and we backed off before the court hearing on legal advice that we would lose ... Wherever we went on the Island, a group of opponents would spring up, form a residents' association, get some money together and start taking out injunction proceedings, and or, threatening the farmer. Quite a lot of farmers were threatened and we were getting rather desperate."

July 11th, 1970.

MYSTERY OF POP FESTIVAL SITE
SELECT COMMITTEE DECIDE ON ACTION

DEVELOPMENTS continued to see-saw during the week over the proposed pop festival. Anxiety among Island residents about the site continued to be unallayed, although tension appeared to have been eased for those living in the Wootton area. The Select Committee of the County Council took a firm step on Monday when they decided to seek an injunction restraining the promoters from holding the festival on a site at Staplers.

Another injunction, being sought by the Wootton and Fairlee Ratepayers' and Residents' Association, is due to be heard in the High Court on Monday but in view of a written undertaking from solicitors acting for Fiery Creations stating that the festival would not take place within the area, it is likely that the petition will be withdrawn ...

———————————————◆———————————————

So far, Fiery Creations' intention had always been that the festival would take place in the East Wight, but with only four weeks to go, the plan was changed ...

> Ray Foulk : "We'd always, for some reason, had a mental block, which said that this thing has got to be near to Ryde because of the ferries. We couldn't see that you could move out of the East Wight, because most festivalgoers are going to come down on the Portsmouth route and come over to Ryde, but the moment somebody suggested the site at Afton, and we found that there was a very friendly farmer that was up for it, that suddenly changed our thinking; and it was an absolute master stroke to go for that ... There were very few residents that could complain and as West Wight residents ourselves, we were on home territory."

July 25th, 1970.

AGREEMENT SIGNED FOR POP FESTIVAL
WEEK OF NEGOTIATIONS

SHORTLY before midnight on Thursday, after negotiations lasting more than 24 hours, agreement was reached between officers of the County Council and the Rural District Council and representatives of Fiery Creations Ltd., over the pop festival being held at East Afton Farm, Freshwater ... With little more than a month to go, the Island was still in a state of flux throughout the week as to what exactly was happening, although assurances were given by the promoters that the site would definitely be in the West Wight ... Radio and national Press reports on Thursday indicated that whether or not agreement was reached, the promoters intended carrying on with the festival, regardless of obstacles and local feeling.

◆

Now that the site of the festival had changed from East to West Wight, the concerns of local residents were to be addressed at a public meeting at Freshwater Memorial Hall. There was initial friction at the meeting as a County Hall faction, comprising an Admiral, a Rear-Admiral and a Brigadier, seem to have automatically assumed that one of their number should take the chair ...

Ray Foulk : "The Memorial Hall meeting was fraught. It was set up by a group of local residents. I say local residents; they were Island residents that had come from the other side of the Island to show the Freshwater people how to do it; and the idea is that you create a residents' association and you appeal to everyone for money, and you take out proceedings in the High Court. They were just trying the same routine. They'd done it several times by now, but our people rather took over the meeting. More than half the people in the room were either people who were friends or relatives working for us, or friends and relatives who lived in the neighbourhood that were there to support us, and they weren't having any of it, so the meeting was on our side and that scotched their plans immediately.

It started off and Laurie Say started speaking. He was a councillor at Newport with Daisy Krishnahma, also a councillor, and they were our liaison officers with the local authorities ... Laurie stood up at the beginning of the meeting and yelled out, 'Is this a constitutional meeting?' and that was ignored and he kept repeating the question. In the end the guy on the stage shouted out, 'Sit down and shut up!' whereupon he then said, 'I'd like to propose the Reverend Bowyer chairman of this meeting.' Well, it all quickly degenerated into mayhem and it wasn't long before they decided to pack it in and they left the stage, and our people all traipsed onto the stage and we just ran the meeting.

I remember at one point, Rikki Farr, before they left the stage, managed to get the microphone and he said, 'My father fought in the war for people like you.' Now these were all ex-military people, retired Colonels and Admirals, and here is a 29-year-old saying his father fought in the war 'for people like you.' It was good old Rikki Farr at his best!"

July 25th, 1970.

ANGRY SCENES

On Friday week, a meeting of Freshwater, Yarmouth and Totland people was broken up in disorder. A crowd of more than 650 filled the Memorial Hall and overflowed into the car park and street. Loudspeakers were erected outside. There were angry scenes at the door when local people were refused admission because it was full. They pointed out that many inside came from places other than the West Wight. In the hall itself, the left side was taken mainly by pro-festival younger people in their colourful clothes, and the right side by older residents.

Often wrongly described as one of the festival promoters, Rikki Farr acted as compere for the festivals and in his capacity as concert tour promoter was able to secure appearances at the festival for acts he represented. His effusive and emotional stage announcements are a central feature of the film 'Message To Love.'

When Brigadier C. G. Phipps, County Council representative for Freshwater, took the stage there was uproar. Among those with him were Admiral Sir Manley Power and Rear-Admiral N. E. H. Clarke (a member of the County. Council Select Committee) and Mr. R. W. Cawdell (secretary of the Vectis Nationalist Party).

There were loud objections to the Brigadier's chairmanship by the younger group, who called for the Rev, R. J. Bowyer (rector of Brook) to be chairman. A message was passed to the stage and Brigadier Phipps announced that the rector did not wish to take the chair. As he tried to explain why the meeting of local people had been called, he was drowned by shouts, catcalls and a constant stream of interruptions. Someone proposed, without success, that Mrs. J. Cooper be allowed to take the chair and the brigadier put the matter to the vote — should he remain as chairman or not? There was a show of hands and he continued.

Brigadier Phipps said there was no reason why they should not have the pop festival in the West Wight. He could see no reason against it as such and he and his daughters would probably attend anyway. There had to be proper safeguards, however. One of the loudest objectors to the chairmanship was Mr. L. Say, a Newport Borough councillor. At one stage a woman in the audience ran to him and shouted "Let the man (Brigadier Phipps) speak." "I am very sorry a Newport councillor should behave in this way in our village — it is really most extraordinary," said Brigadier Phipps. He went on to say that the site at East Afton was a fine site and Mr. Clarke, the owner, was with them that evening. The site had been inspected by the County Council and Mr. Clarke had made it quite clear that he did not intend to have the festival on his land unless all officials were satisfied. Fiery Creations Ltd., had said they were prepared to provide all the required facilities. "We hope this has been said in good faith," he said

Mr. Rikki Farr, who had been continually objecting, got on the stage. He stood in front of the brigadier, who was still trying to talk, and finally left the stage. In another incident he was offered the microphone but it was taken from him after a few minutes when Brigadier Phipps accused him of talking propaganda. Conditions were now so bad that the brigadier announced "This meeting is out of hand and I greatly regret that it is closed."

After the brigadier and his party left the hall, Mr. Farr took over the microphone and was joined on stage by some of the promoters, including Mr. R. Foulk* and Mr. P. Harrigan. Mr. Farr admitted "I have no real right to stand here ... I feel a complete pirate. If I can, I appoint myself chairman." He said there had been a huge investment in the festival, at which there would not be as much pop as last year. "We have, in a way, worked against ourselves by the action taken tonight."

Mr. D. Clarke joined the party on stage and Mr. Bowyer came forward to take the chair. By this time more than half the people had left, including most of the festival's opponents. The rector said he thought he was going to be chairman at the meeting. He was neither for pop nor against it. People were his concern. He had been on a committee for six months considering the question of having a large number of people on the Island.

A member of the audience shouted "I have been on this Island for 20 years —

---

*   Dr Douglas Quantrill, the Island's Medical Officer of Health in 1970, described the meeting in 1994 interview for the book 'Isle Of Wight Rock' by Vic King, Mike Plumbley and Pete Turner, at the public meeting, Ray Foulk stayed on the platform with his hands in his pockets. He floored everyone with his standard of logic, argument and intelligence. He shot down absurd questions."

who, are the unfamiliar faces I see here tonight?" Mr. Bowyer said they all should be Islanders and should stop divisions. Mr. Clarke said he wanted to hear from people who did not want the pop festival. "The organisers are here to allay their fears — that is what it is all about really," he said.

Mr. Gordon Kay, described as local manager of a catering company, promised that they would supply every item of food and drink required and prices would be in line with normal High Street prices.

Mr. P. Harrigan spoke of sewage disposal and said there would be 1000 gallon tankers from the mainland working night and day. The company concerned would also deal with litter problems. Toilets would be erected en route to the site ... Southern Vectis Bus Company were confident they could handle the numbers expected and British Rail had agreed to run a night and day ferry shuttle service for the five days of the festival. Captain Wheeler (British Rail) had said there were two boats in Scotland they were prepared to bring down.

Mr. Cawdell, who also joined the group on stage, said he had a petition of over 25,000 signatures protesting against the festival. A woman in the audience stood up and produced some papers saying she also had a petition for the festival. Mr. Cawdell said there were widespread fear of trespass, violation of property and lack of proper hygiene. If these questions could all be answered and the numbers were limited to about 50,000, some of the fears would be allayed. The second, impromptu meeting ended at 10 p.m. and Fiery Creations later announced they would hold a public meeting in the hall on Tuesday.

All through this period, Mark Woodnutt continued his attempts to control and regulate the festival ...

> Ray Foulk : "We knew what his views were because he'd written that dreadful leading article (*What Price Pop?*) He made it plain that he was not in favour of festivals on the Isle of Wight, but if they were going to take place it was important that they had proper facilities and they were regulated to some extent ... He was polite and pragmatic, but he made his views known. He was willing to talk things through and help come to some sort of arrangement between the promoters and the council, to safeguard the local interests ... I thought he was all right. I didn't ever feel that he was duplicitous particularly, because he said openly what his position was! ... This is Woodnutt talking to the Guardian, *'An Island full of long-hairs is damaging to the normal tourist trade of families and elderly retired couples. I'm not against festivals as such, but cannot see even one advantage to the Island from such happenings. The people here are not the sort that appreciate hippies and layabouts.'* He's prejudiced about the people that are coming over; not just the numbers, but what kind of people they are, and the fact that they've got long hair."

July 25th, 1970.

MEMBER AND POP FESTIVAL

Mr. Mark Woodnutt, M.P., has written to Freshwater Parish Council regarding the pop festival. He writes:

"I thank you for your letter about the proposed pop festival and I share your concern. Doubtless you will know that local authorities have no statutory power to ban or permit such festivals and that I am trying to obtain the powers required by the introduction of new legislation ... On Saturday morning I was informed by the promoters that they were considering an alternative site at Churchill's Farm. I have obtained a verbal undertaking from the landowner that he will not permit the use of his land unless the promoters sign the agreement prepared by the two councils. However, if preparations for the festival continue and the promoters do not sign the agreement, proceedings will be commenced immediately to obtain an injunction from the High Court. Solicitors and senior counsel are already briefed. This is the best we can do to safeguard the Island, its residents and the people who will be attending the festival.

I am sorry you have not had an earlier reply to your letter. Very nearly the whole of my time has been spent on this wretched business for the last three weeks, including Sundays. It is a great worry."

Aug 1st, 1970

Pop festival

Now that the pop festival is to be held near Freshwater, may we hope that the Department of Social Security will rise nobly to the occasion. Surely it would be a humane and generous act on their part to open a temporary office on Yarmouth quay? This would enable the young fans to draw their pay and supplementary benefit en-route without making a long trudge into Freshwater. A great boon, especially should the weather be wet and windy (for which we fear some misguided souls are already praying!) After all, few of us would begrudge these youngsters their innocent fun and games and it would be an affront to their dignity if a large number of them had to crawl through a hedge to gain admittance instead of walking tall through the paying entrance. And surely a puff or two of "pot" would not harm anyone? We are convinced that those old age pensioners who might feel the pinch this coming winter, owing to the high price of coal, will not consider the money lavished on these young fans a waste of resources.

THREE OLD LADIES OF FRESHWATER.

East Afton Farm was now the official festival site, but the proximity of the nearby hill, with its obvious potential as a free viewpoint, was causing concern for Fiery Creations so when nearby Churchill's Farm became available they invoked a clause in their agreement with the Council that allowed them to suggest it as an alternative site ...

Ray Foulk : "No sooner had the Afton site become available than we looked at another West Wight site at Calbourne. That was Churchill's farm, owned by David Spence, and that seemed to us to be a more suitable site in that you didn't have the problem of the hill, but the Council were either getting so fed up with us moving around the place, or they saw it as a good idea to force us to keep to the Afton site and suffer the consequences of the hill. There were certainly elements within the authorities that would have thought like that and would have been that vindictive; there's no question about that ... We went back to the various Councils with Churchill's Farm and said, "Look, we'd rather use Churchill's, can you appraise this and approve this as an alternative?" The Rural District Council and Freshwater Council approved it but the County Committee disapproved of it and their reasons were clearly spurious. We were very upset at that point. We felt we were being forced onto this other site which we didn't like very much ... Afton was forced on us eventually."

Aug 1st, 1970.

POP FESTIVAL SITE
SELECT COMMITTEE REJECT CHURCHILL'S FARM

A Select Committee of the County Council did not approve the use of the land at Churchill's Farm, Calbourne, for the 1970 pop festival, despite the opinion of the Rural District Council that it was acceptable on public health grounds. The committee have told Fiery Creations, organisers of the proposed festival, that land at East Afton, Freshwater, is still available.

The letter, signed by Mr. L. H. Baines, clerk of the County Council, states: "The Select Committee have today considered your application for approval to the use of a site at Churchill's Farm for the proposed Festival of Music ... I am to convey to you their decision that they are unable to approve the site at Churchill's for a number of reasons which, singularly or cumulatively, in their opinion make the Churchill's site unsuitable for the holding of the proposed festival.* ...The position, therefore, remains that under the agreement the site at East Afton Farm is available and in respect of the general layout of the site the committee have no comments to offer. Details must, of course, be agreed with the officers named in the agreement in accordance with the terms of the agreement.

---◆---

Letters to the Editor

Aug 8th, 1970.

Pop festival

I feel it would be fair if any Island residents are asked by visiting pop festival fans to suggest reasonable bed and breakfast accommodation, they should refer them to Inglefield, Madeira Road, Totland Bay,† as there appears to be ample space there both inside and out. It could even be courteous to have small cards printed with this information to hand to the fans as they arrive tired and hot (or wet) from the mainland. It could even be that there is room in the garden of this same property for the empty bottles, tins and other less pleasant rubbish that will doubtless be collected on the Warren, Tennyson Downs, and the beaches at Compton, Brook, Freshwater, Colwell and Totland Bay.

JOHN SCOTCHER. Debourne Manor, Cowes.

---

* The reasons cited were, "fire brigade access, the size of the site, the fact that crops were still in situ, and that the site was "windy and damp." Despite this clear refusal, in an open letter to the County Press some months later, the Council subsequently claimed that "the choice of site was at all times left to the promoter." (See page 220.)

† The headquarters of Fiery Creations.

With only three weeks to go, Fiery Creations and the Council entered into an agreement spelling out the terms and conditions under which the festival would take place ...

Ray Foulk : "Well, the officials and the health people we dealt with were fairly relaxed. The medical officer of health, Doctor Quantrill was more than relaxed, he was actually a positive supporter. He famously said to the newspapers and television, "There is no known disease that you can get from urine*." He was so laid back about things ... He didn't want doors on the toilets. He said, "That's not a health issue, you don't need doors on there," and we said, "Well, we're going to put doors on anyway because we're sure people will want them! ... The toilets, I thought, were very imaginative and they were devised by Ron Smith, with George Weeks who had Golden Hill Fort in those days ... The wall was eight foot high corrugated iron. The double wall system was our idea. You can have your security within the double wall zone so nobody sees your security unless they're in the business of trespassing, and you've got a roadway all the way around the site to service your shops and toilets and backstage ... I think the dogs were unfortunate but at the time we believed we had to have dogs."

Aug 8th, 1970.

POP FESTIVAL PROMOTERS' AGREEMENT
WITH COUNTY COUNCIL

The County Council issued a Press statement on Monday giving details of their agreement with Fiery Creations, Ltd., promoters of the festival of music.

The statement says the agreement entered into by the local authorities and the promoters in no way indicates approval of the holding of an event of this size for so long a period in the Island. Indeed, no local authority has the power to prevent a festival being held. Moreover, existing legislation gives only very limited powers of control to any public authority and derisory penalties for any breach. It was in these circumstances that the promoters were invited, and agreed in principle, to enter into an agreement regulating a number of aspects of the proposed festival this year as long ago as March 31st ...

The agreement which is in force provides (inter alia) for the following requirements: ... Double walls around the arena site and a high fence between the site and the adjoining footpath and National Trust land.

Control of the volume and timing of noise.

The provisions of parking on the site and access routes to various parts of the site, with clearance for fire appliances, ambulances, etc.

The provision of an adequate number of toilets (1200 closets as compared with the 80 that were provided at Wootton last year) as well as 1800 feet of urinals.

An adequate water supply with not less than 90 self-closing taps, drains, soakaways, etc. [For the protection of local users the pumping of water to the festival site will take place only at night and the promoters are required to provide water storage to cover the expected demand.]

Strict compliance with food hygiene regulations, etc., and proper provision of toilets and washing facilities for catering staff.

Adequate arrangements for daily refuse and litter collection.

Suitable lighting at all times.

All the works must be ready for inspection by Monday, August 17th ...

---

* Urine is medically sterile.

In a letter to the County Press the previous year, Peter Harrigan, press officer for Fiery Creations, had written of "the unhappy barrier between the age groups." Many who grew up as teenagers in the late 1960s will recognise the truth of that statement. Parents lived on one planet, teenagers lived on another and rarely, if ever, did the twain meet - and if they did, it was certainly not going to be in the pages of the County Press, as this first major report of the 1970 festival makes clear. For the record, the other main stories attracting the attention of the County Press that week were the straightening of a double-bend in the road at Cowleaze, events at the Bembridge and Folly regattas, a bowling tournament at Sandown and poor attendance figures for the Carisbrooke garden show.

For the most part, the festival report confined itself to a reasonably factual, if openly cynical account of what had taken place. Whilst not openly negative, the report contained liberal doses of inference and sarcasm but it was remarkable for the one thing it did not contain. During the past eight months barely a week had gone by when the subject of the festival had not appeared in the pages of the County Press. The lengthy, almost obsessive, coverage had microscopically examined every aspect of the event, in every degree of light and shade. It had dominated their pages like no other subject in the paper's history, filling page after page and column after column but astonishingly, nowhere in this marathon coverage of one of the biggest events in the Island's history could one single performer's name be found. Not one of the world's biggest musical acts now appearing on the Island was ever referred to. It was an extraordinary omission and an act of selective reporting taken to absurd lengths. It was also a gesture that spoke volumes ...

Aug 29th, 1970.

TRANSFORMATION OF FRESHWATER.
POP FESTIVAL CREATES NEW ATMOSPHERE

The face of Freshwater and much of the West Wight has undergone a transformation in the past seven days with the arrival of hordes of pop fans and itinerant followers for the controversial festival at East Afton. On Wednesday, the opening day, police made 34 arrests for drug offences and on the same day four students appeared in court at Newport for stealing food from a Freshwater supermarket.

In the words of the local biographer, Hester Thackeray Fuller, "Memories quickly pass away, changes arrive with such unexpected and diabolic force that tradition vanishes." This has been discovered by those in Freshwater who find themselves unable to accept invasion. Holidaymakers, too, have been affected, for at Compton Bay this week hippies were seen swimming and sunbathing in the nude. Some parents with small children packed their things and moved to other places.

For others, however, the encampment at East Afton has proved to be a tourist attraction — which has only added to the already onerous task of the police, who have had to enforce parking restrictions in the vicinity and to make frequent appeals for sightseers to keep away.

For days now, garishly dressed individuals have been arriving at the various ferry terminals; from thereon it has been a question of reaching Freshwater by any possible means. Although many had the money to pay bus fares, there were equal numbers using the thumb, some displaying placards indicating the travellers

The front page of the County Press for the week of the festival.

country of origin. Instances have been reported from Ryde of hippies stopping people in the streets and asking for money. Some of those travelling to the festival have been 9 to 5 London office workers who changed from natty suits to pop gear in the train; while on television more than one hippy interviewed has admitted that he was present for the purpose of selling or passing "pot."

One thing that has rankled some Island people and holidaymakers is the express bus service being operated by Southern Vectis direct from Ryde to Freshwater, 24 hours a day. "Why cannot we have such a service, throughout the season?" The same attitude has applied with some people towards the temporarily improved ferry services.

THREATENED BATTLE

There was an awesome incident at the festival site on Tuesday night when a militant section of hippies threatened a miniature battle as they demanded that the event should be free. A red flare was suddenly emblazoned on the ridge of "Devastation Hill," a signal for hundreds of fans to pour down the hillside, some waving lighted torches and candles. Then they marched on the site, pelting officials, Press and television men with stones, bottles and cans; they pounded the fence, breaking it down at several points. They finally dispersed after it was pointed out that the first two days of the festival would be free.

At a police Press conference on Thursday, Inspector G. Cutliffe said that 34 arrests had been made the previous day for drug offences; analyses had been made in 27 cases, and 20 had been confirmed. Six arrests had been made for minor thefts in the village, although a greater theft problem faced the police from a gang operating inside the arena. On the first day, 11 thefts were made from campers on the site and in some cases people lost all their belongings.

HELICOPTER WATCH

Throughout the festival the police have hired a helicopter to provide aerial observation over the site. During its first day in operation it swooped down to assist in the arrest of a suspected drug possessor.

The National Trust announced on Thursday that the closing of all car parks, at the request of the police, had effectively stopped parking on the downs; the object is to minimise the number of sightseers. (This objective was rather nullified the same day when a national newspaper came out with an editorial article exhorting people "Come out and watch ... get a panoramic view of a whole breakaway generation!").

The Trust confirmed that the festival organisers would be depositing £500 with the County Council for the protection of the hill on the downs overlooking the site. This hill has been taken over by a breakaway group of hippies who consider that their type of music should be free, although they have been warned of an adder infestation.

Mr. F. W. Bright, secretary of the Island National Trust, emphasised that Freshwater Golf Club have their land on lease from the Trust; the two rights of way across the course, one at the top and the other at the bottom immediately behind the festival site, remain open and can still be used by the public. In order to reduce, as far as practicable, pressure from the general public, arrangements had been made for a large part of the downs to be fenced off, but should there be any trouble in an emergency, the police may allow patrons into the fenced-off area as a safety measure and this is the only circumstance when the downs would be used by the pop fraternity. As to the hippies who are encamped in hedgerows — known as "Desolation Row" on the edge of the site — Mr. Bright said they would all be flushed out as soon as the fencing was finished.

CASUALTY SERVICE
St. Mary's Hospital, Newport, has been providing a night cover casualty service since last night and continues to do so for today and tomorrow to deal with emergencies from the pop festival site.

MARRIED AT MOTTISTONE
Two hippies attending the pop festival were married at the Church of St. Peter and Paul, Mottistone, on Thursday. They were both dressed in hippie gear. They were Alan Tunnell, (23), from New Zealand, and Carol Kelly, of Edinburgh, who was barefoot. The Rev. R. J. Bowyer, rector of Brook with Mottistone, officiated.

POLICE PREPARED
Up to yesterday (Friday) the police said there had been 63 confirmed cases of people in possession of drugs and 24 for petty thefts.

On Thursday night at the site, about 200 fans, believed to be French Algerians, tried to stop the organisers completing the building of fences. After a slight disturbance between them and private security guards, the fencing was completed. The police were not called.

An invasion by Hell's Angels was stopped at mainland ferry terminals by the police. Some of the Angels left their motorcycles on the other side and came over to the Island on foot, but weapons were confiscated beforehand. Police have also been warned that gangs of skinheads were on their way from London. The police said they were prepared to deal with any kind of trouble from these people or any other troublemakers.

Douglas Osmond, the Chief Constable of Hampshire, who has been on the Island since Wednesday said today, 'One of the good things has been the absence of violence. There is far less violence here than at a normal league football match.' He criticised the lunatic fringe and he blamed them for attacks on the wall and their attitude towards the police. Mr Osmond said he had gone, in casual clothes, to sit on the downs among the people to listen to the music, "and I found it very pleasant," he said ...

———————————◆———————————

Ray Foulk - "The police were great. Fantastic. We had nothing but good relationships with the police ... By and large, without them I don't think we'd ever have got the festival on ... They were very supportive. They didn't have any objections. They reported that there hadn't been trouble at the previous festival and they didn't see why there would be trouble here, and from a policing point of view they didn't see any problems."

The coverage of the festival weekend itself appeared the following week. Events that weekend gave rise to several myths and falsehoods that persist to this day. "Give a lie a headstart and the truth will never catch up," goes the saying, and that is certainly true of the myths and innaccuracies surrounding the 1970 festival that now seem destined to be copied and pasted on the internet for all eternity.

In an effort to lay some to rest, firstly the festival was not attended by 600,000. The probable truth, stripped of nostalgic wishful thinking, is that about 300,000 attended. Estimates at the time by the County Press, police and national press all agree on a figure of between 250 and 350,000, and that was to remain the accepted figure for 25 years until the film of the festival, 'Message to Love,' was released in 1995. It was this film, directed by Murray Lerner, that gave birth to the 600,000 legend - an unfounded myth based on nothing more than one stage announcement. In the film, festival compere Rikki Farr, described by the Times as, 'a man not given to understatement,' tells the crowd, "British Railways have told us that over 600,000 people have come to the Isle of Wight." Where Mr Farr got this information from is a mystery. British Rail themselves, made no such claim in their statement to the County Press that week; indeed their Captain Wheeler speaking back in March, had been quite clear, "The ferry service," he told the Council, "could (only) move 60,000 a day." That being so, even allowing for the services of Red Funnel, it would have required nine or 10 days to get the festivalgoers onto the Island and the same time to get them off, a transport epic that quite clearly did not take place.

A comparison of an aerial photograph of the 2010 Festival, where 55,000 are known to be in attendance, with one of the 1970 festival crowd, settles the matter once and for all. The Afton crowd is not by any stretch of the imagination 10 or 12 times the size of the Seaclose one and finally, Ray Foulk, a man who should know, says "I personally have never gone along with the 600,000 figure. I think that's absurd ... It couldn't have been 600,000."

It is also often claimed that the 1970 festival was the last ever performance for Jimi Hendrix. It was not. His last paid performance was in Germany, one week later, at the Isle of Fehmarn festival on September 6th, while his last ever public appearance was a jam at Ronnie Scott's Club, on September 17th, just a few hours before his death.

Finally, many accounts of the festival portray it as five days of chaos and riot. This myth has its roots in events on the Tuesday night prior to the festival, when a short-lived attack was made on the arena fence. The County Press decided the attack was of little consequence, devoting only one paragraph to it, but in 'Message to Love," it took on a new significance when the Tuesday night's events were edited into the Saturday night footage, leading viewers to believe, quite wrongly, that the attack took place in the course of the main festival, during the Doors performance of 'When the Music's Over' ...

Ray Foulk : "It's a myth. The myth has been built up much further by the Murray Lerner film that came out in 1995. Absolutely absurd stuff. The film was an essay in conflict. It built a narrative based on cutting up the chronology to exaggerate the minority conflict"

In a telephone interview with Tom Stroud in 2010, for an Isle of Wight Radio documentary, Murray Lerner disagreed :

"People are gonna have different attitudes. I don't know whether that was a mistake or not, but that's the way I make films. I don't go for literal replications of an event. I'm not making newsreel."

THE ISLE OF WIGHT COUNTY PRESS, SATURDAY SEPTEMBER 5 1970

THE POP SCENE IN PICTURES

"A period of tranquility, oblivious to their surroundings."

"Pop fans sleeping outside the Red Funnel offices at Cowes, as they waited for the first morning ferry."

Earning Their Bus Fare
"Pop festival fans playing the guitar at Ryde Esplanade to raise the bus fare to East Afton."

Spiritual Counsellor
Rev. Robert Bowyer, rector of Brook Mottistone, tries to sort out hippies' les. He organised and co-ordinated the tian counsellors on the pop site."

"A general scene at the site, some taking a brief rest."

Perhaps sensing that this would be the last festival, the County Press reporting had become noticeably more hostile. Over the last two years, although plainly opposed to the festivals, the County Press had by and large confined its disapproval to editorials but as this report makes abundantly clear, the disparaging remarks had now well and truly spread to the news pages. With a distinct lack of objectivity and more than a whiff of prejudice, the festivalgoers are described as "a horde of unwelcome guests" while the air at the festival is described as"polluted with the stench of sweat." Quotes from Fiery Creations, which would have offered some balance and right of reply to the ill-disposed County Press stance, are conspicuous by their absence. The reason is simple, says Ray Foulk:

"They never sought quotes from us. And they were extremely selective in their coverage of the more negative and 'legalistic' issues, to the exclusion of what was an unprecedented phenomenon taking place on the Island."

Through today's eyes this next account reads more like an opinion column than a news report. It is a blend of innuendo and exaggeration, with a dash of snobbery. The reporter introduces hearsay as fact and has been unable, or unwilling, to find anything positive to say about the event. As for the music, the sole reason for the festival, there is no mention whatsoever.

In an odd turn of events, on March 18th, 1971, during the second reading of the Isle of Wight Bill, Mark Woodnutt told the House of Commons: "I spent two days at this festival, incognito in my hippie outfit, and the scene both during and after the festival was one of indescribable squalor and filth." Why Mr Woodnutt chose to keep this tale of undercover bravado to himself for so long, rather than reveal it here, is a matter of conjecture ...

Sept 5th, 1970.

POP FESTIVAL DISORGANISES ISLAND
VISIT OF NOTORIOUS 'HELL'S ANGELS'

THE organisers of the pop festival at East Afton, Freshwater, stated at the weekend that it would be the last such event they would hold on the Island.

Estimates of the attendance varied from 150,000 to 400,000. The presence of so large a gathering disorganised life in the Island, particularly in the West Wight, where many people are angry at the intrusion of such a horde of unwelcome guests, against their expressed wishes.

The organisers blamed a minority group who tried to wreck the festival in support of their plea for free entertainment, which the promoters were forced to grant at certain times. Other things were also free, including mass nude bathing at Compton Bay, one of the many dubious aspects which gained nationwide publicity for the Island through the national press and television.

It was estimated that by Sunday morning there were 300,000 people in the vicinity of the site at Freshwater. Although praising the police, Mr. Mark Woodnutt, M.P., said that such an event on such a scale prevented them carrying out their duties properly. He vowed that so far as he was concerned, there would never be another similar function in the Island. Tension mounted throughout the week preceding the opening day when the first drug and theft cases were heard at special courts at Newport. These went on during the weekend, including Sunday, and continued into this week.

At the back of the stage, away from the main festival, Hawkwind gave free performances outside 'Canvas City,' an inflatable tent city.   *[Photograph by Harry Matthews]*

y Creations offered free tickets to festivalgoers who had arrived without any, in exchange for 'ing sections of the fence. Tickets and paint were handed over but it soon became apparent that ing meant different things to different people. "I sent down 200 gallons of paint and 300 es and everything, and they're all painting swastikas all over the place." - Ronnie Foulk in lm "Message To Love."   *[Photograph by Alan Stroud]*

Although those who favoured the festival claimed there was little or no trouble, as did the police, many reports were to the contrary. For instance, the Island had its first major visit from the mainland of the notorious Hell's Angels, who banded together with French and Algerian students to disrupt the event, causing considerable damage to site property. The nude bathing, too, on a public beach, did not go down at all well with holidaymakers or local residents. On Sunday many left the area as hundreds of hippies descended on Compton, stripped and stretched on the sands; then they cavorted and bathed naked. At one stage, our photographer was the only man with his trousers on. Some French students told him they had never seen anything like it before, adding that such a thing would not be allowed by the police on their beaches.

Not only in Freshwater but in other Island towns people objected to hippies squatting on the pavements in groups, causing everyone to step over them. "They seem too lazy even to stand up," said one elderly woman from the West Wight. "Why the police never moved them on for causing an obstruction I do not know. If I sat in the middle of the pavement I would soon get shifted by the law."

LAW UNENFORCEABLE

Mr Woodnutt said situations had been created whereby it was impossible to enforce the law; there had been very little trouble because the police had to exercise their discretion and not enforce the law. He was not criticising the police, as he thought they acted admirably in the circumstances. With 500 bathing naked and thousands smoking drugs round camp fires, there would have been a riot if they were all arrested. The Member has written to the Home Secretary, seeking Government legislation enabling councils to say whether or not festivals should be held in their areas.

Licensees in the West Wight admitted they had done record business but were not keen on another festival because they had suffered losses through theft and damage. Several complained about the foul language used by male and female fans in bars. One publican said that she had lost not only her own supply of pint glasses but others loaned to her by friends. Some of the hippies were not averse to going behind the bar and serving themselves if the landlord was busy. It was not unusual for a guest house proprietor who had let a room to a fan to find in the morning several more present - they had come through the windows during the night!

As was expected, one of the biggest aftermath problems was litter — cans, bottles, discarded clothing, toilet paper, pieces of corrugated iron. On Tuesday the task of quick removal appeared to be an impossibility. Apart from the rubbish, hedges had been stripped and trees damaged in the area known as "Desolation Row." The sight was not much better on "Devastation Hill" where the renegades against paying encamped. The air was polluted with the stench of joss sticks, marijuana and sweat. Some of the improvised toilets were torn down by hippies, which did not seem to deter some, who relieved themselves in fields or against fences. Taken comparatively, it could be said that the number of arrests for drug offences was small, but "pot" was openly peddled and smoked, especially at night around the camp fires. Quite a few of those apprehended were allowed to go after a caution from the police, who were after more serious offenders, particularly "pushers" of drugs. The scenes at Compton attracted crowds of onlookers and

3 ☆ FREEk PREESS ☆ PASS IT ON
Friends - Oz - InK - Friday Afternoon

BUST FUND

sometime later today a bust fund will be announced from the stage. It's being organised by Friends-Oz-Ink. So far it's only been broadcast at Canvas City so you may not know about it. If you want any information, come over to the Friends Tent.

FRIENDS EDITOR TO BE RELEASED!!!!!!!!!!!

It seems that the labs on the island have not been able to confirm what it was Allan Harcusson was busted for. He's applied for for legal aid and at 9:30 this evening he can no longer be detained. He has yet to appear in court because of the inconclusive lab reports.

HEAVY CHARGE FOR INJURY

Dr. Kennedyof St. John's Ambulance and Festival official doctor arrived back again at the Festival to insist that National Health forms be filled out , so he gets 22/6 for every patient that comes in for treatment. St. John's ambulance, who have been doing all the hard work and getting nothing, think this isevery unfair.

A young kid fell off a cliff today. After enquiries at S.J.A. no one knew mcuh, but we were later told by them that he is in critical condition at Southampton Neurological Hospital.

STOP PRESS!!!!!!!!!!!!!!!!!!!!!!!!!!!!!!!!!!!

The FREEk correspondent predicts that the fence separating the people from the VII's will be torn down by the end of the festival. First stirrings of violence occurred at 6 P. . last night when an angry hail of beercans greeted attempts to erect the news tower. following this barrage, people in the front row attempted to rip down the fence. "Why should we be divided!" shouted the people as they repeatedly charged the fence. Some of the stewards guarding the fence as well as some VIP's were visibly shaken by the incident. If feeling is already running so high against the absurd amount of space taken by the VIP's, press and other groupies, it is bound to explode well before Sunday. Fiery Creations must also be feeling the heat. Extra scaffolding is now reinforcing the existing division the people and the parasites.

HARRISON IN AUDIENCE TONITE

American co-ordinators have confirmed that George Harrison is arriving on the island at Bembridge airport at 7.30 this evening. Nobody has any idea as yet when he is going to arrive at the Festival or whether he might play. Could happen. The same sources have told us that the difficulties the management had in getting Crosby Stills Nash and Young in have not been overcome, and Neil Young is coming on his own instead. He will play 6th place Saturday evening.

Miles Davis is having a great hassle over passports and getting his equipment together. Nobody seems to know why; if he does appear, it will be Sunday night. Cat Mother have been really hung up at customs and won't be appearing at all.

FRENCH BUST

Those who have been arriving at the Festival today tell us that French kids are being searched on the Lymington Ferry. There's a heavy concentration of plain clothes cops on board and Securicor guards with their dogs at this end of the ferry. They were apparently tipped off that these kids were bringing in heavy quantities all day yesterday.

HANDCUFFED AUDIENCE

People arrested have asked to come to the campsite to collect belongings or get bread, but the fuzz are not prepared to bring them out to the site. They would have to be handcuffed, and police fear a riot. Generally though the fuzz are being very good. Some people busted for small amounts have been discharged, but foreigners and people with no fixed abode are being fined £40 or 30 days and then kept in custody until they can raise the funds.

FINAL (?) FOOTNOTE TO ROBIN F.'S ARREST!!!!

Before he was taken off in the Guards' land-rover, the Young Liberals managed to convince three Hell's Angels who were being assaulted by Robin to get in the Liberals' van "Giggles in Your Eyes". The angels responded with remarkable composure and nobody was hurt. At this stage no one knows Robin's whereabouts.

The leading underground magazines of the day collaborated on a daily festival news sheet, Freek Press, this edition complete with mis-spelling of its own title. Given away on site, this one issued on the Friday afternoon wrongly predicts the arrival of George Harrison but correctly predicts the tearing down of the fences.

traffic was halted for about two miles as binoculars and telescopes were brought into play. By Compton Steps dozens of hippies frolicked naked beneath a miniature waterfall, making "Oh, Calcutta" look like "Alice in Wonderland." More than one naked couple were seen walking along roads and across the Downs.

FRIGHTENING EXPERIENCE

Marching behind a Nazi style swastika banner, Hell's Angels, together with the anarchists from Devastation Hill, made a foray against catering stalls and fences surrounding the arena. They caused much damage and for a time terrorised the more passive element. "It was a frightening experience for those of us who simply came to hear the music," said one young girl

Itinerant traders took advantage of the tremendous influx, and temporary stalls appeared on the most unexpected sites. A cheese roll could be bought for 3s. and a pint of milk for 2s.— although quite a few people missed their pinta from the doorstep in the mornings!

On television and in various sections of the Press, some local people expressed the view that everything went off fine, the fans were well-behaved and there was no trouble; it transpired later, however, that most of these people had a minor, vested interest as traders in one form or another and welcomed the extra cash.

At one stage during the actual performance (by the artists) the police appealed to those taking part not to aggravate the drug situation by giving encouragement from the stage; this applied particularly to comperes.

GENUINE FANS UPSET

Some of the genuine fans, upset by the intrusion of troublemakers, began to leave on Sunday, although the main exodus did not begin until the following day. Many of the young people, especially foreigners, were by now penniless and various organisations, including the police, raised money for fares home after reassuring parents and obtaining guarantees from them and foreign embassies and consulates. Hundreds had not eaten for many hours and a free soup kitchen was set up. The National Voluntary Civil Aid Service reported that the telephone service was becoming overloaded and bread was in short supply; fresh water points and toilet facilities appeared to be inadequate. They said they had handled communications and emergency soup kitchens — services which had proved invaluable at previous festivals, according to their statement.

Ferries and bus services were stretched to the limit on Monday in an attempt to get the thousands back to the mainland. At one time there was a mile-long queue for buses at the site and one nearly as long at Yarmouth for the ferry. The site itself looked like the retreat from Moscow with a straggling, dejected line of hippies shuffling through the snow-like debris. Boat owners took advantage of the situation by operating a service from Yarmouth to Lymington for those who could pay — anything from 6s. to 16s. for the trip. Not unexpectedly, some of the hippies tried to hitch a lift across the water. Boatmen came from as far afield as Poole to cash in. Whether or not they approved of the invasion, Island people took compassion on the penniless and bedraggled mob; there were many gestures of kindness, including the offer of food and sometimes money, not to mention car lifts to ferry terminals.

The problem now is to clean the site of debris in the allotted time and to make the Down at least presentable again for the remainder of the season. Police were

e view from the hill on the Sunday afternoon. Already, sheets of corrugated iron, 'liberated' from
e perimeter fencing, are being used as windbreaks and makeshift accomodation.

[Photograph by Reg Davies]

The view from the stage three days later.　　　*[Photograph by Alan Stroud]*

expected to stay on the site for a few days during the mopping-up operations and to supervise several hundred remaining campers. Inspector G. Cutliffe said that any hippies who planned to stay for the rest of the summer would probably be "elbowed out."

Not a few of the fans left disillusioned by the whole affair. Said one: "The festival was sour, it was too commercial. The hippy bond was missing, we are not used to thieving and selfishness in our ranks — and that was the case at Freshwater." The punch line was provided by a hippy girl who summed up to the 'County Press'; "It was great, man, but I am glad it did not happen on my doorstep."

Police said on Wednesday that there were an estimated 2000 fans remaining on the festival site. Mr. A. Pemberton, owner of Freshwater Golf Club, on Wednesday told the 'County Press': "I think it is highly probable that we will only be able to play ten holes for the rest of the year. I can say nothing definite until all the litter is cleared away."

Ray Foulk : "By the Sunday it was clear there wouldn't be another festival in this format ...There was a move on the part of our press department to make something of this for the benefit of the film, like declaring it a free festival. It was at a time when we'd stopped taking money so I don't think it was of much financial consequence at that point. What was of financial consequence was for the Press department to announce to the world that we'd lost money like that, because that then put financial pressure on us that we would have been able to handle in a more orderly fashion ... I don't think the hill or anything stopped it working, because the festival did work. If you mean working financially, making a profit, yes, the hill was a massive contributory factor. We were overbudget, we'd piled in more groups than we probably needed to and we'd built more facilities than we could probably afford to, but in terms of the thing working as an event, I think it worked pretty well. It was a very smooth-going festival. Most people who went to it got enough toilets and they got enough food. Every band that was booked, appeared and performed, and some of them were memorable performances, so in terms of working for our public, it was great.

On the Tuesday morning, in sheeting drizzle, the clearing up of the site began and the two brothers began to take stock of their financial situation ...

... It was quite a wet day on the Tuesday and I was in a marquee backstage for the whole of the morning, and we were counting money and paying staff and that was a fairly dispiriting job, knowing in the back of my mind that this is not a very good financial result for us. We didn't know at that point what the ticket sales returns, still in the ticket shops, was going to be. We didn't know whether it was going to be miniscule or massive, we just didn't have a clue at that point and it was probably some days before we started really getting the feedback. But at that moment, on the Tuesday morning, we still had money from the turnstiles on the site and we were able to pay everybody that needed paying on-site ... We didn't know what the financial ramifications were until afterwards. We had an inkling that it was not going to be very good .... Certainly on the day, we would still be living in hope that the thing would be rescued by the ticket sales returns yet to come in. A week later we would have known that the thing was in trouble" ...

The volume of letters received regarding the festival was the greatest the paper had ever received on one subject in its entire history. Some of those letters are extraordinary. It is worth quoting the editor's statement on the 'Letters' page three weeks after the previous year's festival, when he wrote, "This event, and its repercussions, have brought a record number of letters to the editor on any one topic. He has tried to present a fair balance of opinion in choosing those published."

While there seems no reason to doubt that that remained the policy for the 1970 festival, Mr. Ash certainly chose some extremely prejudiced letters for publication and allowed some absurd untruths in them to go unchallenged ...

Sept 5th, 1970.

Pop festival

We are now told that, financially, the pop festival was a disaster. The problems of the site had not been met, nor even (until too late) perceived. Throughout, despite security guards with Alsatian dogs and Land-Rovers, and many hundreds of police, for whom the ratepayer must pay, there was intermittent violence, culminating in an organised attempt by many hundreds, by night, to loot the caterers. The violence in fact reached such a pitch that the promoters were forced to give free entry to the huge enclosure walled with a double fence of corrugated iron 10 feet high; thus incidentally, defrauding those who had purchased tickets. The element with tents numbered some 10,000 to 20,000, reckoning two or three to a tent; the rest, to the number of more than 200,000, slept on the bare ground, and had the weather turned wet the desperate search for shelter would have led to violence throughout the West Wight.

Twelve hundred lavatories — sufficient for about one in five of those present — were provided; the rest fouled some thousands of acres of private land, including part of Freshwater golf course and some National Trust property; I myself saw 50 to 100 at a time squatting in standing corn. Protective fences that had been erected were at once torn down to build shacks. So little were many of them concerned to hear the performers that throughout Saturday and Sunday morning, before the star bookings had appeared, tens of thousands were leaving, feeling apparently, that they were over-policed. A proportion of the faces were depraved almost beyond belief, and in many cases clearly drug-ridden; scores had such faces as might be seen in a criminal lunatic asylum; many seemed to be adenoidal, with mouths hanging open, slouched shoulders, and pitiful physiques; in the unceasing procession along the roads the occasional "fellow-traveller" or half-hippy, looking both healthy and clean, numbered less than one in six.

Several square miles of country will now be affected for some years with litter than can never be wholly gathered, human excrement equivalent to almost the whole output of Southampton for several days and hedges ravaged for fuel or by fire. The police made more than 100 arrests for theft or drug-offences, and it is reasonable to suppose that for one case that they detected under such impossible conditions 20 went undetected. As to "pot," the police threw their hand in (vide statement in Press); had the law been enforced as to this, arrests must have run into scores of thousands; thus once again the law is brought into contempt.

If anyone was ever in any doubt about the festival, their doubts, presumably, are now resolved; but at what a cost!

S. E. SCAMMELL. Longs Wharf, Yarmouth.

Pop Festival

Sept 5th, 1970.

I was at the first meeting in Freshwater Memorial Hall as an impartial witness. I impartially listened as some of the noisier elements of the crowd chanted for Mrs. Cooper to be chairman of the meeting. I tried to remain impartial when Mr. Rikki Farr took over the microphone and completely disrupted the meeting. Since then I have tried to remain impartial when men have urinated in front of me and in front of young children, without even the common decency to turn their backs to the road. I tried to remain impartial when I saw people throwing bottles into the water at Freshwater Bay, causing untold dangers to young children paddling. I tried to remain impartial when I saw hippies occupying a whole seat by lying down, thus making it impossible for elderly people to sit down. I tried to remain impartial when I wandered round the festival site on the Monday following the festival and saw the filth and was nauseated by the stench of human excreta from Desolation Row (would someone please convince me that the thousands who camped on the once beautiful Afton Downs made the trek down to use the site toilets). I tried to remain impartial when I was approached by people, begging for money for food. I am afraid my impartiality was finally exhausted.

I will admit that I spoke to some very nice hippies, and some not so nice, one of whom told me that we have just got to accept their behaviour and their way of life. I will also admit that I stood to gain nothing, either directly or indirectly, from the festival. However, people of Freshwater, a whole new way of life has now opened up for us. We can now urinate where and when we please, we can lie down on the pavements when we feel weary of our daily toil. We can throw empty bottles into the Bay without fear of reprisals.

I would like to take this opportunity of praising the manager and staff of a Freshwater supermarket who did a wonderful job and who realised that the local people will be using the store for 52 weeks of the year and not one week. I would add that I am not a tired old man (as suggested by Mr. Rikki Farr) nor am I a retired brigadier or colonel and, Mrs. Cooper, I am quite a few years younger than you so even if I am in the minority I must accept the fact that I am, as you state, a "reactionary" and proud of it.

RATEPAYER. Name and address supplied.

———————◆———————

Not surprisingly, a considerable number of minor crimes took place at the festival and within days, special courts were held at Newport. The details of every prosecution were faithfully recorded in the 'Courts' columns of the County Press and shed some light on subsequent claims that the festival was the scene of widespread drug abuse.

Although it should be made clear that the County Press had no direct hand in cultivating the drugs myth, it is not entirely blame free in the matter and did little to correct those correspondents to the paper who did. For the record, over 1200 festivalgoers were checked for drugs, resulting in 70 prosecutions and 31 cautions. Fifty four of those convictions were for the possession of cannabis, 13 for LSD, two for heroin and six for possession of methadone and amphetamines. There were no convictions for the possession of cocaine.

The following cases are a representative sample of the prosecutions that took place ...

Sept 5th, 1970.
MAGISTRATES' COURTS - SPECIAL WEEKEND COURTS
MANY DEFENDANTS FACE DRUG CHARGES
Magistrates sitting at special courts at the Guildhall, Newport, during the pop festival period dealt with nearly 100 people, many facing drug charges.

Between Wednesday week and Tuesday, 69 appeared for a variety of drug offences — including possessing cannabis, L.S.D., amphetamine, and heroin* — and others were charged with shoplifting and theft.

Trevor Ellis (19), of 41, Icen Road, Radipole, Weymouth, pleaded not guilty to possessing L.S.D. He was remanded on bail until September 18th.   Alan David Pitcher (24), labourer, of 21, Powys Square, London, W.I, was fined a total of £70 for possessing L.S.D. and cannabis at Ryde. Bruce Sher (24), unemployed American citizen, c/o Pickwick Hotel, Notting hill Gate, London, was fined £40 for possessing cannabis at Yarmouth. Michael John Trill (24), assistant, of 31, Cumberland Terrace Mews.-London, N.W.I, was fined £40 for possessing cannabis at Fishbourne.   Jonathan Bruce Park, freelance architect, of 68b, Belsize Park Gardens, London, N.W.3, was fined a total of £70 for possessing L.S.D. and cannabis at Cowes.   Lee Feld (24), self-employed decorator, of 69, Bartholomew Road, Kentish Town, London, N.W.5, was fined £40 for possessing cannabis at Ryde.   Julie Webb (19), film actress, of 1159 Monument Street, Pacific, Palisades, California, was fined £40 with an alternative of 30 days for possessing cannabis at Ryde.   Derek Alexander Neal (21), unemployed welder, of 255, Greenway Road, Rumney, Cardiff, was given a conditional discharge for 12 months for the theft of 12 cans of beer and two bottles of cider from the Freshwater Bay Hotel. Colin James Toomey (29), docker, of 36, Langthorney Street, Fulham, London, S.W.6, was fined £40 for possessing cannabis at Fishbourne. Michael Baar Winter (25), department store buyer, of 1100 West Avenue, Miami Beach, Florida, was fined £40 with an alternative of 30 days for possessing cannabis at Yarmouth.   Allan William McKelvie (17), student, of 30, Chohan Park Avenue, South Croydon, Surrey, was fined £10 for the theft of chocolate, soup, two tins of beans and a packet of peanuts from the Richway Supermarket at Freshwater. John William (21), manager, of Half Way Garage, Taffs Well, Cardiff, and Phillip Davies (19), driver, of 17, Calewid, Tontwynlon, New Cardiff, South Wales, were each fined £10 for taking a dinghy without consent from Yarmouth.   Patrick Micoin (18), student of 149 Rue Pierre Lati, Le Havre 76, France, was fined £10 for the theft of biscuits and nuts from Richway Supermarket, Freshwater.   Barry Blades, unemployed, of Oak Cottage, Ashey Road, Ryde, was fined £20 for using abusive words and insulting behaviour likely to cause a breach of the peace at Ryde on August 28th.   John Mc Parland (33), magazine distributor, of 33, Oakley Street, London, S.W.3, was charged with possessing cannabis, stated to be worth £1500 on the retail market, methadine hydrochloride and L.S.D. Bail was refused and Mc Parland was remanded in custody until 7th of September ...

---

* Though not a strict, nor perhaps fair, comparison, the Hampshire Police statement accompanying the 2009 IW Festival application stated "In 2008, of the 781 people searched as they entered the arena, 512, or nearly two thirds, were found to be either in possession of drugs or admitted to having recently used drugs. £77,350 worth of drugs were seized, predominantly cocaine, cannabis and ecstasy."

Despite presenting no supporting evidence, the County Press had always maintained that most Islanders were opposed to the festival. Vectensis also claimed to know the minds of "the vast majority" of his fellow Islanders ...

September 5th, 1970

AN ISLANDER'S NOTES
[BY VECTENSIS]

"POP UTOPIA," - This was the heading of a comment in Tuesday's "Daily Telegraph" about the pop festival at East Afton. Not a very appropriate title. There was nothing utopian about the event. In the opinion of most Islanders it was a perfect nuisance, as they feared it would be ... The law has been flouted by hundreds of nude bathers at Compton Bay and, in force of numbers also, by drug takers at the festival ... While the police have done a difficult job in an admirable manner, it was impossible for them to impose the full rigour of the law on masses of offenders, as it would be imposed on the individual.

This travesty of justice should alone be sufficient ground on which to base action to prevent any such pop extravaganzas happening in the Island again ... I am sure that the vast majority of Islanders prefer 'Garden Isle' to 'Pop Island.' It is high time that their wishes were respected.

Sept 12th, 1970

Pop Festival *

I was one of the many who attended the pop festival. I met very nice people. Most of us were there for the music. The people leaving early were ones who had run out of money for food or who had been awake since early Friday. As for violence, I myself never saw any; consider the size - over three times that of any football match at which there is violence and quite a few arrests. The site which Fiery Creations had as a last resort, had the hill which acted as a grandstand. If they had been given the choice of a better site the troublemakers, finding it impossible to see or get in, would have left us alone. Hippies threw things in the sea but our holidaymakers do that and leave their rubbish on the downs and beaches, the only difference being they scatter theirs all over the Island.

S. SEXTON (Mrs) 34, Sandcroft Avenue, Ryde.

As co-ordinator of Christian Counsellors at the pop festival, and of the ad hoc committee formed late on the Sunday night to help the needy, may I express appreciation of all who gave their money, time or services; both the many Islanders and the hundreds of young visitors. Especially distinguished was the co-operation of the police and their courteous treatment of everyone ... Fiery Creations gave generous help throughout. Those of us involved in caring for these young people have been enriched by the experience. We all know this is the last Island pop festival on this scale; let us give thanks to God for all we have learned.

ROBERT BOWYER. The Rectory, Mottistone Manor

---

* An 'Editor's Note' that week brought the festival correspondence to an end, "About 40 letters were received dealing with the pop festival this week. As it is impossible to use this many here, this correspondence is now closed."

Not all the discussions regarding the festival were carried on in a state of high excitement or confrontation. Councillor Quick, at the Rural District Council meeting, indulged in a flight of whimsy, or 'poetic effusion' as it was referred to ...

October 3rd, 1970

POP FESTIVAL INQUEST
R.D.C. CHAIRMAN'S ANNOUNCEMENT

At the Rural District Council meeting on Tuesday ... Mr. W. H. Quick, C.C., said he thought that the time was right for comment on the event so far as it affected the West Wight. It was now a memory, to some a bad dream, an experience that would probably never be felt again in the Island or the whole country. Good, bad or indifferent, it was the greatest advertisement in the Island for all time. Many people in Freshwater had never seen the outside world, so the world came to Freshwater and Freshwater was amazed; it was an experience never to be forgotten, with conventions flung to the winds, the winds of change that stirred the imagination. There had been a lot of idle talk about the festival, with contradictory utterances. The Member of Parliament talked on television about the ruderies and nuderies; but were there no nuderies in Bembridge and no ruderies on the beach there? ... Totland was not affected because they had their usual aloofness of the vulgar scene! When Mr. Quick sat down, he was congratulated by Mr. F. Hollis, C.A., on his "poetic effusion." ...

Six weeks after the festival, creditors of Fiery Creations applied for the winding up of the company ...

October 10th, 1970

PETITION AGAINST FIERY CREATIONS

Creditors for more than £30,000 appeared on a High Court petition on Monday for the compulsory winding-up of Fiery Creations, Ltd. Mr. Justice Megarry adjourned the case for three weeks after the petitioners, I.P.C. Magazines, Ltd., judgment creditors for £1012, said that they wished to amend the petition and add a further debt of £2240. Creditors supporting the petition were the National Trade Press, Ltd., of London (£730); Watney Mann (London and Home Counties), Ltd., of London (£9900); George Cohen Sons and Co., Ltd., of London (£1403); and Frederick Wain, of Portsmouth (£17,711).

Fiery Creations have called a meeting of creditors to be held at Southsea, next Wednesday.

The subsequent creditors' meeting was held in the ballroom on Clarence Pier, Southsea. It was a lively affair ...

Ray Foulk: "It was a matter of a lot of people in a public hall, and I had to take to the microphone, with a solicitor and a barrister either side of me, and read out a statement to say, "I have no comment to make at this time" and I was not allowed to say anything more than this, and I had to repeat it several times, whenever I was being pressed."

October 17th, 1970
CREDITORS' MEETING ENDS IN UPROAR
NO FIRM PROPOSALS FROM FIERY CREATIONS

A MEETING of 30 creditors of Fiery Creations, Ltd., promoters of the Island pop festival, ended in uproar at Southsea on Wednesday after they were told that the company had no firm proposals to make to them at that stage.

Creditors rose in protest as the representatives of Fiery Creations closed the meeting after five minutes and attempted to leave. A 75-year-old Andover businessman, shouting abuse, had to be restrained from reaching Mr. Raymond Foulk, a director and shareholder of Fiery Creations, as he was hustled from the meeting. Held in the ballroom, Clarence Pier, the meeting lasted just long enough for Mr. Raymond Foulk to read a prepared statement. He told the creditors that his brother, Ronald, who was accompanying him, was the only other director and shareholder in the company. He stated: "Since the company experienced financial difficulties in respect of its commitments arising out of the I.W. festival, my brother and I have done everything in our power to safeguard the position of the company's creditors. When we convened this informal meeting of creditors, we had hoped to be in a position to lay before you certain concrete proposals upon which to seek your approval to a moratorium in respect of the company's debts. We had hoped, and confidently expected, that such proposals, which could be related to royalties to fall due to the company under an agreement by which the company is entitled to a percentage of the profits derived from the distribution of a film which was made of the festival would, if accepted by the creditors, result in the latter being paid at the rate of 20 shillings in the pound on their debts.

MUCH REGRET

"In spite of the efforts of my brother and myself and our lawyers, however, we very much regret that in view of certain difficulties with regard to the film, we are not at this stage in a position to put forward such concrete proposals as we had hoped, though we are confident that we shall be in such a position in the very near future. The situation with regard to the exploitation of the film of the festival is not at present as clear as we had hoped, with the result that we are not in a position to put forward concrete proposals today ... My brother and I are confident that within five weeks of today, the arrangements with regard to the distribution of the film will have been finalised, or at any rate sufficiently advanced, so that we shall be able to lay before the creditors at that meeting proposals for a moratorium which, if accepted, we hope will result in the creditors ultimately realising 20 shillings in the pound on their debts — instead of merely the small dividend which we fear they might receive in the event of the company being placed in liquidation ..."

LEGAL ADVICE

He said that acting on legal advice, they regretted that they did not intend to answer any questions at that informal meeting nor go into the details of the company accounts. They regretted any inconvenience to those people who had travelled a long way, but they had only received their legal advice the previous day, when it had finally become apparent that they were not in a position to put forward concrete proposals for creditors' approval.

Mr. Foulk declared the meeting closed and he and his party attempted to leave. Solicitors for the larger creditors jumped to their feet and pointed out that although he had said a further creditors' meeting would be held in five weeks' time, a petition had been presented last week in the High Court for the compulsory winding up of Fiery Creations. The case had been adjourned for three weeks, and so was due to be finalised before the next creditors' meeting took place.

The creditors then began to shout, some demanding to know when they would be paid. For five minutes chaos reigned as the two Foulk brothers had to "run the gauntlet", of creditors — some of whom were obviously heated.

At one point Mr. Rikki Farr (producer of the festival) and Mr. Peter Steggles, a solicitor acting for Fiery Creations, attempted to pacify an irate Andover businessman who had tried to grasp Mr. Raymond Foulk. The man shouted that the company owed him over £3000 for fencing equipment.

Mr. Farr said later that Fiery Creations did not set out to lose money. Their intention was to give entertainment for people of a certain type, age and generation, and people had come to the festival in their thousands. Unfortunately a small minority, — which was large in numbers because of the massive attendance at the festival — had caused considerable damage. "They (Fiery Creations) did not work for three years to produce a festival for Chairman Mao's boys to come over from France to break down their walls and fences."

> Ray Foulk : "That was a fairly horrendous occasion but probably not as bad as it sounds there. I don't remember being physically frightened at all, I think that might be an exaggeration. I think there were a few people shouting things. The most aggrieved creditor of all was the guy who'd hired us the corrugated iron which had been destroyed. It was just destroyed and it was thousands of pounds worth that he'd hired to us. It was terrible."

———————————————◆———————————————

A common festival myth is that Mark Woodnutt's Isle of Wight Act banned the festivals. It did not. The Act simply put in place a series of controls for future promoters to abide by if they wished to hold an overnight gathering of more than 5000 people on the Isle of Wight.

The requirements of the Act were indeed irksome, requiring amongst other things, four months notice of the location of the event, but they were manageable. Indeed Ray Foulk is quite sure that had the law been in place in 1970, the Afton festival would have met all of its requirements. In 1971, Richard Roscoe, a London promoter, was planning what would have been the fourth festival, and of all the things that did stop him, the Isle of Wight Act was not one of them - it was not passed until the December of that year. However, Roscoe was prepared to meet all the conditions of the forthcoming Act, as indeed the festivals at Seaclose do to this day.*

* Most provisions of the IOW Act were repealed after being superceded by legislation which now applies the same controls nationally, but Section 5 of the original 1971 legislation, relating to overnight gatherings, was unaffected and remains in place. The Act remained unused until 1982, when the annual scooter rallies on the Island began. Following public order problems at the 1986 rally, the 1971 Act was amended to become the Isle of Wight Act of 1990. The word 'overnight' disappeared from the new Act, and the legislation now covers "gatherings of more than 5000 in the open air at any one time," not just within the hours of darkness. The 1971 requirement that organisers of a festival must give the Council at least four months prior notice of the event, still remains in place.

On the face of it the 1971 Act seems a minor piece of legislation but it had some very important implications for civil liberties. Tom Driberg, MP, told the Commons during a debate on the Bill, "It is undesirable that we should have sweeping local legislation creating new offences which are not offences anywhere else in the country ... Whatever one may think, for or against pop festivals, much more important is the general issue of the right of assembly. So many episodes in the history of this country are concerned with the right of assembly."

Back on the Island at a public meeting, Mr Catchpole of Freshwater tried his best to make that very same point ...

October 31st, 1970

'BIGGER AND BETTER POP FESTIVAL'

MR. R. D. Way (chairman of the West Wight Ratepayers' Association) told members that a recording company intended holding a bigger pop festival next year. The company would engage Fiery Creations to run the festival for them ... Mr. B. E. Catchpole, of Court Road, Freshwater Bay, said that he wished to make a statement and was invited on to the stage. He said that he had talked to about 80 or 100 fans at the festival and it was inescapable that the majority of them were perfectly decent people assembled for a lawful purpose. If the new Bill went through Parliament he thought it would be morally wrong ... He thought the ratepayers should say that they welcomed another pop festival with the provision that the promoters had to advertise certain conditions, and the fans had to observe them. Uproar greeted his remarks and he was not allowed to finish ...

———————————◆———————————

Financially, the choice of Afton as a site had clearly worked against Fiery Creations, but to what degree remains an unknown quantity. There certainly were those on the hill who had not bought a ticket, but equally certainly, there were many who had. What is not in doubt is that Afton had not been the preferred choice of Fiery Creations. There was no question that the Council had been instrumental in forcing Fiery Creations' hand to accept the flawed site by refusing the application for the alternative location of Churchill's Farm.

This refusal was something the Council were quite happy to admit to back in August, but something they now denied in a defensive statement issued in response to a Fiery Creations press release ...

October 31st, 1970

COUNTY COUNCIL AND POP FESTIVAL

....Attention was drawn to a statement circulated to the Press by Fiery Creations Ltd., and reported in an evening newspaper on October 15th, which attributed the company's present misfortunes to the County Council. The committee decided that in the public interest the main points of this statement should be summarily refuted. The facts, which the Council can fully substantiate, are as follows:

The choice of site was at all times left to the promoters,* who eventually

---

* Not according to the article dated August 1st (see page 198) and certainly not according to Mark Woodnutt. Speaking in the Commons on the 18th of March 1971, during the second reading of the Isle of Wight County Council Bill, he told the House, "On the last occasion, the County Council had only seven weeks' notice of the site. When the agreement was signed, the promoters rang me up, as chairman of the committee, the very next day and wanted to change the site about 28 days before the date of the event, and of course we would not let them do so."

disclosed their option on the East Afton site only on July 14th ... It subsequently became apparent that the promoters had obtained an option on the Churchills Farm site ... A technical study of the site was started at once and put before a special Select Committee meeting on July 30th when it was decided that the Churchills site was unsuitable ... Whether, from Fiery Creations' Limited standpoint of profitability, the Churchill's site would have been more satisfactory must remain a matter for speculation. The Select Committee were, and remain, convinced that from the standpoint of the general public, their decision was correct ...Fiery Creations cannot now expect public sympathy, nor can they reasonably pass blame elsewhere, for the consequences of a private agreement with the County and Rural District Councils ... Full responsibility for the festival and its aftermath must rest on its promoters.

The lingering death throes of the festival continued to be acted out in public, as more companies joined the list of creditors ...

November 7th, 1970
FIERY CREATIONS CASE ADJOURNED
Five more creditors of Fiery Creations, Ltd. applied in the High Court on Monday to be added to the list of those seeking to have the company compulsorily wound-up ... They were: City Electronics, Ltd. (with a debt of £268); Burgess Bros., Ltd. (£3084); Messrs. James Gilbert and Son (£240); Messrs. R. C. Gray £849); and Mole-Richardson (England), Ltd. (£1156).

The petition has been supported by I.P.C. Magazines, Ltd., creditors for £3250, and is supported by four other creditors whose debts total nearly £30,000.

The film of the Woodstock festival had been a box-office success and partly with that in mind, Fiery Creations had hired an American film director, Murray Lerner, to film the entire 1970 festival with a view to producing their own film for cinema release. It was to be a film which Rikki Farr confidently predicted would "take more money than Gone With The Wind." The resulting footage ran to 175 hours, covering virtually every performer at the festival, and tantalisingly, much of it featuring the Island and its inhabitants filmed in the weeks leading up to and following the festival. Negotiations had recently begun to obtain artists' releases to enable the film to go ahead, and on that basis the creditors had been persuaded to hold their collective fire for the moment ...

Ray Foulk : "Everything was riding on the film - that was the thing. It was probably that that bolstered up our morale - that we thought we had a very valuable film in the can and that it was just a matter of time before we could afford to pay off everything in full and get some profit."

November 28th, 1970
THREE MONTHS GRACE FOR FIERY CREATIONS

Fiery Creations, the company which organised the Isle of Wight pop festival, was given three months' grace by more than 150 creditors at Portsmouth on Monday. The creditors agreed to a three-month deferment of payment and empowered a committee to extend the time if necessary.

The company owes the creditors £105,000. After Monday's three-hour meeting at the Chamber of Commerce offices at Portsmouth, Mr. Ron Foulk, a director of the company, said the chances were good that the creditors would get 20 shillings in the pound. Creditors had shown faith in the company ... Mr. Leonard Gold, the company's accountant, said the festival had been a financial disaster. The latest balance sheet showed assets of only £12,000 and a cash balance of £169. There was also some 200 hours of film of the festival.

Mr. Cameron, public relations officer for the company, said after the meeting that the company placed great hope in the film rights. The film would be ready for distribution within the next five to six months* ...

It was not to be ...

> Ray Foulk : "Well, the trouble with the artists was that you had so many of them saying they were the biggest star in the film, and they wanted a thirty per cent cut or something. The Hendrix estate was saying they were the biggest, the Who were saying they were the biggest and the Doors were saying they were the biggest. You couldn't make any sense of it at all. Nobody was willing to sign, nobody was willing to concede that this was a kind of joint effort and that they maybe get two or three per cent each or something, instead of wanting something like 20 or 30 per cent. So there was complete deadlock ... The biggest problem was creditors to be paid. We spent the next two or three years paying back people, earning and paying back what we could, and a lot of it was paid back ... and we did work very hard for a period of years to regroup and carry on with our careers."

And with that - the festivals were over. Ray and Ronnie Foulk carried on as promoters throughout the early 1970s, putting on highly successful concerts and one-day festivals featuring such diverse acts as Emerson, Lake and Palmer, Chuck Berry, Led Zeppelin and Frank Zappa. Ronnie went on to manage a chain of shops retailing furniture manufactured on the Island while Ray worked in the arts, assisting in the creation of Milton Keynes before going on to become a successful architect.

In the early 1970s, the Conservative Government proposed national legislation along the lines of Mark Woodnutt's Isle of Wight Act, which would regulate and restrict subsequent festivals. However, in what Ray Foulk describes as an 'extraordinary irony,' evidence submitted to the Government's Stevenson Committee by both the Chief Constable of Hampshire, Sir Douglas Osmond, and the Island's Medical Officer of Health, Dr Douglas Quantrill, led directly to the failure of such authoritarian measures being enacted.

---

* The film would not see the light of day until 1995, by which time the footage, originally conceived and commissioned by the Foulk brothers, had passed into the hands of film director, Murray Lerner. This unique footage of the Island forty years ago is currently in storage in New York, where it seems destined to remain.

Both men were sufficiently positive about the 1970 festival for the Committee to recommend in 1973 that no additional powers were necessary. The Chief Constable told the Committee: "It is easy to become emotional about pop festivals. The world's press was present in considerable numbers. They sought sensation but in the main were disappointed... By the end of the festival the Press representatives became almost desperate for material and they seemed a little disappointed that the patrons had been so well behaved. It is essential to explode the myth that all patrons of pop festivals are undesirables. The vast majority are perfectly decent, well-behaved youngsters, courteous and considerate. The desire on the part of the Press to sensationalise such functions by over-emphasis on drugs and immorality is to be deplored and only creates unnecessary anxiety in the minds of parents."

Ray Foulk : "So in what is almost the punch-line to the whole story, try as he did to rubbish the festival, Woodnutt was finally defeated in his attempt to close off festivals nationwide, because the most authoritative voice of all, the police, said that the IOW Festival was orderly and successful from their point of view."

◆

The final word in the festival saga goes to Ray Foulk, in an anecdote which perfectly captures the bravado and self-assured confidence of youth that drove Ray and his brothers to put the festivals on :

"I think that I benefited from the festival. It gave us the confidence to do almost anything. I remember at one point sitting in the office, I think it was the winter of '69, in between the two festivals, and Peter Harrigan and a couple of other people were discussing some projects we might go in for - One of them was to go and raise some money to raise the Titanic."

Photo : Harry Matthews

1971 Postscript

January 23rd, 1971

FORTNIGHT IN WHICH TO SELL FILM RIGHTS — A further adjournment was granted in the High Court on Monday of a petition for the compulsory winding-up of Fiery Creations, Ltd., organisers of last summer's pop festival. Mr. Justice Brightman gave the company another fortnight in which to sell its rights in a film of the festival, its one substantial asset ...

February 6th, 1971.

COMPULSORY WINDING UP — Fiery Creations, Ltd,, the company which organised last summer's I.W. Pop Music Festival, was compulsorily wound up in the High Court on Monday without opposition. Counsel for petitioners, I.P.C. Magazines, Ltd., creditors for £3250, who were supported by a large number of other creditors, told Mr. Justice Brightman that negotiations for the sale of the company's rights in a film of the festival had come to nothing ...

April 10th, 1971.

CHIEF CONSTABLE AND POP FESTIVAL
NEED FOR IMPROVED ORGANISATION

Many valuable police lessons were learned as a result of the 1970 pop festival, the most outstanding one being that in future there must be regular police patrols within the site perimeter to prevent crime and ensure that troublesome situations did not arise. The organisers must be expected to pay for this service. These views were expressed in the annual report of Sir Douglas Osmond, chief constable, presented to the Hampshire Police Authority at Winchester on Monday ... The attendance at the third festival was higher than ever. No precise figures were available, but it was unlikely that on the three main days the average attendance was less than 200,000 and at its peak may well have been of the order of a quarter-of-a million. The vast majority of those attending were young people.

DISLOCATION OF NORMAL WORK

Police arrangements for an event of such a size caused heavy dislocation to normal work of the force. Numbers of officers, varying between 300 and 650, were employed in the Island throughout the week of the festival. Cost to the Police Authority - which would not have been incurred had the festival not been held - was of the order of £70,000. The behaviour of those attending was, in the main, extremely good. There was, however, a substantial element of extremists, mainly anarchists, many of them foreigners, amounting to perhaps 10,000 to 15,000, who were intent on provoking disorder. Their attempts met with little response from the main body of those attending, and prompt deployment of police officers at potential trouble spots prevented any serious trouble.

Sir Douglas said that, as was to be expected, the event attracted many from the drug-taking fraternity. Special police arrangements were made to ensure that these people were as far as possible identified and checked on landing in the Island. More than 1000 were checked and about 120 arrests made. These figures did indicate, however, that drug taking was not as prevalent as had been suggested in some quarters, for with the likely persons producing only a ten per cent yield of offenders, the percentage of all attending who participated in drug abuse was probably far less.

NUDE BATHING

Sir Douglas referred to the world Press coverage of the event and said there was a scarcity of the sensationalism anticipated by news media. Much was made of the fact that a contingent of more than 100 patrons regularly bathed in the nude at Compton Beach. The nude bathing was not, however, the subject of any complaint to the police. There were less than 50 complaints of various kinds from residents during the week of the festival. These were mainly trivial and promptly attended to. There was, however, a considerable amount of larceny - about 600 cases on the site ... Contrary to popular expectation, police officers were well received and the only antagonism expressed was by those who were intent on causing disorder. Relations between police and patrons were extremely cordial throughout and officers involved in the exercise much enjoyed the experience, which undoubtedly helped to promote understanding between the police and the thousands of young people attending.

EXPENSIVE OPERATION

Although the whole operation was expensive, there were no grounds on which the police could advocate that such festivals should be banned ... The police had no mandate, and should have no mandate, for causing widespread disruption of an event by unnecessary infiltration into a crowd in an overzealous hunt for offenders. Such action could well lead to disturbances and violence and would defeat the main purpose of police deployment, which was to keep the peace. On the whole, it could be claimed that the peace was kept in 1970, that offenders were identified and action taken, and that their achievements were as much due to the restraint and courtesy of those attending as to the good humour and understanding of what, in the context of the enormous mass of people living in a confined space for a protracted period was, relatively, only a handful of police officers ... Sir Douglas said that 70 prosecutions and 31 cautions arose from the Island pop festival, compared with about 25 offenders at the festival the previous year. Drug squad officers checked 1244 at the pop festival.

April 17th, 1971.

BOTH POP FESTIVALS MADE LOSS

The Isle of Wight pop festival lost about £61,000 last year even though ticket sales amounted to £197,000, creditors of the festival's organisers, Fiery Creations Limited., were told at a meeting in London on Thursday ... Mr. A. Cheek, senior official receiver, said a film had also been made in colour of the festival and the company appeared to have an interest in the film's net receipts. The Foulk brothers had estimated the company's interests in the film at £28,000, but so far it had not been submitted to distributors. The Foulks had been paid a total of £8900 as sole directors.

April 17th, 1971.

PLANS FOR THIS YEAR

Not only have brothers Raymond and Ronald Foulk - formerly of Fiery Creations - announced plans for a "gentler" pop festival over the Summer Bank Holiday but a 29-year-old London music promoter has revealed that he too is hoping to stage a three-day festival beginning on August 27th. Mr. L. H Baines, clerk of the County Council, said Mr. Richard Roscoe contacted the council several weeks ago, but had asked that it should not be made public at that stage. He had been told that the council would be acting as if their Bill were already law. This would give four months' notice of proposed site or sites. The council would then examine them and indicate if they were suitable..

August 7th, 1971.

ISLAND LEADS THE WAY

Mr. Mark Woodnutt's success in the small hours of Tuesday, when he led 108 MP's through the division lobby on the final stage of the Isle of Wight County Council Bill, was historic. The cheers from both sides of the House when the majority of 101 was announced were well deserved and reflect the admiration and gratitude which the Island feels for the Member for his persistence, ability and never-failing courtesy in piloting the Bill through all its stages until it had reached the Statute Book. The Isle of Wight County Council Act, 1971, is an outstanding example of co-operation between the Member, the County Council, the district councils and other Island organisations. To Mark Woodnutt, who has devoted months of his time and effort to such a successful outcome, the result must be especially gratifying. The Act has national as well as local significance. The unprecedented controversial clause to control large overnight gatherings in the open not only gives the Island the protection it needs, it sets the pattern for national legislation which should follow in the next session of Parliament. The Island has given the lead for the rest of the country.

ISLE OF WIGHT REVISITED

Most of the photographs in this book were taken nearly a hundred years ago. All the photographs were taken on glass negatives and, apart from a handful, have not been seen since the day they were first printed. All the photographs in this book have been produced by returning to the original glass plate negatives to produce stunning new prints from them, modern technology allowing them to be carefully and sensitively restored. The result is a unique collection of photographs of the Island, all of the highest quality.

By Colin Fairweather & Alan Stroud.

Oakwood Press. ISBN 978 0 85361 642 9 *Hardback* **£19.95**

RYDE REVISITED

Postcard collectors on the Isle of Wight will be familiar with the name of William R. Hogg. This book celebrates Hogg's work by reproducing over a hundred of his photographs, in large format and in the highest possible detail, to a degree unavailable until now. Without exception they have all been produced from Hogg's original glass negatives. Mr Hogg would be pleased and proud to see his photographs published today.

By Colin Fairweather & Alan Stroud.

Oakwood Press. ISBN 978 0 85361 660 3 *Hardback* **£19.95**

ISLAND VOICES

In the early 1980s, the authors carried out a series of recorded interviews with Islanders talking about their working lives and childhood in the early part of the 20th century. All were in their seventies or eighties at the time of recording and some of them are speaking of Island life over 100 years ago. Nine Islanders recount the intimate details of everyday life that no-one will live again.

By Alan Stroud & Colin Fairweather

Now and Then Books. ISBN 978 0 95650 760 0 **£11.95**

YESTERDAY'S PAPERS Vol 1:   *Life in Late Victorian England, 1884 - 1901*

With the passing of time, journalists' work, originally meant to have a life of only seven days, has become a valuable history resource. These first-hand accounts of the day-to-day life of Victorians, written with few inhibitions and often in the smallest and most revealing detail, provide a history not found in textbooks. This is the Victorians writing about themselves, uncluttered by today's attitudes and opinions, and with no other agenda than to provide a straightforward account of the week's news.

Oakwood Press. ISBN 978 0 85361 671 9   **£11.95**

YESTERDAY'S PAPERS Vol 2 :   *Life in Edwardian England, 1901 - 1918*

Volume 2 dips into the County Press archive to present a selection of cuttings from 1901 to 1918 which give a flavour of life on the Island, covering the Edwardian era and World War I. By their very nature all the items have historical interest. Some of them are amusing while some of them are not so amusing - on occasions they are both at the same time. This is pure and undiluted history; Island news, told every seven days, as it happened.

Oakwood Press. ISBN 978 0 85361 6849   **£12.95**

YESTERDAY'S PAPERS Vol 3 :   *Life in England between the wars, 1918 - 1934*

While the Victorian way of life was a whole world away from today, the same is not true for the inter-war years. Much of what is familiar now was familiar then. By the 1930s the car, the telephone, electrical appliances of every type and even air travel, had become a part of everyday life for those able to afford them. For many others the 1930s were not so cheerful. Long-term unemployment became a way of life for thousands, especially on the Island.

Oakwood Press. ISBN 978 0 85361 6931   **£13.95**

YESTERDAY'S PAPERS Vol 4 :   *Life on the Island, 1935 - 1949*

For the second time in many people's lifetimes, Britain and Germany went to war. With its shipyards, aircraft manufacturers and proximity to Portsmouth's dockyards, the Island was an important military target and suffered heavy bombing raids. Overnight the County Press found itself at the centre of Island life, recording the highs and lows of Islanders' lives week after week; accounts of the lives of long-suffering, but always resilient, Islanders

Now and Then Books. ISBN 978 0 95650 7617   **£11.95**

YESTERDAY'S PAPERS Vol 5 :   *Life on the Island in the Fifties*

"You've never had it so good" said Harold Macmillan. It's farewell to three of the Island's railway lines while the rise in car ownership continues. The arrival of television saw many Island cinemas close their doors for good. The Island's tourist industry finally established itself as a multi-million pound business and ever larger holiday camps opened. The Fifties also saw the development of many of the Island's coastal resorts. Unemployment was low and jobs were created at Somerton's Decca Radar factory and also in the East Cowes hovercraft factories of Saunders-Roe. This is the story of Britain and the Isle of Wight in the 1950s, written by the County Press, to the soundtrack of Victor Sylvester and Rock Around The Clock.

Now and Then Books. ISBN 978 0 956507624   **£11.95**

Index